THE BREVIARIUM GLOSSATUM

The Hymns of the Divine Office

Latin Text Edited with Vocabulary and Notes
by

Hugh Ballantyne

Also Available

<u>The Psalms and Canticles of the Divine Office</u>
Latin Text Edited with Vocabulary and Grammatical Notes

<u>The Oratory Guide to Reading the Greek New Testament</u> (in 10 fascicules)

1 Matthew
2 Mark
3 Luke
4 John
5 Acts
6 Romans and Galatians
7 I Corinthians, II Corinthians
8 Ephesians, Philippians, Colossians
I Thessalonians, II Thessalonians
Titus, Philemon
9 Hebrews, James
I Peter, II Peter
I John, II John, III John
Jude
10 Apocalypse

Index

31 Beata caeli gaudia
32 Beata nobis gaudia
33 Beate pastor Petre
34 Bella dum late furerent
35 Caelestis Agni nuptias
36 Caelestis aulae nuntius
37 Caelestis urbs Jerusalem
38 Caeli Deus sanctissime
39 Caelitum Joseph
40 Caelo Redemptor praetulit

41 Christe Redemptor omnium, Conserva
42 Christe Redemptor omnium, Ex patre
43 Christe sanctorum decus (M)
44 Christe sanctorum decus (R)
45 Christo profusum sanguinem
46 Claro paschali gaudio
47 Conditor alme siderum
48 Consors paterni luminis
49 Cor arca legem continens
50 Corpus domas jejuniis

51 Creator alme siderum
-- Crudelis Herodes (R)
Cf Hostis Herodes impie
52 Custodes hominum
53 Decora lux aeternitatis
54 Deus tuorum militum
55 Doctor egregie Paule
56 Domare cordis
57 Dum nocte pulsa
58 Ecce jam noctis (M)
59 Ecce jam noctis (R)
nn Egregie Doctor Paule (R)
Cf Beate Pastor Petre (R)
60 En clara vox redarguit (R)

61 En ut superba criminum
62 Ex more docti mystico
63 Exsultet caeli laudibus
64 Exsultet orbis gaudiis
65 Festivis resonent compita vocibus
66 Fortem virili pectore
67 Gentis Polonae gloria
68 Haec est dies
69 Hominis superne conditor
70 Hostis Herodes impie

71 Huius obtentu (M)
72 Huius oratu (R)
73 Immense caeli conditor
74 Inclitos Christi famulos
75 In monte olivis consito
nn. Invicte martyr unicum (R)
Cf Martyr Dei qui unicum (M)
76 Ira justa conditoris
77 Iste confessor Domini (M)
78 Iste confessor Domini (R)
79 Iste quem laeti
80 Jam bone pastor Petre (M)

81 Jam Christe sol justitiae
82 Jam Christus astra ascenderat
83 Jam lucis orto sidere
84 Jam morte victor obruta
85 Jam sol recedit igneus
86 Jam toto subitus vesper
87 Jesu corona celsior
88 Jesu corona virginum
89 Jesu decus angelicum
90 Jesu dulcis memoria

121 O nimis felix meritique celsi (M)
122 O nimis felix meritique celsi (R)
123 Opes decusque regium reliqueras
124 O prima Virgo prodita
125 O quot undis lacrimarum
nn Orbis patrator optime (M)
cf Aeterne Rector siderum
126 O sola magnarum urbium
127 O sol salutis intimis
128 Pange lingua gloriosi Corporis
129 Pange lingua gloriosi Proelium (Lauream)
Note on Meter: Trochaic tetrameter
130 Paschale mundo gaudium

131 Pater superni luminis
132 Petrus beatus catenarum laqueos
Note on Meter: Iambic trimeter
133 Placare Christe servulis
134 Plasmator hominis Deus
135 Plenis resultet vocibus
136 Praeclara custos virginum
137 Primo die quo Trinitas
138 Primo dierum omnium
139 Quem terra pontus aethera
140 Quicumque Christum quaeritis

141 Quodcumque in orbe
nn Quodcumque vinclis
142 Rector potens verax Deus
143 Regali solio fortis Iberiae
144 Regis superni nuntia
145 Rerum creator optime
146 Rerum Deus tenax vigor
147 Rerum supremo in vertice
148 Rex gloriose martyrum
nn Rex gloriose praesulum
149 Rex sempiterne caelitum
150 Rex sempiterne Domine

151 Sacra iam splendent decorata lychnis
152 Sacris solemniis juncta sint gaudia
153 Salutis aeterne dator
154 Salutis humanae sator
155 Salvete Christi vulnera
156 Salvete flores martyrum
    Note on meter: Iambic dimeter
157 Sanctorum meritis inclita gaudia (M)
    Note on meter: Asclepiadic
158 Sanctorum meritis inclita gaudia (R)
159 Sedibus caeli nitidis receptos
    Note on meter: Sapphic stanza
160 Si lege prisca fortibus

161 Sic patres vitam peragunt in umbra
162 Solis O Virgo radiis amicta
163 Somno refectis artubus
    Note on meter: Iambic dimeter
164 Splendor paternae gloriae
165 Summae Deus clementiae (15 September, Lauds)
166 Summae Deus clementiae (M, Saturday Matins)
167 Summae Parens clementiae (R, Saturday Matins)
168 Summae Deus clementiae (M, Trinity Sunday)
    Summae Parens clementiae (R, Trinity Sunday)
169 Summi Parentis unice
170 Surge iam terris fera bruma

171 Te deprecante corporum
172 Te dicimus praeconio
173 Te gestientem gaudiis
174 Te Joseph celebrent
    Note on meter: Asclepiadic
175 Telluris ingens conditor
176 Te lucis ante terminum
177 Te mater alma Numinis
178 Te pater Joseph opifex colende
    Note on meter: Sapphic stanza
179 Te saeculorum principem
180 Te splendor et virtus Patris

181 Tibi Christe splendor Patris
Note on meter: Trochaic tetrameter catalectic
182 Tristes erant Apostoli (M)
183 Tristes erant Apostoli (R)
184 Tu Trinitatis unitas (feria sexta ad Matutinum)
185 Tu Trinitatis unitas (in festo sanctissimae Trinitatis)
186 Urbs Jerusalem beata
187 Ut queant laxis
188 Veni creator Spiritus
189 Verbum supernum prodiens, A Patre (M)
190 Verbum supernum prodiens, E Patris (R)

191 Verbum supernum prodiens, Nec Patris
192 Vexilla Christus inclita
193 Vexilla regis prodeunt (M)
Note on meter: Iambic dimeter
194 Vexilla regis prodeunt (R)
195 Virginis proles opifexque matris (M)
Note on meter: Sapphic
196 Virginis proles opifexque matris (R)
197 Vox clara ecce intonat
198 Vox sonat sponsi

Supplementum Monasticum

Starts on page 365

1. Adeste sancti plurimo
2. Ad sacros Virgo thalamos
3. Anglorum jam apostolus
4. Aurora surgit aurea
5. Avete solitudinis
6. Fortis en praesul
7. Gaude mater Anna
8. Gemma caelestis pretiosa Regis
9. Gertrudis arca numinis
10. Hymnis angelicis ora resolvimus

11. Inter aeternas superum coronas
12. Jam noctis umbrae concidunt
13. Jam regina discubuit
14. Jesu corona caelitum
15. Jesu salvator saeculi
16. Jucunda patrum rediit
17. Lacte quondam profluentes
18. Laudibus cives resonent canoris
19. Mella cor obdulcantia
20. Mira nocturnis modulante lingua

21. Omnis sanctorum concio
22. O vos unanimes Christiadum chori
23. Puellus Placidus quem pater obtulit
24. Quiquid antiqui cecinere vates
25. Qui te posthabitis omnibus
26. Sacrata nobis gaudia
27. Salvete, cedri Libani
28. Signifer Invictissime
29. Succedit nocti lucifer
30. Te beata Sponsa Christi

    Note on Meter: Trochaic tetrameter catalectic.

Introduction

1. This volume presupposes the vocabulary of the Latin psalms. The student who has not yet assimilated that vocabulary should start with the preceding volume: *The Psalms and Canticles of the Divine Office.*

2. The hymns of both the Breviarium Romanum (1960) and the Breviarium Monasticum are included in alphabetical order by *incipit*. Consonantal J is retained and it follows vocalic I. Thus for example, we spell *Jerusalem* rather than *Ierusalem*. This is useful for Hebrew words. In a Latin word like *ejus* it is a matter of indifference.

3. The reader should note that there are often two different versions of a given hymn: the Monastic and the Roman. The editio typica of the Roman Breviary in 1632 under Pope Urban VIII included for the first time the so-called "humanist" revision of the post-classical and medieval hymns. These humanist hymns are now to be found in almost all editions of the Roman Breviary.

The Monastic Breviary never adopted the humanist revision. It likewise never adopted the revision of the Latin psalter under Pope Pius XII. Nor has it adopted the Nova Vulgata. And it was untouched by the reform of the Roman office under Pius X in 1910. In this way the Breviarium Monasticum represents the purest and oldest stream of the divine office in the western church.

4. We are here concerned with the liturgical text. However, in a small number of cases the abbreviation *Mss* will be used to refer to a variant literary reading, when that reading seems helpful.

The abbreviation R will refer to the Roman text of a hymn. The abbreviation M will refer to the monastic text.

Where the two versions of a hymn are very different, they are given separately with a cross reference.

Where the two versions are very similar, the variations are shown on the same page in a second column. In these cases the vocabulary for both is supplied.

The abbreviation V will mean either *Versio* or *Variationes*. Hence accordingly, VR and VM.

The symbol Δ means "distinguish" or "do not confuse with".

5. Where a hymn occurs only in the monastic office, and a cognate *versio Romana* does not exist, the hymn will not be found in the main list. It will instead be listed in the *Supplementum Monasticum* at the end of this volume.

6 Final strophes, whether *doxologia* or *conclusio*, are generally omitted. They are, however, included if they display any lexical or grammatical difficulty.

7. After Vatican II the editors of the new *Liturgia Horarum* reversed the humanist revisions of the Roman hymns. In many cases, therefore, users of LH will be able to employ this volume by consulting the *versio monastica* of a given hymn.

8 Useful References:
Joseph Connelly, *Hymns of the Roman Liturgy* (New York 1957)
Matthew Britt, *The Hymns of the Breviary and Missal* (New York 1948)

For older hymns newly introduced into the office by LH:
Anselmo Lentini, *Hymni instaurandi Breviarii Romani* (Libreria Editrice Vaticana 1968)
Martin O'Keefe, *Exsultemus* (Saint Louis 2002)

9 A question: What happens if I forget a word?
Nothing happens. It is normal to forget vocabulary. You may even find that you look the same word up more than once. If you are studying a hymn, and you encounter a word that you cannot remember, just add an appropriate note by hand.

10 Always read the text out loud. If possible sing it. If you want to study the meters, Matthew Britt's book is a good place to start.

12 Long vowels are occasionally marked in these notes. The absence of the macron means nothing. Thus *mensa* with no mark might be ablative, but *mensā* with the mark can only be ablative.

11 Comments, questions, and notices of errata may be sent by email to hugh.ballantyne@sympatico.ca.

1. <u>A solis ortus cardine</u>
   Sedulius c.450 → Variationes Romanae

A solis ortūs cardine
Ad usque terrae limitem,
Christum canamus principem,
Natum Maria virgine.

Beatus auctor saeculi
Servile corpus induit,
Ut carne carnem liberans
Ne perderet quos condidit.

Castae parentis viscera
Caelestis intrat gratia;
Venter puellae bajulat
Secreta, quae non noverat.

Domus pudici pectoris
Templum repente fit Dei;
Intacta nesciens virum
Verbo concepit filium. Concepit alvo filium

ortus, -us: rising

servilis: of a slave, humble, servile
ut….ne: *so that…. not* (Neg purpose clause)

castus: chaste
viscera (viscus): belly, guts, innards, interior
gratia: (nominative)
venter, ventris: womb, belly
intro, intrare: enter, go into (+acc)
bajulo: carry (a heavy load)

pudicus: modest, bashful, pure
pectus, pectoris: chest, (metaph) heart
repente: suddenly
intactus: untouched, unbroken, intact
alvus: belly, womb (*alvo = in her womb*)

1. <u>A solis ortus cardine</u>

Enixa est puerpera	Enititur puerpera
Quem Gabriel praedixerat,	
Quem matris alvo gestiens	Quem ventre matris gestiens
Clausus Johannes senserat.	Baptista clausum senserat.[1]
Foeno jacere pertulit;	
Presepe non abhorruit;	
Parvoque lacte pastus est,	Et lacte modico pastus est [2]
Per quem nec ales esurit.	
Gaudet chorus caelestium	
Et angeli canunt Deo,	
Palamque fit pastoribus	
Pastor, creator omnium.	

enitor, eniti, enixus: bring forth, bear (Cf Introitus: *Salve sancta parens*)
puerpera (Adj): child-bearing, in travail
gestio, gestire: leap, exult

perfero: endure, accept
praesepe (Neut): stable, stall
abhorreo: shrink from, disdain
pascor, pasci, pastus: be fed, be nourished
ales, alitis: bird, a winged creature (Δ *ala*)
nec: not even

palam: openly, in front of

[1] *Baptista* is masculine nominative. The VR transfers *clausum* from John to Jesus.
[2] Hypermetric. We must scan *Et lacte mod'co pastus est*.

2. Ad cenam Agni providi (M)
   Anon c. 550   Cf *Ad regias Agni dapes* (R)

Ad cenam Agni providi,
Et stolis albis candidi
Post transitum maris Rubri
Christo canamus principi.

Cujus corpus sanctissimum
In ara crucis torridum,
Cruore ejus roseo   mss. Sed et cruorem roseum
Gustando vivimus Deo.

Protecti Paschae vespere
A devastante angelo,
Erepti de durissimo
Pharaonis imperio.

Jam Pascha nostrum Christus est,
Qui immolatus agnus est,
Sinceritatis azyma,
Caro ejus oblata est.

providus: foreseeing
stola: robe, gown, stole
albus: white
candidus: bright, shining

torridus: burning, parched
cruor: blood, bloodshed (Ablative where accusative might be expected.)

Pascha, Paschae: (neuter)
azyma: unleaven, unleavened bread (cf I Cor 5:8)

2. Ad cenam Agni providi (M)

O vere digna hostia,
Per quam fracta sunt tartara,
Redempta plebs captivata,
Reddita vitae praemia.

Consurgit Christus tumulo[1],
Victor redit de barathro,
Tyrannum trudens vinculo,
Et Paradisum reserans.

Quaesumus, auctor omnium,
In hoc paschali gaudio,
Ab omni mortis impetu
Tuum defende populum.

tartara: the lower regions, the underworld
captivatus: in bondage, captive
praemium: reward, recompense

tumulus: grave, burial mound
barathrum: abyss, chasm
trudo: drive, press upon, confine
resero: unlock

[1] Ablative without a preposition to express place from which. Rare in classical Latin, but common in later Latin hymnography.

3. <u>Adoro te devote</u> [1]

Adoro te devote, latens Deitas,
Quae sub his figuris vere latitas:
Tibi se cor meum totum subjicit,
Quia te contemplans totum deficit.

Visus, tactus, gustus in te fallitur,
Sed auditu solo tuto creditur;
Credo quidquid dixit Dei Filius:
Nil hoc verbo Veritatis verius.

In cruce latebat sola Deitas,
At hic latet simul et humanitas;
Ambo tamen credens atque confitens,
Peto quod petivit latro paenitens.

adoro: worship, adore
devote: bowing down, with devotion
latens (< lateo): hidden, unseen
figura; form, shape, figure
latito: lie hid, be concealed
subjicio: submit, be subject to, follow

visus, tactus, gustus (Nouns): sight, touch *and* taste
fallo, fallere, fefelli, falsus: deceive, elude, mislead
tuto (Adv): safely, reliably
creditur: (Impersonal)

sola: *sola deitas*, not *in cruce sola*
at: but (Mss *sed*)
ambo (Here indeclinable): both

---

[1] This *rhythmus*, or poem, by Thomas Aquinas is not a liturgical hymn. It may be sung at Benediction. It is included in the Missale Romanum and in many editions of the Breviary *pro opportunitate sacerdotis*. There is no concluding doxology. For the symbolism of the pelican in Christian art, cf *Oxford Dictionary of the Christian Church*.

3. Adoro te devote

Plagas, sicut Thomas, non intueor;
Deum tamen meum te confiteor;
Fac me tibi semper magis credere,
In te spem habere, te diligere.

O memoriale mortis Domini!
Panis vivus, vitam praestans homini!
Praesta meae menti de te vivere
Et te illi semper dulce sapere.

Pie pellicane, Jesu Domine,
Me immundum munda tuo sanguine;
Cujus una stilla salvum facere
Totum mundum quit ab omni scelere.

Jesu, quem velatum nunc aspicio,
Oro fiat illud quod tam sitio;
Ut te revelata cernens facie,
Visu sim beatus tuae gloriae.

sicut: as Thomas *did*, unlike Thomas
intueor: inspect, observe

praesto: show, assure, offer, grant
illi: (ie *meae menti*)
dulce: agreeably, delightfully
sapio: taste *of*, savor *of* (*te* = subj of *sapere*)

immundus: unclean
mundo, mundare: cleanse, clean
queo, quire: be able (= *possum*) [1]
scelus, sceleris: crime, sin

cerno, cernere: discern, perceive

[1] Queo, quis, quit, quimus, quitis, queunt. Cf Hymnus *Ut queant laxis resonare fibris* in festo Praecursoris.

4. Ad regias Agni dapes (R)
   Cf. *Ad cenam Agni providi* (M)

Ad regias Agni dapes,
Stolis amicti candidis,
Post transitum Maris Rubri,
Christo canamus Principi :

Divina cujus caritas
Sacrum propinat sanguinem,
Almique membra corporis
Amor sacerdos immolat.

Sparsum cruorem postibus
Vastator horret Angelus:
Fugitque divisum mare;
Merguntur hostes fluctibus.

Jam Pascha nostrum Christus est,
Paschalis idem victima,
Et pura puris mentibus
Sinceritatis azyma.

regius: kingly, royal
daps, dapis: feast, banquet
stola: robe, gown, stole
amictus (< amicio): clothed in, wearing
candidus: bright, shining, white

propino, -are: pledge, yield, offer, shed
almus: nourishing, bountiful, loving

spargo, spargere, sparsi, sparsus: sprinkle, spread, moisten
cruor: gore, blood
postis, -is: door-post, door, post
vastator: ravaging, *angel* of devastation
horreo + acc: shudder at, shrink from, stay away from
mergo, mergere, mersi, mersus: sink, engulf, overwhelm

Pascha: (Neuter)
puris mentibus: *to pure minds, for those whose souls are pure*
azyma (Neut nom plu): unleaven, unleavened bread

4. Ad regias Agni dapes (R)

O vera cæli victima,
Subjecta cui sunt tartara;
Soluta mortis vincula,
Recepta vitæ præmia.[1]

Victor, subactis inferis,
Trophæa Christus explicat;
Cæloque aperto, subditum
Regem tenebrarum trahit.

Ut sis perenne mentibus
Paschale, Jesu, gaudium,
A morte dira criminum
Vitæ renatos libera.

recipio: regain, take back, bring back

subigo, subigere, subegi, subactus: overcome, subjugate, conquer
inferi, -orum: the underworld, the demons of the underworld
trop(h)aeum: victory, trophy, flag of victory
explico, -are: unfold, unfurl, display
subdo, subdere, subdidi, subditus: subject, bring down, defeat
traho, trahere: drag away, haul away

dirus: fearful, dread
crimen, criminis: fault, offence, wrong-doing

---

[1] Poetic ellipsis. Since *soluta cui* and *recepta cui* would here be ungrammatical, the reader must mentally supply *a quo* or *per quem*. Alternatively, start a new independent clause at *Soluta* and supply *sunt*. Here is a rigid translation which will display the problem in English. *O true heavenly victim, to whom the nether regions are made subject.....(by whom) the chains of death are sundered, (and) the rewards of life regained.* The reader will also note that the second line is one syllable too long, so that *cui* must be sung as *qui*.

5. <u>Aeterna caeli gloria</u>
Anon, c. 500. Revised 1632 → VR

Aeterna caeli gloria,	
Beata spes mortalium,	
Celsi Tonantis Unice	Summi Tonantis Unice,
Castaeque proles Virginis:	
Da dexteram surgentibus,	
Exsurgat et mens sobria.	
Flagrans et in laudem Dei	
Grates rependat debitas.	
Ortus refulget lucifer,	
Sparsamque lucem nuntiat	Praeitque solem nuntius;
Cadit caligo noctium	Cadunt tenebrae noctium;
Lux sancta nos illuminet.	

tono, tonare, tonui: thunder, resound (Mss *parentis*)
celsus: lofty, towering, high
proles, prolis: offspring, child

flagrans (< flagrare): burning, ardent, passionate
sobrius: sober, moderate, sensible
grates, gratium: thanks, thanksgiving
rependo, -ere: pay, repay

orior, oriri, ortus: rise
refulgeo: shine again
lucifer: light-bearer, morning star
prae-eo: precede, go before (+ acc)

5. Aeterna caeli gloria

Manensque nostris sensibus,	
Noctem repellat saeculi,	
Omnique fine diei	Omnique fine temporis,
Purgata servet pectora.	
Quaesita jam primum fides	
Radicet altis sensibus	In corde radices agat
Secunda spes congaudeat,	
Qua major exstat caritas.	

omnis: whole, complete
pectus, pectoris: chest, *metaph* heart

primum: first of all, firstly
radices agat: strike root, take root
radico, radicare: take root (as if *radicet in sensibus nostris profundis*)
exsto, -are: stand out, be prominent

6. Aeterna Christi munera (M)
Saint Ambrose 339-397 Cf *Aeterna Christi munera* (R)

Aeterna Christi munera,
Apostolorum gloriam,
Laudes canentes debitas,
Laetis canamus mentibus.

Ecclesiarum principes,
Belli triumphales duces,
Caelestis aulae milites,
Et vera mundi lumina.

Devota sanctorum fides,
Invicta spes credentium,
Perfecta Christi caritas
Mundi triumphat principem.

In his Paterna gloria,
In his voluntas Spiritus,
Exsultat in his Filius,
Caelum repletur gaudio.

Te nunc, Redemptor, quaesumus,
Ut ipsorum consortio
Jungas precantes servulos
In sempiterna saecula.

munus, muneris: gift
cano, canere, cecini: sing *of* (*munera* and *gloriam* = dir obj of *canamus*)

aula: court, hall

triumpho, -are: triumph *over*, defeat, lead in triumph

consortium: company, fellowship

Note on Meter

Aeterna Christi munera is in the classical iambic dimeter. A Latin hymn in this meter is called "Ambrosian", regardless of who wrote the words. As it happens, all of the hymns by Saint Ambrose are in the Ambrosian meter.

Iambic dimeter is a doubled meter, and so it is the same as an English iambic tetrameter. The line consists of four feet of two syllables each. The foot may be strictly iambic (short-long), or spondaic (long-long), and the final syllable of the line is *anceps*, or optional. Thus the final two syllables can actually be short-short, eg *(lu) mi-ne*, *(mu) ne-ra.*

Until about 500AD Latin meters were quantitative rather than accentual. In a quantitative meter a syllable is long if it contains a long vowel or a diphthong, or if the vowel is followed by two consonants. The accented—or loud—syllable will have no bearing on the meter.

Aeter na Chris tī mū nera
— — | ∪ — | — — | ∪ ∪
Apos tolō rum glō riam
∪ — | ∪ — | — — | ∪ ∪
Laudēs canen tēs dē bitās
— — | ∪ — | — — | ∪ —
Laetis canā mus men tibus.
— — | ∪ — | — — | ∪ ∪

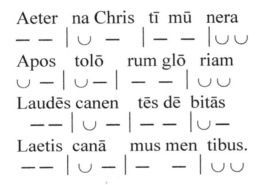

In the third line an alternative manuscript tradion has

laudes ferentes debitas

with the same scansion. This has been adopted by LH.

In 1632 the editors altered the third line to

palmas et hymnos debitos

perhaps in order to avoid "canentes…. canamus".

7. Aeterna Christi munera (R)
Saint Ambrose 339-397

Cf *Aeterna Christi munera* (M)

Aeterna Christi munera,
Apostolorum gloriam,
Palmas et hymnos debitos
Laetis canamus mentibus.

Ecclesiarum principes,
Belli triumphales duces,
Caelestis aulae milites,
Et vera mundi lumina.

Devota sanctorum fides,
Invicta spes credentium,
Perfecta Christi caritas
Mundi tyrannum conterit.

In his Paterna gloria,
In his triumphat Filius,
In his voluntas Spiritūs,
Caelum repletur gaudio.

Patri simulque Filio,
Tibique Sancte Spiritus,
Sicut fuit, sit jugiter
Saeclum per omne gloria.

munus, muneris: gift
palma: palm, (symbol of) victory, song of victory
cano, canere, cecini: sing *of* (*munera*, *gloriam,* etc = dir obj of *canamus*)

aula: court, hall

jugiter: continually, without interruption

8. Aeterna Christi munera, Et martyrum victorias (M)
Saint Ambrose 339-397 Cf *Christo profusum sanguinem* (R)

Aeterna Christi munera
Et Martyrum victorias,
Laudes canentes debitas,
Laetis canamus mentibus.

Terrore victo saeculi
Poenisque spretis corporis,
Mortis sacrae compendio
Vitam beatam possident.

Traduntur igni Martyres
Et bestiarum dentibus;
Armata saevit ungulis
Tortoris insani manus.

cano, canere (+ acc): sing *praises*, sing of , sing about

sperno, spernere, sprevi, spretus: disdain, despise
compendium: short-cut, swift path

armo, armare: arm, equip with weapons (*armata….manus* subj of *saevit*)
saevio, saevire, saevii : rage, be fierce, be wild, be savage
ungula: claw, hook (instrument of torture)
tortor: executioner, tormenter, torturer
insanus: mad, raging, frantic

8. <u>Aeterna Christi munera, Et martyrum victorias</u> (M)

Nudata pendent viscera,
Sanguis sacratus funditur;
Sed permanent immobiles,
Vitae perennis gratiā.

Te nunc, Redemptor, quaesumus,
Ut Martyrum consortio
Jungas precantes servulos,
In sempiterna saecula.

nudo, nudare: expose, lay bare, strip open
pendeo, pendére (intrans): hang out, hang down (Δ *pendo, péndere*)
sacratus (< sacrare): hallowed, consecrated
immobilis: unmoving, steady, persevering, constant

consortium: company, fellowship

9. Aeterna Imago Altissimi
c. 1925, in festo DNJC Regis

Aeterna Imago Altissimi,
Lumen, Deus, de Lumine,
Tibi, Redemptor, gloria,
Honor, potestas regia.

Tu solus ante saecula
Spes atque centrum temporum
Cui jure sceptrum gentium
Pater supremum credidit.

Tu flos pudicae Virginis,
Nostrae caput propaginis,
Lapis caducus vertice,
Ac mole terras occupans.

regius: kingly, royal

centrum (Gk κέντρον): mid-point, center, origin
jus, juris: right
jure: by right, rightly
sceptrum: royal staff, sceptre
credo, credere: entrust, confide, bestow

propago, propaginis: off-spring, family, race
lapis: stone, precious stone
caducus: falling, fallen
vertex, verticis: high-point, summit (*A stone fallen from the summit*)
moles, molis: vastness, magnitude (*And filling the earth with its immensity*)

9. Aeterna Imago Altissimi

Diro tyranno subdita,
Damnata stirps mortalium,
Per te refregit vincula
Sibique caelum vindicat.

Doctor, Sacerdos, Legifer
Praefers notatum sanguine
In veste: "Princeps principum
Regumque Rex Altissimus".

Tibi volentes subdimur,
Qui jure cunctis imperas;
Haec civium beatitas
Tuis subesse legibus.

Jesu, tibi sit gloria, Gloria tibi, Domine VM
Qui sceptra mundi temperas,
Cum Patre et almo Spiritu Cum Patre et Sancto Spiritu
In sempiterna saecula.

stirps, stirpis: race, breed, family
refringo, -ere, refregi: break apart, break anew
vindico, -are (+ acc): claim *as one's own*, claim title to

praefero, -ferre: display, show forth, present
noto, notare: write, mark
notatum: *adj* written, *noun* emblem, writing, motto
vestis: garment, vesture
You display, written in blood upon your garment, (the words): Prince etc.

cunctus, -a, -um: all
impero, -are (+ dat): hold sway over, command
civis: citizen
beatitas: happiness, felicity (= *beatitudo*)

tempero, -are: govern, rule, moderate

10. <u>Aeterne Rector Siderum</u>
Saint Robert Bellarmine 1542-1621 →VM

Aeterne Rector siderum, — Orbis patrator optime
Qui, quidquid est, potentiā
Magnā creasti, nec regis
Minore providentiā.

Adesto supplicantium
Tibi reorum coetui,
Lucisque sub crepusculum
Lucem novam da mentibus.

Tuusque nobis Angelus,
Electus ad custodiam, — Signatus ad custodiam
Hic adsit, a contagio
Ut criminum nos protegat. — Qui criminum nos protegat

patrator: author, composer, maker
qui…. regis: *who rulest, you who rule*

supplico, are: kneel down, humbly pray, entreat, beseech
reus, -a, -um: guilty
coe-tus, -ūs: assembly, crowd, company, gathering
crepusculum: twilight, dusk

nobis (dat): *for us*
signatus (<signare): marked, sealed
ad custodiam: *for (the purpose of) guarding, to guard*
contagium: infection, taint (Δ *contagio, contagionis*)
crimen, criminis: fault, offence, sin

10. Aeterne Rector siderum

Nobis draconis aemuli
Versutias exterminet,
Ne rete fraudulentiae
Incauta nectat pectora.

Serpentis nobis aemuli
Calumnias exterminet

Metum repellat hostium
Nostris procul de finibus:
Pacem procuret civium,
Fugetque pestilentiam.

Metum propellat hostium

Deo Patri sit gloria,
Qui, quos redemit Filius
Et Sanctus unxit Spiritus,
Per Angelos custodiat.

nobis: *for us*
aemulus: jealous, envious, greedy
extermino, -are: expel, drive away
versutiae, -arum: tricks, trickery, cunning
calumnia: slander, trickery
rete, retis: net
fraudulentia: cheating, dishonesty
incautus: careless, heedless, unguarded
necto, nectere, nexui, nexus: capture, bind, imprison

propello: push away, drive off (transitive)
procul: far
procuro, -are: take care of, manage, attend to
fugo, fugare, fugavi: rout, put to flight (Δ *fugio, fugere, fugi*)

ungo, ungere, unxi: anoint
qui….custodiat: And may he (*qui*) with angels guard those whom etc

11. <u>Aeterne rerum conditor</u>
Saint Ambrose ob 397 → VR

Aeterne rerum conditor,
Noctem diemque qui regis,
Et temporum das tempora,
Ut alleves fastidium.

Praeco diei jam sonat,
Noctis profundae pervigil,
Nocturna lux viantibus
A nocte noctem segregans.

Nocturna lux viantibus
A nocte noctem segregans
Praeco diei jam sonat
Jubarque solis evocat

Hoc excitatus lucifer
Solvit polum caligine;
Hoc omnis erronum cohors
Viam nocendi deserit.

temporum tempora: *the change of seasons, the changes of time*
allevo, -are: relieve, lighten, diminish, dispel
fastidium: aversion, ennui, boredom

praeco, praeconis: cryer, herald, (ie the rooster)
noctis profundae: *in deep night, during the dark night*
pervigil, -is: ever watchful
lux: light, guide (Figurative: refers to the rooster at cock-crow.)
viantes: wayfarers, pilgrims
nox: time of night, night-watch
a nocte noctem segregans: *marking off the watches of the night*
jubar, jubaris: radiance, sunshine, light

hōc: *by this*
excito, -are: summon, awake, call forth
lucifer: morning star, day-break
polus: pole, sky, the heavenly vault
solvo, -ere: clear, release, free
caligo: mist, fog, dark
solvit…. caligine: *clear of darkness, release from dark*
erro, erronis: vagabond, bandit
cohors, cohortis: gang, group, cohort
desero, deserere, deserui, desertus: abandon, forsake, desert

11. Aeterne rerum conditor

Hoc nauta vires colligit
Pontique mitescunt freta;
Hoc ipsa Petra Ecclesiae
Canente culpam diluit.

Surgamus ergo strenue.
Gallus jacentes excitat,
Et somnolentos increpat;
Gallus negantes arguit.

Gallo canente spes redit,
Aegris salus refunditur,
Mucro latronis conditur,
Lapsis fides revertitur.

nauta: sailor
vires, virium: strength
colligo, -ere: gather
pontus: the sea
freta (fretum): strait, straits, narrows
mitesco, -ere: be calmed, become gentle
hoc (gallo)....canente: (The sound of dawn is a figure of the Resurrection.)
diluo, -ere, dilui, dilutus: wash away, remove

strenue: quickly, promptly
nego, -are: deny (ie deny the Lord)
arguo, -ere: accuse, denounce

aeger, -gra, -grum: sick, unwell
salus: health, safety, salvation
refundo, -ere: restore
mucro, -onis: blade, sharp tip, edge of a sword
latro, latronis: thief, robber, bandit
condo, condere: put away, sheathe (a weapon)
labor, labi, lapsus: fall, lapse (Δ *labor, laboris* and *lapsus, -us*)

Note
For the symbolism of the *gallicinium* see bibliography sv *Aeterne rerum conditor* in *New Catholic Encyclopedia* (Washington 1967). Cf likewise Matt 26: 30-35 and 69-75. The word-play in this hymn repays careful study.

11. <u>Aeterne rerum conditor</u> → VR

Jesu, labentes respice,	Jesu, labantes respice
Et nos videndo corrige;	
Si respicis, lapsi stabunt,	Si respicis labes cadunt
Fletuque culpa solvitur.	

Tu lux refulge sensibus,
Mentisque somnum discute,
Te nostra vox primum sonet
Et vota solvamus tibi.

labentes: (present participle of *labor, labi, lapsus = fail, fall*)
labo, labare: hesitate, waver, be weak (hence *labantes*)
labes, labis: stain, blemish (cf *sacrificia il-libata* in Canone Missae)
cado, cadere: fall off, disappear
solvo, -ere: dissolve, wash away

refulgeo: shine again
discutio, discutere, discussi: dispel, remove
primum: first of all, before all else
sono, sonare, sonui (+ acc): sing of, celebrate, sound out, make heard
votum: prayer, promise, vow
solvere vota: fulfill, discharge, make good on

12. Aeterne Rex altissime (R)
Anon, c. 450

Cf *Aeterne Rex altissime* (M)

Aeterne rex altissime,
Redemptor et fidelium,
Cui mors perempta detulit
Summae triumphum gloriae.

Ascendis orbes siderum,
Quo te vocabat caelitus
Collata, non humanitus,
Rerum potestas omnium:

Ut trina rerum machina,
Caelestium, terrestrium,
Et inferorum condita,
Flectat genu jam subdita.

Tremunt videntes angeli
Versam vicem mortalium;
Peccat caro, mundat caro;
Regnat Deus Dei caro.

perimo, perimere, peremi, peremptus: reverse, undo, end
defero, detuli: bring, carry, usher in

sidus, sideris: star
quo: whither
caelitus (adv): in heaven, in a heavenly manner, celestially
confero, collatus: unite, assemble
humanitus (adv): humanly

trinus: three-fold
machina: structure, artifact
conditus (< condere): buried, concealed *neut plu* the buried depths
flecto, flectere, flexi, flexus: bend (subj of *flectat* is *machina*)
genu, genus: knee

(vicis) vicem: fate, vicissitude, status (*vicem* is obj of *videntes*)
verto, vertere, versus: reverse, transform
mundo, mundare: cleanse, purify
regnat etc: *reigns (as) God, the Flesh of God.*

12. <u>Aeterne Rex altissime</u> (R)

Sis ipse nostrum gaudium,
Manens olympo praemium,
Mundi regis qui fabricam,
Mundana vincens gaudia.

Hinc te precantes quaesumus,
Ignosce culpis omnibus,
Et corda sursum subleva
Ad te supernā gratiā.

Ut, cum repente coeperis
Clarere nube Judicis,
Poenas repellas debitas,
Reddas coronas perditas.

olympo: *upon Olympus, in Heaven*
praemium: reward (ie *nostrum praemium, our reward*)
fabrica: structure, design, fabric (*tu qui regis fabricam mundi*)

hinc: from here, hence, but here
sublevo: lift up, raise up
supernus: celestial, heavenly, sublime

(coepio) coepere, coepi: begin, commence
clareo: shine, be luminous, be bright
nubes, nubis: cloud, thunder-cloud
judex: judge

Cf Luke 21: 27, *Videbunt filium hominis venientem in nube cum potestate magna.* In the NT there are many references to a *cloud* as the sign of divine presence and of the return of the Lord. In this context the cloud, far from being dark, shines luminously.

13. Aeterne Rex altissime (M)
Anon, c. 450 Cf *Aeterne Rex altissime* (R)

Aeterne rex altissime,
Redemptor et fidelium,
Quo mors soluta deperit,
Datur triumphus gratiae.

Scandens tribunal dexterae
Patris: potestas omnium
Collata Jesu caelitus,
Quae non erat humanitus:

Ut trina rerum machina,
Caelestium, terrestrium,
Et inferorum condita,
Flectat genu jam subdita.

Tremunt videntes angeli
Versam vicem mortalium;
Culpat caro, purgat caro
Regnat Deus, Dei caro.

soluta (< solvere): dissolved, resolved, reversed
de-pereo, deperire, deperii: be undone, be overcome, perish

scando, scandere: mount, ascend
tribunal, -alis (n): judgment seat, tribunal
Jesu: (case uncertain; abl, dat, or voc all possible) *gathered celestially unto Jesus*
caelitus (adv): celestially, in a heavenly manner
humanitus (adv): humanly

Strophes *Ut trina* and *Tremunt videntes:* cf 12 VR supra.

Note that *erat* is singular. Antecedent of *quae* is *potestas*, not *omnium*. Thus (*potestas) quae non erat humanitus* means "a power which humanly was not", or "which did not humanly exist", or "which was not human".

13. <u>Aeterne Rex altissime</u> (M)

Tu esto nostrum gaudium
Manens olympo praeditum,
Mundi regis qui fabricam,
Mundana vincens gaudia.

Hinc te precantes quaesumus,
Ignosce culpis omnibus,
Et corda sursum subleva
Ad te supernā gratiā.

Ut, cum repente coeperis
Clarere nube judicis,
Poenas repellas debitas,
Reddas coronas perditas.

Gloria tibi Domine,
Qui scandis super sidera,
Cum Patr*e* et Sancto Spiritu
In sempiterna saecula.

praeditus –a, -um: endowed, presiding over, placed upon

Strophes *Hinc te* and *Ut cum*, cf 12 VR supra.

scando, ere: rise, ascend
sidus, sideris: star

Note: The syntax of *praeditum* is unclear. The Roman editors replace it with *praemium.* If it is an adjective—in effect a perfect participle— then it modifies *gaudium*. Thus:

> Be thou our joy, which is
> Ever (*manens*) placed upon (*praeditum*) Olympus,
> (You) who rule the fabric of the world, etc.

Another solution would be to read *praeditum* as a noun. Thus

> Be thou our joy,
> Abiding (*manens*) as a gift (*praeditum*) from olympian heaven,
> (You) who rule the fabric of the world, etc

In the latter case, *manens* might modify either *Tu* or *gaudium*.

14. Aeterni Patris Unice (M)
c. 1175, attrib Alan de Lille Cf. *Summi Parentis Unice* (R)

Aeterni Patris Unice,
Nos pio vultu respice,
Qui Magdalenam hodie
Vocas ad thronum gloriae.

In thesauro reposita
Regis est drachma perdita;
Gemmaque luce inclyta
De luto luci reddita.

Unicus: Only *Begotten*, Only *Son*

repono, -ere: place, keep, preserve
in thesauro…. regis: *in the treasury of the King*
perditus (< perdere): lost, missing
gemma: jewel, gem-stone
inclytus: brilliant, glorious, renowned
lutum: mud, mire, muck
redditus (< reddere): restored

14. Aeterni Patris Unice (M)

Jesu dulce refugium,
Spes una paenitentium,
Per peccatricis meritum
Peccati solve debitum.

Pia mater et humilis,
Naturae memor fragilis,
In hujus vitae fluctibus
Nos rege tuis precibus.

Uni Deo sit gloria
Pro multiformi gratia,
Qui culpas et supplicia
Remittit, et dat praemia.

peccatrix: woman sinner, sinful woman

memor: mindful, recalling, reminder *of*
fragilis: weak, frail, fragile
fluctus, -us: wave
rego, regere: guide

unus, unius, uni, unum, uno: One, alone, only
multiformis (Adj): multiform, diverse, various
supplicium: torment, punishment
praemium: reward

15. Ales diei nuntius
Prudentius c. 400

Ales diei nuntius
Lucem propinquam praecinit;
Nos excitator mentium
Jam Christus ad vitam vocat.

Auferte, clamat, lectulos,
Aegro sopore desides;
Castique, recti ac sobrii
Vigilate; jam sum proximus.

ales, alitis: *adj* winged, *noun* bird
praecino, -ere, praecinui: sing forth, announce
excitator: awakener
mens, mentis: soul (This use of the word is common in the hymns.)

aufero, auferre: pick up, put away
lectulus: bed, couch
sopor, soporis: deep sleep, slumber, laziness
aeger, aegra, aegrum: sick, sickly
(deses), desidis (Adj): idle, lazy, indolent

Note

The meter requires an elision: vig*i*late.

15. Ales diei nuntius

Jesum ciamus vocibus,
Flentes, precantes, sobrii;
Intenta supplicatio
Dormire cor mundum vetat.

Tu, Christe, somnum discute,
Tu rumpe noctis vincula,
Tu solve peccatum vetus,
Novumque lumen ingere.

cieo, ciere + acc: call upon, appeal to (Irreg form *ciamus*, "let us call upon")
intentus (< intendere): attentive, earnest, watchful
mundus, -a, -um: clean, pure
veto, vetare: forbid

(somnum) discutio: dispel, remove (sleep)
vetus, veteris: old (*vetus* here = neut acc sing)
ingero, ingerere, ingessi, ingestus: pour forth, infuse

16. Alto ex Olympi vertice (R)
 1632. Cf. *Angularis fundamentum* (M)

Alto ex Olympi vertice
Summi Parentis Filius,
Ceu monte desectus lapis
Terras in imas decidens,
Domūs supernae et infimae
Utrumque junxit angulum.

Sed illa sedes Caelitum
Semper resultat laudibus,
Deumque trinum et unicum
Jugi canore praedicat:
Illi canentes jungimur
Almae Sionis aemuli.

ceu: as, like
deseco, -secui, -sectus: cut off, cut away
angulus: corner, angle

Caeles, Caelitis: dwelling in heaven, heavenly being
resulto, -are: reverberate, resound
jugis, -is (adj): perpetual
canor, -oris: melody, tune, song
praedico, -are: proclaim, declare, announce
aemulus + gen: eager for, longing for, desiring

16. Alto ex Olympi vertice (R)

Haec templa, Rex caelestium,
Imple benigno lumine:
Huc, o rogatus, adveni,
Plebisque vota suscipe,
Et nostra corda jugiter
Perfunde cæli gratiā.

Hic impetrent fidelium
Voces precesque supplicum
Domūs beatae munera;
Partisque donis gaudeant:
Donec, soluti corpore,
Sedes beatas impleant.

Decus Parenti debitum
Sit usquequaque Altissimo,
Natoque Patris unico,
Et inclito Paraclito,
Cui laus, potestas, gloria
Aeterna sit per sæcula.

haec templa: these sacred precincts, *pl for sing* this temple
huc: hither, here
advenio, -ire: come, arrive
votum: prayer
jugiter: continually

impetro, -are: obtain, get
supplex, supplicis: bowing, begging, entreating
munus, muneris: gift, blessing
partus (< pario,parere): gained, acquired, obtained
impleo, -ēre: fill, occupy

decus, decoris (neut): honor, glory
usquequaque: at all times

17. Amor Jesu dulcissime (M)
Jacobus Gilius, ob 1456 Cf. *Lux alma Jesu mentium* (R)

Amor Jesu dulcissime,
Quando cor nostrum visitas,
Pellis mentis caliginem
Et nos reples dulcedine.

Quam felix est quem satias!
Consors paternae dexterae,
Tu vere lumen patriae,
Quod omne sensum superat.

Splendor paternae gloriae,
Incomprehensa bonitas,
Amoris tui copiam
Da nobis per praesentiam.

pello, pellere, pepuli, pulsus: dispel, drive off

consors, consortis + gen: sharer in, sharer of, consort of
paterna dextera: *the Father's right hand, the Father's might*
patria: father-land, home-land
supero, -are: exceed, transcend

copia: abundance
incomprehensa: *unknown, unknowable*
praesentia: nearness, presence

18. <u>Angularis fundamentum</u> (M)
Anon c. 700   Cf *Alto ex Olympi vertice* (R)

This hymn *Angularis fundamentum* consists of stanzas 5 – 9 (including an original doxology) of the longer work *Urbs beata Jerusalem*, the first four stanzas of which constitute a separate monastic hymn. The Roman equivalent thereof is *Caelestis urbs Jerusalem.*

Angularis, fundamentum,
Lapis Christus missus est,
Qui parietum compage
In utroque nectitur,
Quem Sion sancta suscepit,
In quo credens permanet.

angularis, angulare (adj): corner *stone*, of an angle, at the angle
fundamentum: foundation
paries, parietis: wall, walls, building
compages, compagis: joining, joint, structure
qui parietum compage: *who by the joining of the structures*
necto, nexui, nexus: bind, join, connect
in utroque nectitur: *is connected to both, is bound to both*
credens: = *ille qui credit*, the believer

Note:

Angularis is not a noun in the genitive case, but an adjective in the nominative case. We must take *angularis* with *lapis*. The actual noun-phrase is *angularis fundamentum lapis*, "the cornerstone, the foundation".

The phrase *lapidem angularem.....in fundamento fundatum* is found at Isaiah 28:16, and cited with a variant reading at I Peter 2: 6. See also Eph 2:20.

18. <u>Angularis fundamentum</u>

Omnis illa Deo sacra
Et dilecta civitas,
Plena modulis, in laude
Et canore jubilo,
Trinum Deum unicumque
Cum fervore praedicat.

Hoc in templo, summe Deus,
Exoratus adveni;
Et clementi bonitate
Precum vota suscipe;
Largam benedictionem
Hic infunde jugiter.

modulus: melody, rhythm, musical measure
canor, canoris: melody, tune, song
jubilus, -a, -um: exultant, rejoicing
unicus: single, only
unicumque: = *et unicum*
fervor: passion, enthusiasm, fervor
praedico, -are: proclaim, declare, announce

exoro, exorare: move, induce, prevail upon, appease
precum vota: *the offering(s) of prayers*
largus: abundant, plentiful, large
infundo, -ere: pour out, radiate
jugiter: continually

18. Angularis fundamentum

Hic promereantur omnes
Petita acquirere,
Et adepta possidere,
Cum sanctis perenniter
Paradisum introire,
Translati in requiem.

Gloria et honor Deo
Usquequaque altissimo,
Una Patri, Filioque,
Inclyto Paraclito,
Cui laus est et potestas
Per aeterna saecula.

promereor, -mereri, -meritus: be worthy, deserve, merit
petita (< petere): *what they seek, what they have asked*
acquiro, -ere: obtain, gather
adipiscor, adipisci, adeptus: get, obtain, reach
possideo, -ere: hold, keep, possess
perenniter: permanently, forever
trans-fero, ferre, tuli, latus: carry over, transport

usquequaque: always, at all times, forever
una (adv): at the same time, at once, together

19. Antra deserti teneris sub annis

Attrib Paul the Deacon c 775 AD

This hymn is composed of verses 5-8 of the longer work *Ut queant laxis*, the first 4 verses of which are employed as a different hymn.

Antra deserti teneris sub annis,	→ VR
Civium turmas fugiens, petisti,	
Ne levi saltem maculare vitam	Ne levi posses maculare vitam
Famine posses.	Crimine linguae.
Praebuit hirtum tegumen camelus	Praebuit durum tegumen camelus
Artubus sacris, strophium bidentes;	
Cui latex haustum, sociata pastum	
Mella locustis.	

antrum: cave, cavern
tener, tenera, tenerum: tender, young
sub + abl: during, within, in the time of
cives, civium: citizens, fellows, townsmen
turma: throng, crowd
levis, levis: light, slight, trifling
saltem (Adv) : at least, anyway
ne….saltem: *so that….not even*
maculo, -are: stain, defile, pollute
famen, faminis: talk, speech, words (VR expands as *crimen linguae*)
crimen: offence, sin
ne….posses: *lest you be able*, ie: *so that you would be unable*

praebeo, praebēre, praebui: offer, furnish, supply
hirtus, -a, -um: rough, shaggy
durus: hard, harsh
tegumen, tegminis: covering, cover
camelus: camel
artūs, artuum (pl): limbs (*for your holy limbs*)
strophium: band, cincture, girdle
bidens, bidentis: calf (*bidentes praebuerunt strophium*)
cui (= *et tibi*): *for whom, you for whom, for you*
latex, laticis: water, spring-water (*latex praebuit haustum*)
haustus, -us: drink (*water furnished your drink*)
sociatus (+ dat): taken with, eaten with, joined with
pastus, -us: food (*mella praebuerunt pastum*)
mel, mellis (*plu* mella, mellum): honey (plu for sing)
locusta: locust, grasshopper

19. Antra deserti teneris sub annis →VR

Ceteri tantum cecinēre vatum
Corde praesago jubar affuturum;
Tu quidem mundi scelus auferentem
Indice prodis.

Non fuit vasti spatium per orbis
Sanctior quisquam genitus Joanne,
Qui nefas saecli meruit lavantem
Tingere lymphis.

Gloria Patri genitaeque Proli,	Sit decus Patri genitaeque Proli
Et tibi, compar utriusque semper	Et tibi, compar utriusque virtus,
Spiritus alme, Deus unus omni	Spiritus semper, Deus unus omni
Tempore saecli.	Temporis aevo.

tantum (Adv): only
cano, canere, cecini (+ acc): sing of, sing about (cecinēre = cecinērunt)
vates, vatis: foreteller, prophet
ceteri…. vatum: *others of the prophets, other prophets*
praesagus: prophetic, foreseeing, farseeing
jubar (neut): radiance, splendor
scelus, sceleris: sin, crime
aufero, auferre: remove, take away
index, indicis: finger, index finger
prodo, prodere, prodidi: indicate, point out (Δ *prodeo, prodis, prodit*)

non fuit (True perfect, not aorist): *there has not been*
quisquam: anyone, any man
sanctior….Joanne: *holier than John*
nefas (indecl, here acc): wickedness, unholiness
mereo, merere, merui: be worthy
tingo, tingere, tinxi: moisten, wet (vb), bathe
lympha: water, clear water, running water

proles, prolis (fem): Son, Offspring
compar, comparis (+gen): like, equal to
virtus, Spiritus, Deus: (All in vocative case)
aevum: age, expanse (of time), period

20. Athleta Christi nobilis
Anon, c. 1650

Athleta Christi nobilis
Idola damnat gentium,
Deique amore saucius
Vitae pericla despicit.

Loris revinctus asperis,
E rupe praeceps volvitur;
Spineta vultum lancinant;
Per saxa corpus scinditur.

athleta (Masc): athlete, champion
idolum: idol
damno, -are: condemn
saucius a um: wounded, smitten
pericla: = pericula

revincio, -īre, revinxi, revinctus: tie up, bind, fasten
lorum: thong, strap
asper, aspera, asperum: harsh, tight
rupes, rupis: rock, cliff
praeceps, praecipitis: headlong, abrupt (*prae* + *caput, capitis*)
volvo, -ere: roll, toss
spinetum: thorn-bush, thorn
lancino, -are: damage, pierce
scindo, -ere: tear, tear apart

20. Athleta Christi nobilis

Dum membra raptant martyris,
Languent siti satellites;
Signo crucis Venantius
E rupe fontes elicit.

Bellator o fortissime,
Qui perfidis tortoribus
E caute praebes poculum,
Nos rore gratiae irriga.

rapto, raptare: ravage, tear off
membrum: limb, member
langueo, ēre: be faint, be weary
sitis, sitis: thirst
satelles, satellitis: companion, follower
elicio, -ere: draw out, bring forth, produce

bellator: warrior, fighter
perfidus: faithless, perfidious
tortor, tortoris: tormenter, torturer, executioner
cautes, cautis: rock, crag
praebeo, ere: supply, furnish
poculum: drink, cup
ros, roris: dew, moisture
irrigo, āre: water, irrigate, flood (*irriga* is imperative)

21. <u>Auctor beate saeculi</u>
Anon c. 1750

Auctor beate saeculi,
Christe redemptor omnium,
Lumen Patris de lumine,
Deusque verus de Deo.

Amor coegit te tuus
Mortale corpus sumere,
Ut novus Adam redderes
Quod vetus ille abstulerat.

Ille amor almus artifex
Terrae marisque et siderum,
Errata patrum miserans
Et nostra rumpens vincula.

auctor, auctoris: builder, founder
sumo: take on, assume, accept
reddo, reddere, reddidi: restore, give back
aufero, auferre, abstuli, ablatus: tale away

artifex, artificis: maker, author, designer
miseror, miserari, miseratus: lament, take pity (+acc)

21. Auctor beate saeculi

Non corde discedat tuo
Vis illa amoris incliti;
Hoc fonte gentes hauriant
Remissionis gratiam.

Percussum ad hoc est lanceā,
Passumque ad hoc est vulnera,
Ut nos lavaret sordibus,
Unda fluente et sanguine.

Jesu, tibi sit gloria,	VM Gloria tibi Domine
Qui corde fundis gratiam,	
Cum Patre et almo Spiritu,	Cum Patre et Sancto Spiritu
In sempiterna saecula.	

vis, vis, vi, vim, vi (fem): power
inclitus a um: renowned, glorious
haurio, haurire: draw, take (water)

lancea: lance, spear
percutio, -ere, persussi, percussus: strike (Subj is "it", ie "cor tuum")
ad hoc: *for this reason, to this end*
patior, pati, passus (+acc): suffer
sordes, sordium: filth
unda: wave, water
fluo, fluere, fluxi: flow

fundo, fundere, fudi, fusus: pour, pour out

22. Audi, benigne conditor
St Gregory the Great, ob 604 → VM

Audi, benigne conditor,
Nostras preces cum fletibus,
In hoc sacro jejunio
Fusas quadragenario.

Scrutator alme cordium,
Infirma tu scis virium;
Ad te reversis exhibe
Remissionis gratiam.

Multum quidem peccavimus,
Sed parce confitentibus;
Ad nominis laudem tui — Ad laudem tui nominis
Confer medelam languidis.

prex, precis: prayer, supplication
jejunium: fast, fasting, time of fasting
quadragenarius: of forty *days*, lasting forty *days*
fundo, -ere, fudi, fusus: pour out, pour forth
preces.... fusas: *prayers.... poured out*

scrutator: examiner, searcher
vires, virium: strength
infirma etc: *you know the weakness of our strength, you know our weak points*
revertor, reverti, reversus: return, come back
ad te reversis: *to those who have returned to you*
exhibeo, exhibēre: show, grant

multum (Adv): greatly, a lot, much
parco, parcere, peperci (+dat): spare, show mercy, pardon
ad: for, in answer to
confero, conferre: grant, give, confer
medela: remedy, cure, medecine
languidus: weak, feeble, powerless

22. Audi, benigne conditor

Concede nostrum conteri
Corpus per abstinentiam,
Culpae ut relinquant pabulum
Jejuna corda criminum

Sic corpus extra conteri
Dona per abstinentiam,
Jejunet ut mens sobria
A labe prorsus criminum.

Praesta, beata Trinitas,
Concede, simplex Unitas,
Ut fructuosa sint tuis
Haec parcitatis munera.

Jejuniorum munera

concede, dona: (+ Acc and infin)
extra: outwardly, outside
contero, -ere: beat, bruise, perh *discipline*
pabulum: food, nourishment
culpae.... pabulum: perh *the nourishment of sin*
jejunus (+ gen): abstinent, fasting from
labes, labis: stain, blot
prorsus: utterly, entirely, in fact
crimen, criminis: sin, offence

fructuosus a um: fruitful
tuis: (scil *tuis fidelibus, tuis populis*)
parcitas: smallness, insufficiency, niggardliness

23. Audit tyrannus anxius
Prudentius 348-410 → Mss

Audit tyrannus anxius Adesse regum principem, Qui nomen Israel regat Teneatque David regiam.	
Exclamat amens nuntio: "Successor instat, pellimur. Satelles, i, ferrum rape, Perfunde cunas sanguine."	 Ferrum, satelles, corripe
Quid proficit tantum nefas? Quid crimen Herodem juvat? Unus tot inter funera Impune Christus tollitur.	Quid proficit tantum nefas? Inter coaevi sanguinis Fluenta, solus integer Impune Christus tollitur

regia, -ae: royal house, royal throne (Δ *regius, -a, -um*)

amens, amentis: mad, frantic
nuntius: messenger
insto, instare, institi: be at hand, draw near, be here
satelles, satellitis: companion
ferrum rape: *take iron! grab a sword*
cunae, cunarum: cradle
perfundo, -ere: drench

quid: how?, what?
quid proficit: *what is the gain? how does he profit (from)?*
nefas (indeclinable): evil, wickedness
juvo, juvare: help, benefit
fluenta, -orum: flood, river
funus, funeris: funeral, death, murder
impune: safely, unharmed (*Christ alone is safely removed...*)

24. Aurea luce et decore roseo (M)
    Attrib Elpis c. 500, also attrib Paulinus of Aquileia c. 800
    Cf *Decora lux aeternitatis auream* (R)

Aurea luce et decore roseo
Lux lucis omne perfudisti saeculum,
Decorans caelos inclyto martyrio
Hac sacra die, quae dat reis veniam.

Janitor caeli, doctor orbis pariter,
Judices saecli, vera mundi lumina;
Per crucem alter, alter ense triumphans,
Vitae senatum laureati possident.

O felix Roma, quae tantorum principum
Es purpurata pretioso sanguine,
Non laude tua sed ipsorum meritis
Excellis omnem mundi pulchritudinem.

Sit Trinitati sempiterna gloria,
Honor, potestas, atque jubilatio,
In unitate, cui manet imperium,
Ex tunc et modo, per aeterna saecula.

roseus: rosy, rose-colored
decor, decoris: beauty, loveliness
perfundo, -ere: drench, bathe, wash
decoro, decorare: adorn, beautify
inclytus a um: glorious, renowned
venia: pardon, forgiveness

janitor: door-keeper, gatekeeper
judex, judicis: judge
ensis: sword
vitae senatum: *the senate of true life*
laureatus: prize-winner, laureate, having won
possideo, -ēre: occupy, have gained, have reached

purpuratus: ennobled, clad in purple, empurpled
excello, -ere: exceed

ex tunc: cf *ex hoc nunc et usque in saeculum*
modo: now

25. Aurora caelum purpurat (R)
Anon c. 400 Cf *Aurora lucis rutilat* (M)

Aurora caelum purpurat,
Aether resultat laudibus,
Mundus triumphans jubilat,
Horrens avernus infremit,

Rex ille dum fortissimus
De mortis inferno specu
Patrum senatum liberum
Educit ad vitae jubar.

purpuro, -are: make purple, empurple, redden
aether, aetheris: air, sky, firmament
resulto, -are: resound
horreo, -ēre: tremble, shudder
avernus: the lower world, the region of death
infremo, infremere, infremui: growl, bellow

infernus, -a, -um: lower, bottom, infernal
specus, -us: chasm, cavern
patrum senatum: *senate of (our) (fore)fathers, senate of the patriarchs*
liber, -a, -um: free
jubar, jubaris (neut): radiance

25. Aurora caelum purpurat (R)

Cujus sepulchrum plurimo
Custode signabat lapis,
Victor triumphat; et suo
Mortem sepulchro funerat.

Sat funeri, sat lacrimis,
Sat est datum doloribus;
Surrexit exstinctor necis,
Clamat coruscans angelus.

Ut sis perenne mentibus
Paschale, Jesu, gaudium,
A morte dira criminum
Vitae renatos libera.

custos, custodis: guard, sentry
plurimus: many a (guard), a large number of (guards)
signo, -are: seal, designate, seal up
funero, -are: bury
suo sepulchro: *by his own grave, in his grave*

sat (indeclinable): enough, sufficient
funus, funeris: funeral(s), death
sat est datum: *enough has been given*
dolor, doloris: pain, sorrow
exstinctor: annihilator, suppressor
nex, necis: death, murder
coruscans <coruscare: brilliant, flashing, glittering

perennis, perenne: permanent, perpetual
mens, mentis: (In the hymns often a synonym of *anima*, meaning "soul".)
dirus a um: dread, fearful
crimen, criminis: sin, crime
renascor, renasci, renatus: be reborn
libera: (Imperative)

26. Aurora jam spargit polum
Anon c. 400, attrib St Ambrose → VR

Aurora iam spargit polum;
Terris dies illabitur;
Lucis resultat spiculum;
Discedat omne lubricum.

Phantasma noctis decidat;	Phantasma noctis exsulet;
Mentis reatus subruat;	Mentis reatus corruat;
Quidquid tenebris horridum	
Nox attulit culpae, cadat.	

Ut mane illud ultimum,	Ut mane, quod nos ultimum
Quod praestolamur cernui,	Hic deprecamur cernui,
In lucem nobis effluat,	Cum luce nobis effluat,
Dum hoc canore concrepat.	

spargo, spargere, sparsi: strew, sprinkle, bestrew
polus: celestial vault, the heavens, sky
illabor, illabi, illapsus: flow in, settle on, fall upon
spiculum: point, tip
resulto, -are: spring back, rebound
discedo, -ere: go away, depart, withdraw
lubricus a um: slippery, uncertain, hazardous

phantasma, phantasmatis: dream, phantom, image
decido, -ere: fall away, vanish
exsulo, -are: be an exile, be banished
reatus, -ūs: guilt
subruo, -ere: be removed (Transitive verb used intransitively)
corruo, -ere: collapse, tumble down (Intransitive verb)
quidquid….culpae: *whatever….of fault, everything blameworthy which*
tenebris (Adverbial): *in the dark, in shadows*
horridus a um: fearful, awful, nasty
affero, affere, attuli: bring in, introduce
cado, cadere: fall, depart, go away

mane (Adv used as a noun): morning
praestolor, -ari: stand ready for, expect, await
cernuus, -a, -um: with bowed head, bowing down
effluo, effluere, effluxi: flow forth, break out, burst forth
canor, canoris: melody, chant (ie this hymn)
concrepo, -are: resound, harmonise

27. Aurora lucis rutilat (M)
c. 400, possibly St Ambrose Cf *Aurora caelum purpurat* (R)

Aurora lucis rutilat,
Caelum laudibus intonat,
Mundus exsultans jubilat,
Gemens infernus ululat:

Cum rex ille fortissimus,
Mortis confractis viribus,
Pede conculcans tartara,
Solvit a poena miseros.

Ille, qui clausus lapide
Custoditur sub milite,
Triumphans pompa nobili,
Victor surgit de funere.

rutilo, rutilare: redden, glow red, be golden red
intono, intonare, intonui: thunder, resound
gemo, gemere, gemui: sigh, groan, lament
ululo, ululare: howl, shriek

vires, virium: strength, powers
confrango, -ere: smash, destroy
conculco, -are: grind down, crush
tartara (neut plu): hell, the lower regions
solvo, -ere: release

pompa: display, parade
triumpho, -are: triumph, march in victory
funus, funeris: grave, death

27. Aurora lucis rutilat (M)

Solutis jam gemitibus
Et inferni doloribus,
Quia surrexit Dominus,
Resplendens clamat angelus.

Quaesumus, Auctor omnium,
In hoc paschali gaudio,
Ab omni mortis impetu
Tuum defende populum.

solvo, -ere: end, do away with
gemitus, -us: sighing, groaning
resplendeo, ēre: be brilliant, shine

impetus, -ūs: onrush, attack, assault

28. Aurora soli praevia
Anon c. 1900

Aurora soli praevia,
Felix salutis nuntia,
In noctis umbra plebs tua
Te, Virgo, supplex invocat.

Torrens nefastis fluctibus
Cunctos trahens voragine,
Leni residit aequore
Cum transit Arca Foederis.

Dum torret arescens humus,
Tu rore sola spargeris;
Tellure circum roridā,
Intacta sola permanes.

praevius, -a, -um: going before, leading the way for (+ dat)
nuntia, -ae: announcer, messenger

torrens, torrentis: surging waters, torrent (cf Joshua 3:13-17)
nefastus, -a, -um: irreligious, impious, wicked (*fluctibus*, abl of descrip)
vorago, voraginis: whirlpool, abyss, chasm (abl of means)
resido, residere, resedi: grow calm, settle down, abate (Δ *resideo, resedi*)
lenis, lenis: mild, calm, gentle
aequor, aequoris: water, *perh* surface, smooth water (abl of descrip)
Arca Foederis: Ark of the Covenant

torreo, torrere, torrui, tostus: dry up, parch, scorch
aresco, -ere: become dry, dry out
humus, -i (fem): earth, ground, soil
ros, roris (masc): dew
spargo, spargere: sprinkle
tu rore sola spargeris: *you alone are sprinkled by the dew*
tellus, telluris (fem): land, ground
roridus, -a, -um: dewy, bedewed (*tellure rorida*, abl absol)
circum (Adv): round about, all around

28. <u>Aurora soli praevia</u>

Fatale virus evomens
Attollit anguis verticem;
At tu draconis turgidum
Invicta conteris caput.

Mater benigna, respice
Fletus precesque supplicum,
Et dimicantes, tartari
Victrix, tuere ab hostibus.

fatalis, -e: deadly
virus, -i (neut): venom, poison
evomo, -ere, evomui: spit out, spew out
attollo, attollere: raise, lift up
anguis: serpent, snake
vertex: top, head
turgidus: swollen, distended
contero, -ere: crush, step on

supplex, supplicis: kneeling in prayer, begging
dimico, -are: struggle, contend, be in peril
tartarus, -i: tartarus, hell
tueor, tueri: watch over, preserve, defend

29. Aurora solis nuntia
Evaristo d'Anversa, c. 1955

Aurora solis nuntia
Florumque mensi praevia,
Fabri sonoram malleo
Domum salutat Nazarae.

Salve, caput domesticum,
Sub quo supremus Artifex,
Sudore salso roridus,
Exercet artem patriam.

nuntia: announcer, messenger
praevius, -a, -um: going before, ushering in, introducing (+dat)
flos, floris: flower
mensis, mensis: month
faber, fabri: workman, carpenter
sonorus, -a, -um: ringing with (abl), full of the sound of (abl)
malleus: hammer
domum: (fem)
saluto, -are: greet, welcome
Nazara, -ae: Nazareth

salve: hail!, greetings!
domesticus: of the house, of the family, of the household
sudor, sudoris: sweat
salsus a um: salty
roridus: bedewed, moist
exerceo, -ēre: perform, exercise, work at
ars, artis: craft, trade
patrius, -a, -um: of (his) father

Note: This hymn was composed for the Feast of Saint Joseph the Workman on May 1st. The feast was introduced into the liturgical calendar by Pius XII.

29. Aurora solis nuntia

Altis locatus sedibus
Celsaeque Sponsae proximus,
Adesto nunc clientibus,
Quos vexat indigentia.

Absintque vis et jurgia,
Fraus omnis a mercedibus;
Victūs cibique copiam
Mensuret una parcitas.

O Trinitatis Unitas,
Joseph precante, quaesumus,
In pace nostros omnium
Gressūs viamque dirige.

loco, locare: place, establish, settle
sedes, sedis: seat, abode (plu for sing)
celsus, -a, -um: lofty, elevated
sponsa: bride
cliens, clientis: *your* follower, companion
vexo, -are: harass, worry, disquiet
indigentia: need, want, poverty

vis, vis: violence
jurgium: quarrel, strife
fraus, fraudis: cheating, fraud
merces, mercedis: wages, salary
victus, -ūs: victuals, provisions, means of living
cibus, cibi: food, nourishment
mensuro, mensurare: mete out, measure
copia: supply, amount
parcitas, parcitatis: a sparing amount, a frugal quantity

precor, pracari: pray
gressus, -ūs: step

30. Ave maris stella
    Anon c. 700

Ave maris stella,
Dei Mater alma,
Atque semper Virgo,
Felix caeli porta.

Sumens illud Ave
Gabrielis ore,
Funda nos in pace,
Mutans Hevae nomen.

Solve vincla reis,
Profer lumen caecis,
Mala nostra pelle,
Bona cuncta posce.

sumo, sumere: take, accept (*accepting that Ave from the mouth of Gabriel*)

vincla: = vincula
caecus a um: blind
posco, poscere, poposci: beg, ask
cunctus a um: all

Note:

Mutans nomen: By receiving the *Ave* of Gabriel, our Lady changes the name from *Eva* to *Ave*. When we spell the name *Heva*, with an H, this anagram is obscured. There is more. *Maria* (Mary) and *maria* (seas) differ in the quantity of one vowel: hence the image, *Maria = stella maris*. *Porta* means *gate*; but *porto, portare* with the same stem and the same thematic vowel means *carry*, as in *carry a child*. *Malum* means both *evil* and *apple*. The word *tu* or *te* is iteratively embedded in other words, culminating in *collaetemur*.

30. Ave maris stella

Monstra te esse matrem;
Sumat per te preces,
Qui pro nobis natus,
Tulit esse tuus.

Mss Monstra esse matrem;
Sumat per te precem

Virgo singularis,
Inter omnes mitis,
Nos culpis solutos,
Mites fac et castos.

Vitam praesta puram,
Iter para tutum,
Ut videntes Jesum
Semper collaetemur.

Sit laus Deo Patri,
Summo Christo decus,
Spiritui Sancto,
Tribus honor unus.

monstro, monstrare: show, disclose
fero, ferre, tuli: bear, endure, accept (*bore to be thine*)

mitis, mitis: meek, mild
inter omnes: among, ie *beyond* all others
culpa: fault, sin
solvo, solvere: release, free (us from sin)
castus a um: pure, chaste

paro, parare: prepare
tutus, -a, -um: safe, secure

decus, decoris: honor, glory
tribus: (dat of *tres* = *three*)

31. Beata caeli gaudia

Beata caeli gaudia,
Confessionis praemium,
Christi, o fideles asseclae,
Jam possidetis affatim.

Laudes benignis auribus
Audite, quas effundimus
Nos exsules de patria,
Vobis sacrato cantico.

Amore Christi perciti
Crucem tulistis asperam,
Obedientes, impigri
Et caritate fervidi.

praemium: reward
adsecla, -ae (Masc): follower, attendant
affatim: abundantly, sufficiently

percitus a um: moved, roused
asper, aspera, asperum: cruel, harsh, hopeless
impiger, impigra, impigrum: unwearied, willing, diligent
fervidus: burning, passionate, glowing

Note:

This hymn is found in the *Commune Sanctorum pro aliquibus locis*, introduced into the BR in 1914. There were four such Commons, and they were rarely used. They have never been part of the universal liturgical calendar. They are not found in the BM. Some editions of the BR also omit them. Five other hymns in this category are: *Inclitos Christi famulos, Nobiles Christi famulas, Plenis resultet vocibus, Si lege prisca fortibus,* and *Vox sonat Sponsi*, qqv infra.

31. Beata caeli gaudia

Sprevistis artes daemonum,
Saevumque averni principem:
Christum fatendo moribus,
Migrastis inter sidera.

Jam nunc potiti gloriā
Adeste votis omnium,
Ardenter exoptantium
Exempla vestra prosequi.

Ut, Christe, Rex piissime,
Horum precatu, noxia
Nobis remittas crimina,
Clamamus ore supplici.

sperno, spernere, sprevi: disdain, avoid, condemn
avernus: underworld
fateor, fateri, fassus: confess, acknowledge
mos, moris: custom, behavior (*by your way of life, by your actions)*
migro, -are: migrate, travel,voyage

potior, potiri, potitus (+abl): receive, obtain
exopto, -are: desire earnestly, long for

precatus, -ūs: prayer, entreaty
noxius: harmful, injurious, criminal
crimen, criminis: offence, fault, sin
supplex, supplicis: prayerful, submissive
ore supplici: *with prayerful mouth, with words of prayer*

32. Beata nobis gaudia
Anon c. 500 → VR

Beata nobis gaudia
Anni reduxit orbita,
Cum Spiritus Paraclitus
Effulsit in discipulos. Illapsus est Apostolis

Ignis vibrante lumine
Linguae figuram detulit,
Verbis ut essent proflui,
Et caritate fervidi.

Linguis loquuntur omnium;
Turbae pavent gentilium,
Musto madere deputant
Quos Spiritus repleverat.

orbita, -ae: track, path, cycle
reduco, -ere: bring back, restore
effulgeo, effulgēre, effulsi: shine forth, flash out
illabor, illabi, illapsus: flow into, fall on, penetrate (+dat)

vibro, -are: glitter, scintillate
figura: form, likeness
defero, deferre, detuli: bear (*bore the form of, was in the form of*)
profluus, -a, -um: flowing forth, fluent, flowing
fervidus a um: burning, fervent, passionate

paveo, pavere, pavi: be astonished, be amazed, be afraid
gentilis, -e: (*gentilium* here = *gentium*)
mustum: fermenting wine (cf Acts 2:13: *musto pleni sunt*)
madeo, -ēre: be awash in, be full of, be drunk on
deputo, -are: reckon, consider
repleo, ēre, replevi: fill

32. Beata nobis gaudia

Patrata sunt haec mystice,
Paschae peracto tempore,
Sacro dierum numero, — Sacro dierum circulo
Quo lege fit remissio.

Te nunc, Deus piissime,
Vultu precamur cernuo:
Illapsa nobis caelitus
Largire dona Spiritūs.

Dudum sacrata pectora
Tuā replesti gratiā;
Dimitte nostra crimina,
Et da quieta tempora.

patro, patrare: bring to pass, accomplish
perago, peregi, peractus: complete, finish
sacro dierum numero: (in apposition to *tempore*)
circulus: round, cycle
lege: *by law*

cernuus a um: downcast
illabor, illabi, illapsus (+dat): flow into, fall on, penetrate
caelitus (Abv): from heaven
largior, largiri, largitus: give bountifully, lavish

dudum: but now, recently
sacro, sacrare: consecrate, dedicate, hallow
replesti: (= *replevisti*)

33. Beate Pastor Petre (R)
Attrib Elpis, c. 500

Cf *Jam bone Pastor Petre* (M)
Doctor egregie Paule (M)

Beate pastor, Petre, clemens accipe
Voces precantum, criminumque vincula
Verbo resolve, cui potestas tradita
Aperire terris caelum, apertum claudere.

Egregie Doctor, Paule, mores instrue,
Et nostra tecum pectora in caelum trahe;
Velata dum meridiem cernat fides,
Et solis instar sola regnet caritas.

Sit Trinitati sempiterna gloria,
Honor, potestas, atque jubilatio,
In unitate, quae gubernat omnia,
Per universa aeternitatis saecula.

precantum: (Alternative form of *precantium*)
resolvo, -ere: unbind, release
tradita: (scil *est*)
terris: to earth, from earth
apertum claudere: *(and) to close what is ope*n (the Petrine *potestas clavium*)

egregius a um: exceptional, oustanding
mos, moris: custom, behaviour, way of life
mores instrue: *teach (us) how to behave, how to live*
velo, velare: hide, veil
cerno, -ere: discern, see
dum: until (*dum* + subjunc denotes intention or expectation)
meridies: high noon (an eschatological image; cf *solis* in next line.)
instar (indecl): as mighty as, in the form of (+ gen)

guberno, -are: control, direct

Note:

The hagiographic attribution of hymns to Elpis may be problematic. However, the attribution does testify to the possibility that some hymns in the breviary were composed by women.

34. Bella dum late furerent
c. 1900

Bella dum late furerent, et urbes
Caede fraternā gemerent cruentae,
Adfuit Virgo, nova semper edens
Munera Matris.

En vocat septem famulos, fideles
Ut sibi in luctu recolant dolores,
Quos tulit Jesus, tulit ipsa consors
Sub cruce Nati.

Illico parent Dominae vocanti;
Splendidis tectis opibusque spretis,
Urbe secedunt procul in Senari
Abdita montis.

dum: because, while (here *dum* = *cum*)
late: widely, on all sides, everywhere
furo, furere: rage
caedes, caedis: slaughter, carnage
gemo, gemere, gemui: groan, sigh, lament
cruentus a um: bloody, flowing with blood, blood-thirsty (*urbes....cruentae*)
edo, edere, edidi, editus: give out, produce

en: behold!
famulus: servant
luctus, -ūs: sorrow, mourning
recolo, -ere: recollect, recall
consors, consortis: companion (ie the Mother of the Lord)

illico: forthwith, at once, there and then
pareo, parere, parui (+dat): obey
tectum: house, dwelling, roof
opes, opium: riches, wealth
sperno, sprevi, spretus: spurn, despise, reject
secedo, -ere: withdraw, go away
urbe: *from the city*
Mons Senarius: Mount Senarius (*Senari* is genitive)
abdita, -orum: hidden places, remote regions

34. <u>Bella dum late furerent</u>

Corpora hic poenis cruciant acerbis,
Sontium labes hominum piantes;
Hic prece avertunt lacrimisque fusis
Numinis iram.

Perdolens Mater fovet, atque amictum
Ipsa lugubrem monet induendum;
Agminis sancti pia coepta surgunt,
Mira patescunt.

Palmes in bruma viridans honores
Nuntiat patrum; proprios Mariae
Ore lactenti vocitant puelli
Nomine Servos.

crucio, cruciare: torment, torture, rack
acerbus a um: harsh, violent, severe
sons, sontis (Adj): guilty, criminal, evil-doing
labes, labis: stain, blot, fault
pio, piare: atone for, expiate
Numen, Numinis: Divinity

perdoleo, ēre: grieve deeply, be profoundly sorrowful
lugubris, -e: of mourning, mournful
amictus, ūs: cloak, garment (*warns that her cloak of mourning must be put on)*
agmen, agminis: band, cohort, group
(coepio), coepi, coeptus: commence (*devout deeds once begun*)
surgo, -ere: rise up, swell, increase
patesco, patescere, patui: become visible, be manifest

palmes, palmitis: young branch
bruma: winter-time, the depth of winter
viridor, viridari: grow green, flourish
nuntio, -are: foretell, predict, declare
patrum: *of the Fathers* (ie of the Servite order)
puellus: little boy, baby (*breast-feeding babies cry out that….)*
lacteo, ēre: suckle
ore lactenti: *with suckling mouth*
vocito, -are: name, call, designate (supply *illos esse*)

34. Bella dum late furerent

Sit decus Patri, genitaeque Proli,
Et tibi, compar utriusque Virtus,
Spiritus semper, Deus unus omni
Temporis aevo.

proles, prolis: (This noun refers to the *Son*, but is feminine in gender.)
compar, comparis: like, equal (+ gen)
Virtus, Spiritus, Deus: (all three vocative. cf *alme* in VM.)
aevum: age, expanse (of time), period

The monastic doxology is:

Gloria Patri genitaeque Proli,
Et tibi, compar utriusque semper
Spiritus alme, Deus unus, omni
Tempore saecli.

35. Caelestis Agni nuptias
Francesco Lorenzini, c. 1700

Caelestis Agni nuptias,
O Juliana, dum petis,
Domum paternam deseris,
Chorumque ducis Virginum.

Sponsumque suffixum cruci
Noctes diesque dum gemis,
Doloris icta cuspide
Sponsi refers imaginem.

nuptiae, nuptiarum: wedding, marriage
desero, deserere, deserui, desertus: leave, forsake, abandon
chorus, chori: dance, choir, chorus
(chorum) duco: conduct, lead (cf *uxorem duco = take a wife, marry*)

sponsus: bridegroom, (her) betrothed
suffigo, -figere, -fixus: fasten
cruci suffixus: *crucified, nailed to the cross*
noctes diesque: all day and all night (acc of extent of time)
gemo, gemere, gemui: sigh over, bewail (*sponsum* is dir obj)
cuspis, cuspidis: lance, spear, sting (noun)
ico, icere, ici, ictus: stab, smite, strike
refero, referre: recall, call to mind

35. Caelestis Agni nuptias

Quin septiformi vulnere
Fles ad genu Deiparae;
Sed crescit infusa fletu,
Flammasque tollit caritas.

Hinc morte fessam proximā
Non usitato te modo
Solatur et nutrit Deus,
Dapem supernam porrigens.

Aeterne rerum Conditor,
Aeterne Fili par Patri,
Et par utrique Spiritus,
Soli tibi sit gloria.

quin (in a principal clause): verily, forsooth
septiformis, -is: seven-fold
septiformi vulnere: *with sevenfold wound* (ablative of description)
fleo, flere: weep, cry
ad genu: *at the knee*
Deipara: God-bearing, Theotokos
infundo, -fundere, -fudi, -fusus: pour in, mix, mingle (*caritas infusa fletu*)
tollo: elevate, raise (not *remove. caritas raises the flames of love*)
caritas: (subject both of *crescit* and of *tollit*)

hinc: hence, thereafter
fessus, -a, -um: wearied, weakened, exhausted (*by the approach of death*)
usitatus a um: familiar, usual, customary
solor, solari: comfort, console
nutrio, nutrire: nourish, feed
daps, dapis: feast, banquet
porrigo, porrigere, porrexi: spread out, lay out

par, paris: equal

36. <u>Caelestis aulae nuntius</u>
Eustachius Sirena OP, ob 1796
or Augustine Ricchini, ob. 1779

Caelestis aulae Nuntius,
Arcana pandens Numinis,
Plenam salutat gratiā
Dei Parentem Virginem.

Virgo propinquam sanguine
Matrem Joannis visitat,
Qui, clausus alvo, gestiens
Adesse Christum nuntiat.

Verbum, quod ante saecula
E mente Patris prodiit,
E Matris alvo Virginis,
Mortalis Infans nascitur.

Nuntius: (The angel Gabriel at the Annunciation)
arcanus, -a, -um: hidden, secret, private
pando, pandere, pandi, passus: unfold, lay open
parens, parentis: parent, mother

propinquus: close, related, kindred
qui: (Joannes)
alvus: womb
clausus alvo: *shut up in the womb, enclosed in the womb*
gestio, -ire: leap, leap for joy

prodeo, prodire, prodii: go forth, come forth
nascor, nasci, natus: be born

36. Caelestis aulae nuntius

Templo puellus sistitur,
Legique paret Legifer,
Hic se Redemptor paupere
Pretio redemptus immolat.

Quem jam dolebat perditum,
Mox laeta Mater invenit
Ignota doctis mentibus
Edisserentem Filium.

puellus: little boy
sisto, sistere: convey, bring
pareo, parere, parui (+dat): obey
pauper, pauperis (adj): poor, small, scanty, meagre
immolo, -are: offer, sacrifice

quem: (Redemptor)
doleo: feel pain, be hurt (Transitive. *quem* = direct object)
perdo, perdere, perdidi, perditus: lose
ignota (neut acc plu): *unknown matters, things unknown*
doctus (< docēre): learn-ed, instructed, educated
edissero, edisserui, edissertus: set forth in full, explain

Note:

In what sense is the Redeemer redeemed?

The answer is in the Old Law. See Jerusalem Bible, Luke 2: 22-24, notes h and i. French text, notes d and e. See also New Catholic Encyclopedia, svv *Firstborn* and *Purification of Mary*.

37. Caelestis urbs Jerusalem (R)
Anon c. 700, Revised 1632
Cf *Urbs Jerusalem beata* (M) and *Angularis fundamentum* (M)

Caelestis urbs Jerusalem,
Beata pacis visio,
Quae celsa de viventibus
Saxis ad astra tolleris,
Sponsaeque ritu cingeris
Mille angelorum milibus.

O sorte nupta prosperā,
Dotata Patris gloriā,
Respersa Sponsi gratiā,
Regina formosissima,
Christo jugata Principi,
Caeli corusca civitas.

urbs: (Vocative. There is no main verb in this strophe or the next.)
visio, visionis: vision
celsus a um: lofty, high
saxum, saxi: stone
tollo, tollere: lift, lift up, raise
sponsa, -ae: bride
ritus, -us: ceremony, ritual, rite
cingo, -ere: surround, wreathe, crown

sors, sortis (fem): fate, lot, portion
nupta, nuptae: bride, wife
prosperus, -a, -um: fortunate, favoured, happy
doto, dotare: give as dowry, endow
respergo, -ere: sprinkle, bestrew, spead freely
formosus: comely, beautiful
jugo, jugare: bind, marry, join in wedlock
coruscus, -a, -um: gleaming, glittering

Note

The morphology and syntax of the word *mille* are irregular. Although the core meaning is constant (viz. 1000), the grammatical form is variable.

Mille is an indeclinable adjective, singular in form. *Milia* is an inflected noun, plural in form. It is regularly followed by the genitive.

Here *mille* (the adjective) modifies *milibus* (a noun in the ablative plural). The phrase means, "by a thousand thousands of angels".

37. Caelestis urbs Jerusalem (R)

Hic margaritis emicant
Patentque cunctis ostia;
Virtute namque praeviā
Mortalis illuc ducitur,
Amore Christi percitus
Tormenta quisquis sustinet.

Scalpri salubris ictibus
Et tunsione plurimā,
Fabri polita malleo
Hanc saxa molem construunt,
Aptisque juncta nexibus
Locantur in fastigio.

margarita: pearl
emico, -are: glitter with (pearls)
pateo, -ēre: be open, lie open
ostium: door, entrance, gateway
praevius a um: going before, leading the way, earlier
percitus a um: driven, motivated, aroused
quisquis: everyone who, whoever
sustineo, -ēre: endure, suffer

scalprum, -i: knife, chisel
salubris, -bre: wholesome, salutary
ictus, -ūs: stroke, cut, thrust
tunsio, tunsionis: beating, striking
polio, polire, polivi, politus: refine, smooth, finish, polish
faber, fabri: carpenter, builder
malleus, mallei: hammer
moles, molis (fem): edifice, great structure, building
construo, -ere: construct, assemble, build
aptus, -a, -um: fitted, firm, suitable
nexus, nexibus: connection, interweaving
loco, locare: put in place, arrange
fastigium, fastigii: summit, edge, pediment

38. Caeli Deus sanctissime
Attrib Saint Gregory the Great, c.600.
Possibly earlier. → VR 1632

Caeli Deus sanctissime,	
Qui lucidum centrum poli	Qui lucidas mundi plagas
Candore pingis igneo,	
Augens decoro lumine:	
Quarto die qui flammeam	
Solis rotam constituens,	Dum solis accendis rotam
Lunae ministras ordinem,	
Vagosque cursus siderum:	

centrum, -i: center, mid-point
polus, -i: vault, sky
lucidus a um: light, bright
plaga: region, zone (Δ *plaga=wound*, and *plaga=trap*)
candor, candoris: radiance, brightness, splendor
pingo, pingere, pinxi, pinctus: paint, depict
igneus a um: fiery, flaming, glowing
decorus, a, um: beauteous, lovely
augeo, -ēre: increase, enrich, enhance (Supply a direct object from context.)

quartā die qui: *and who on the fourth day, and on the fourth day you*
flammeus a um: flaming
rota -ae: wheel, disk, orbit
constituo, -ere: set, fix, establish
accendo, -ere: kindle, enflame
ministro, -are: provide, supply, furnish
vagus a um: wandering
cursus, cursūs: course, path

38. Caeli Deus sanctissime

Ut noctibus vel lumini,
Diremptionis terminum,
Primordiis et mensium
Signum dares notissimum:

Illumina cor hominum, Expelle noctem cordium
Absterge sordes mentium,
Resolve culpae vinculum,
Everte moles criminum.

noctibus vel lumini: *to the night-time or to the light of day*
terminus: boundary, limit, border (supply *dares* after *terminum*)
diremptio, -onis: separation
primordia (neut pl): beginnings, commencement
mensis, mensis: month (here the lunar month)
signum.... notissimum: (ie the phases of the moon)

abstergeo, abstergēre, abstersi: wipe away, wash away
resolvo, -ere: release, loosen, unlock
sordes, sordium: filth, corruption
everto, -ere: overturn, destroy, remove
moles, molis: heap, pile, load

Note:

Diremptionis terminum: This is the epexegetic or "explanatory" genitive. For example: *caritatis virtus*.

Diremptionis terminum means a boundary (terminum) which makes a separation (diremptionis).

....noctibus vel lumini
Diremptionis terminum

"....to night and day-light
A border of separation, "

We read *noctibus vel lumini* as a single noun-phrase. The comma after *noctibus*—in some editions—will then seem awkward.

39. Caelitum Joseph
Anon c. 1500

Caelitum, Joseph, decus atque nostrae
Certa spes vitae, columenque mundi,
Quas tibi laeti canimus, benignus
Suscipe laudes.

Te Sator rerum statuit pudicae
Virginis sponsum, voluitque Verbi
Te patrem dici, dedit et ministrum
Esse salutis.

Tu Redemptorem stabulo jacentem,
Quem chorus Vatum cecinit futurum,
Aspicis gaudens, humilisque natum
Numen adoras.

caeles, caelitis: heavenly, celestial being
decus, decoris: grace, glory, honor
columen, columinis: pillar, column

sator, satoris: planter, sower, author
statuo, stauere, statui: set up, establish, ordain
pudicus a um: modest, chaste
minister, ministri: servant, helper, minister

stabulum: stable, stall (*in stabulo*)
jaceo, -ēre: lie
vates, vatis: prophet, seer, foreteller
numen, numinis (neut): divinity, God

39. Caelitum Joseph

Rex Deus regum, dominator orbis,
Cujus ad nutum tremit inferorum
Turba, cui pronus famulatur aether,
Se tibi subdit.

Laus sit excelsae Triadi perennis,
Quae tibi praebens superos honores
Det tuis nobis meritis beatae
Gaudia vitae.

nutus, nutūs: nod
cujus: (Antecedent both of *cujus* and of *cui* is *Deus*)
inferi, inferorum: lower beings, beings below, inhabitants of the underworld
famulor, famulari: be a slave, serve
pronus a um: bowing, bending, abject
aether, aetheris: sky, heaven, firmament
subdit: (Subject of *subdit* is *Deus*)

trias, triadis (fem, Greek): Trinity, Triad
perennis, -e: everlasting, perpetual
superus a um: exalted, heavenly

Note

Throughout this hymn, including the doxology, the pronouns *tu, te, tibi* refer to Saint Joseph.

40. Caelo Redemptor praetulit
Anon, before 1700

Caelo Redemptor praetulit
Felicis alvum Virginis,
Ubi futura victima
Mortale corpus induit.

Haec Virgo nobis edidit
Nostrae salutis auspicem,
Qui nos redemit sanguine,
Poenas crucemque pertulit.

Spes laeta nostro e pectore
Pellat timores anxios;
Haec quippe nostras lacrimas
Precesque defert Filio.

caelo: (Dative)
alvum, alvi: womb
praefero, praeferre, praetuli: prefer (*alvum praetulit caelo*)

edo, edere, edidi: produce, give birth to, beget
auspex, auspicis: founder, author, guarantor
redimo, redimere, redemi: redeem, buy back, recover
perfero, perferre: endure, suffer, accept

pello, pellere: drive, expel
haec: she
quippe: of course, indeed (The *quippe* clause explains the previous clause.)
defero, deferre: carry, bear, give, offer
Filio: *to the Son, to her son*

40. Caelo Redemptor praetulit

Voces Parentis excipit,
Votisque Natus annuit;
Hanc quisque semper diligat,
Rebusque in arctis invocet.

Sit Trinitati gloria,
Quae Matris intactum sinum
Ditavit almo germine;
Laus sit per omne saeculum.

voces parentis: *the words of his mother, the voice of his mother*
excipio, excipere, excepi: receive, hear gladly
votis: *to her wishes, to her prayers*
annuo, annuere, annui: assent, defer, submit (Pres tense, like *excipit*)
quisque: everyone, everybody
hanc: her
artus, -a, -um (arctus): needy, difficult

sinus, sinūs: fold, interior
dito, ditare: enrich
germen, germinis: off-shoot, bud, sprout

41. Christe Redemptor omnium, Conserva (M)
Rabanus Maurus, ob 856 Cf *Placare Christe servulis* (R)

Christe Redemptor omnium,
Conserva tuos famulos,
Beatae semper Virginis
Placatus sanctis precibus.

Beata quoque agmina
Caelestium spirituum,
Praeterita, praesentia,
Futura mala pellite.

Vates aeterni Judicis,
Apostolique Domini,
Suppliciter exposcimus
Salvari vestris precibus.

Martyres Dei incliti
Confessoresque lucidi,
Vestris orationibus
Nos ferte in caelestibus.

placo, placare: appease, pacify (*placatus*, altho nom, modifies *Christe*)

agmen, agminis: multitude, throng, host (*agmina* is voc pl)
mala: *evils* (dir obj of *pellite*)

vates, vatis: Prophet, Speaker (voc plu)
apostolique: *and ye Apostles* (voc)
exposco, -ere: request, beg

in caelestibus: *into (among) the heavenly (multitude)*

41. Christe Redemptor omnium, Conserva (M)

Chori sanctarum virginum,
Monachorumque omnium,
Simul cum Sanctis omnibus
Consortes Christi facite.

Gentem auferte perfidam
Credentium de finibus,
Ut Christo laudes debitas
Persolvamus alacriter

Gloria Patri ingenito
Ejusque Unigenito,
Una cum Sancto Spiritu,
In sempiterna saecula.

consors, consortis: sharer, companion, fellow (supply *nos*)

perfidus a um: unbelieving, faithless, perfidious
fines, finium: lands, territories
persolvo, -ere: give, render, offer, pay
alacriter: gladly, swiftly, with enthusiasm

ingenitus a um: unborn
una cum: *as one with, together with*

42. Christe Redemptor omnium, Ex Patre (M)
Anon, c. 500 Cf *Jesu Redemptor omnium, Quem* (R)

Christe Redemptor omnium,
Ex Patre Patris unice,
Solus ante principium
Natus ineffabiliter.

Tu lumen, tu splendor Patris,
Tu spes perennis omnium,
Intende quas fundunt preces
Tui per orbem famuli.

Memento, salutis Auctor,
Quod nostri quondam corporis,
Ex illibata Virgine
Nascendo, formam sumpseris.

natus: (Nominative for vocative)
ineffabilis: unsayable, inexpressible

intendo, -ere (+acc): hear, hearken to

quondam: once, at an earlier time
corporis: (*nostri corporis….formam*)
sumpseris (<sumere): (Perf subjunc, after *memento quod*)

Note

Natus, ie born of the Father. The earthly birth of the Lord is expressed by the words *Ex illibata Virgine nascendo* in the third strophe.

42. Christe Redemptor omnium, Ex Patre (M)

Sic praesens testatur dies,
Currens per anni circulum,
Quod solus a sede Patris
Mundi salus adveneris.

Hunc caelum, terra, hunc mare,
Hunc omne quod in eis est,
Auctorem adventūs tui
Laudans exsultat cantico.

Nos quoque, qui sancto tuo
Redempti sanguine sumus,
Ob diem natalis tui
Hymnum novum concinimus.

testor, testari, testatus: make known, bear witness, testify
curro, currere: run, pass
circulus: cycle, course
quod: (*dies testatur quod....adveneris*, perf subjunc as above)
salus, salutis: (Pred nom: *you alone.... have come, the salvation of the world*)

hunc....auctorem: (ie *Patris* in previous strophe)
adventus, -ūs: coming, arrival

ob + acc: by reason of, on account of
natalis, -is: birth, birthday (also an adjective, eg *diem natalem*)
concino, concinere: sing together, sing in harmony

43. Christe sanctorum decus (M)
Attrib Rabanus Maurus, ob 856
Cf *Christe sanctorum decus* (R)

Christe, sanctorum decus Angelorum,
Rector humani generis et auctor,
Nobis aeternum tribue benigne
Scandere caelum.

Angelum pacis Michael ad istam
Caelitus mitti rogitamus aulam,
Nobis ut crebro veniente crescant
Prospera cuncta.

Angelus fortis Gabriel, ut hostem
Pellat antiquum, volitet ab alto;
Saepius templum veniat ad istud
Visere nostrum.

decus, decoris: glory, beauty
rector, rectoris: governor, guide
tribuo, tribuere: grant
scando, scandere (+acc): rise up to, mount up to

caelitus (Adv): from heaven
rogito, -are: ask eagerly, keep asking
ad istam.... aulam: *to this church, to this hall*
crebro: frequently, many times
cresco, crescere, crevi: grow, increase
prospera cuncta: *all favorable things, all good fortune*

volito, volitare: fly
ab alto: *from on high, from heaven*
saepius: often, more often, regularly
templum.... ad istud...nostrum: *to this our temple*
viso, visere: behold, survey (Infin to express purpose)

43. Christe sanctorum decus (M)

Angelum nobis medicum salutis
Mitte de caelis Raphael, ut omnes
Sanet aegrotos, pariterque nostros
Dirigat actus.

Hinc Dei nostri Genitrix Maria,
Totus et nobis chorus Angelorum
Semper assistat, simul et beata
Concio tota.

Praestet hoc nobis Deitas beata
Patris ac Nati pariterque Sancti
Spiritūs, cujus reboat in omni
Gloria mundo.

medicus: physician, healer
salutis: *physician of (our) well-being, provider of health*
sano, sanare: heal, cure
aegrotus a um: sick, diseased
pariter: equally, likewise
actus, -ūs: behaviour, acts, life

hinc: hence, next
assisto, assistere (c dat pers): stand near, stand by
concio, concionis (contio): assembly, gathering (ie of all the saints)

rebo-o, rebo-are: resound, re-echo
gloria: (Nominative. subj of *reboat*)
mundo: (*cujus gloria resonat in omni mundo*)

44. Christe sanctorum decus (R)
Cf *Christe sanctorum decus* (M)

Christe, sanctorum decus angelorum,
Gentis humanae Sator et Redemptor,
Caelitum nobis tribuas beatas
Scandere sedes.

Angelus pacis Michael in aedes
Caelitus nostras veniat, serenae
Auctor ut pacis lacrimosa in orcum
Bella releget.

Angelus fortis Gabriel, ut hostes
Pellat antiquos, et amica caelo,
Quae triumphator statuit per orbem,
Templa revisat.

decus, decoris: glory, grace, beauty
sator, satoris: planter, sower, seeder, author
caelites, caelitum (< caeles): heavenly, celestial (beings)
tribuo, tribuere: grant (hortatory subjunctive, as if imperative)
scando, scandere: mount, sit on

aedes, aedis (fem): temple, sanctuary
caelitus (Adv): celestially, from heaven
serenus a um: fair, bright, joyous, serene (*ut auctor pacis serenae*)
orcus, orci: the underworld, the lower regions
lacrimosus: tearful, lamentable, doleful
relego, relegare: banish, exile, expel

Gabriel: (supply *veniat*)
amicus, -a, -um: friendly to, pleasing to, favored of (*templa amica caelo quae*)
triumphator: victor, conqueror (ie the Lord. cf Ant Mag, II Vesp Ascensionis)
statuo, statuere, statui: establish, set up
reviso, revisere (+acc): return to, come back to

44. Christe sanctorum decus (R)

Angelus nostrae medicus salutis,
Adsit e caelo Raphael ut omnes
Sanet aegrotos, dubiosque vitae
Dirigat actus.

Virgo dux pacis Genetrixque lucis,
Et sacer nobis chorus angelorum
Semper assistat, simul et micantis
Regia caeli.

Praestet hoc nobis Deitas beata
Patris ac Nati pariterque Sancti
Spiritūs, cujus resonat per omnem
Gloria mundum.

medicus, medici: physician, doctor
sano, sanare: heal
aegrotus a um: sick, diseased
dubius: uncertain, doubtful, wavering
actus, -us: act

genetrix: (also spelled *genitrix*)
assisto, assistere, astiti: stand by, attend (*nobis*)
micans (< mico): radiant, glittering, luminous
regia, -ae: royal court

resono, -are: resound, echo
gloria: (Nominative)

Note

Deitas beata.... Patris ac Nati, "the blessed Godhead of the Father and the Son", or "the blessed Godhead, namely the Father and the Son". Epexegetic genitive.

45. Christo profusum sanguinem (R)
Cf *Aeterna Christi munera, Et martyrum victorias* (M)

Christo profusum sanguinem,
Et martyrum victorias,
Dignamque caelo lauream
Laetis sequamur vocibus.

Terrore victo saeculi
Poenisque spretis corporis,
Mortis sacrae compendio
Vitam beatam possident.

Traduntur igni Martyres
Et bestiarum dentibus;
Armata saevit ungulis
Tortoris insani manus.

Christo profusum: *shed for Christ*
martyr,martyris: martyr
laurea: prize, reward, honor, laurel
dignam caelo: *deserving of heaven, worthy of heaven*
laetus a um: joyful, happy, rejoicing
sequor, sequi: recount, relate

sperno, spernere, sprevi, spretus: disdain, despise, ignore
compendium: short-cut, swift path

armo, armare: arm, equip with weapons (*armata....manus* subj of *saevit*)
saevio, saevire: rage, be fierce
ungula: hook, claw, talon (instrument of torture)
tortor, tortoris: executioner, torturer
insanus a um: mad, raging, frantic

45. Christo profusum sanguinem (R)

Nudata pendent viscera,
Sanguis sacratus funditur;
Sed permanent immobiles,
Vitae perennis gratiā.

Te nunc, Redemptor, quaesumus,
Ut Martyrum consortio
Jungas precantes servulos,
In sempiterna saecula.

nudo, nudare: expose, lay bare
pendeo, pendēre: hang out, hang down (Δ *pendo, péndere*)
sacratus a um (< sacrare): hallowed, consecrated
immobilis, -e: unmoving, unaffected, steady
perennis, -e: everlasting
gratiā + gen: for the sake of

consortium: company, fellowship

46. Claro paschali gaudio (M)
    c. 400, possibly Saint Ambrose
    This hymn forms part of the complete text of *Aurora lucis rutilat*, qv.
    Cf *Paschale mundo gaudium* (R)

Claro paschali gaudio
Sol mundo nitet radio,
Cum Christum jam Apostoli
Visu cernunt corporeo.

Ostensa sibi vulnera
In Christi carne fulgida,
Resurrexisse Dominum
Voce fatentur publicā.

clarus: bright, shining, brilliant
niteo, nitēre (+dat): shine on, shine over
radius: beam, ray (*radio*: abl of means)
visus, -ūs: sight, appearance
cerno, cernere, crevi, certus: perceive, discern

ostensus a um (late form of *ostentus* < *ostendere*): shown, exhibited
sibi: *to them* (post-classical, not reflexive)
fulgidus: dazzling, radiant, glorious
fateor, fateri: declare, confess, acknowledge

46. Claro paschali gaudio (M)

Rex Christe clementissime,
Tu corda nostra posside,
Ut tibi laudes debitas
Reddamus omni tempore.

Quaesumus, Auctor omnium,
In hoc paschali gaudio:
Ab omni mortis impetu
Tuum defende populum.

clemens, clementis: forgiving, gentle, compassionate
possideo: take possession of, hold
reddo, reddere: render, pay

quaesumus (quaeso): beg, pray, entreat (Defective verb; two forms only)
impetus, -ūs: assault, attack, onrush

47. Conditor alme siderum (M)
Anon, c. 800 Cf *Creator alme siderum* (R)

Conditor alme siderum,
Aeterna lux credentium,
Christe, redemptor omnium,
Exaudi preces supplicum.

Qui condolens interitu
Mortis perire saeculum,
Salvasti mundum languidum,
Donans reis remedium:

Vergente mundi vespere,
Uti sponsus de thalamo,
Egressus honestissimā
Virginis matris clausulā.

supplex, supplicis: kneeling, begging (*of those who beg*)

condoleo (condolesco): suffer, feel pain, be in distress
perire saeculum: *that the world must perish, because the world was perishing*
interitus, -ūs: overthrow, ruin, death
mortis interitu: (*from their ruinous death, from a deathly ruin*)
languidus a um: weak, powerless, sick
reus a um: guilty
remedium: medicine, cure

vergo, vergere: bend, turn (*as the evening of the world was falling*)
uti (ut): as, like (Δ *utor, uti*)
honestus: honorable, virtuous, noble
clausula: enclosure (Poetic abl meaning *from*)

47. Conditor alme siderum (M)

Cujus forti potentiae
Genu curvantur omnia,
Caelestia, terrestria
Nutu fatentur subdita.

Te deprecamur, hagie
Venture judex saeculi,
Conserva nos in tempore
Hostis a telo perfidi.

curvo, curvare: bend
genu, genūs: knee
genu curvantur : *bend the knee, are made to bend at the knee*
nutus, -ūs: nodding, nod (*at your nod, at a nod from you*)
fatentur: *they confess (themselves) defeated, they admit that they are beaten*

hagie: (= *sancte*) (Vocative of Greek *hagios.* Three syllables.)
venture: (vocative of *venturus*, future participle of *venio*)
judex: (vocative)
conservo, -are: save, preserve
in tempore: in season, in time (not *in tempore hostis*)
hostis: (*a telo hostis perfidi*)
telum: spear, weapon
perfidus: faithless, unbelieving, perfidious

Note
Cf Phil 2: 10-11. *Ut in nomine Jesu omne genu flectatur caelestium, terrestrium, et infernorum.*

48. Consors paterni luminis
Anon, c. 500 (Italy)

Consors paterni luminis,
Lux ipse lucis et dies,
Noctem canendo rumpimus;
Assiste postulantibus.

Aufer tenebras mentium,
Fuga catervas daemonum,
Expelle somnolentiam,
Ne pigritantes obruat.

Sic, Christe, nobis omnibus
Indulgeas credentibus,
Ut prosit exorantibus,
Quod praecinentes psallimus.

rumpo, -ere: break, interrupt
postulo, -are: ask, pray

caterva, -ae: crowd, horde
pigritor, pigritari: be slow, be sluggish
obruo, -ere: overcome, overwhelm

indulgeo, indulgēre: be kind, grant, give generously
prosum, prodesse: benefit, do good, be useful
exoro, -are: entreat, appease, move (*nobis te exorantibus*)
praecino, praecinere: make music, sing before *you*
praecinentes psallimus: *we sing forth in music*

49. Cor arca legem continens
Anon, c. 1750

Cor, arca legem continens
Non servitutis veteris,
Sed gratiae, sed veniae,
Sed et misericordiae.

Cor, sanctuarium novi
Intemeratum foederis,
Templum vetusto sanctius,
Velumque scisso utilius.

arca, arcae: Ark
venia, veniae: indulgence, forgiveness, compassion

intemeratus a um: inviolate, pure
foedus, foederis: covenant
vetustus, a, um: aged, ancient, old (*holier than the old one*)
velum: veil, curtain
scindo, scindere, scidi, scissus: tear, cut (*more useful than the torn one*)

Note

Hebrew uses different words for the *ark* of Noah and the *Ark* of the Covenant. Latin uses a single word, *arca*, for both.

49. Cor arca legem continens

Hoc sub amoris symbolo
Passus cruenta et mystica,
Utrumque sacrificium
Christus sacerdos obtulit.

Quis non amantem redamet?
Quis non redemptus diligat,
Et corde in isto seligat
Aeterna tabernacula?

hoc: (*sub hoc symbolo*)
passus < patior: (*Christus passus cruenta*)
cruentus a um: bloody, dripping with blood, stained with blood
offero, offerre, obtuli: offer up, sacrifice

redamo, -are: love in return, love back
redemptus: (*quis redemptus….non diligat?*)
seligo, seligere: choose, select (*quis non seligat?*)

50. <u>Corpus domas jejuniis</u>

Corpus domas jejuniis,
Caedis cruento verbere,
Ut castra poenitentium
Miles sequaris innocens.

Sequamur et nos sedulo
Gressūs parentis optimi;
Sequamur, ut licentiam
Carnis refraenet spiritus.

domo, domare, domui: tame, subdue, master
jejunium: fasting, fast
caedo, caedere: beat, strike (supply *corpus*)
cruentus a um: bloody
verber, verberis: lash, scourge, whipping
castra, -orum (neut pl): camp (singular) (dir obj of *sequaris*)
paenitens, -entis: repentant, penitent
sequor, sequi: follow, go with, *perh* join
innocens, -entis: blameless, harmless, innocent

sedulo (Adv): dilgently, eagerly
gressus, -ūs: step
licentia, -ae: freedom, wantonness, immorality
refraeno, refraenare: check, control, restrain

50. Corpus domas jejuniis

Rigente brumā, providum
Praebes amictum pauperi,
Sitim famemque egentium
Esca potuque sublevas.

O qui negasti nemini
Opem roganti, patrium
Regnum tuere, postulant
Cives Poloni et exteri.

Sit laus Patri, sit Filio,
Tibique Sancte Spiritus;
Preces Joannis impetrent
Beata nobis gaudia.

rigeo, rigēre: harden, stiffen, freeze
bruma, -ae: early winter, winter
amictus, -ūs: cloak, coat
praebeo, -ēre: offer, give
providus a um: caring, provident
sitis, -is: thirst
fames, famis: hunger
egeo, egēre: need, be needy, be in want
sublevo, sublevare: relieve, assuage, mitigate

ops, opis: aid, help, assistance
patrius, -a, -um: ancestral, native
tueor, tueri, tutus: watch over, uphold, defend
Polonus, -a, -um: Polish
exterus, -a, -um: of another land, foreign

impetro, impetrare: obtain, gain by prayer

Note

Providum…amictum: Perhaps a case of transferred epithet. Saint John Cantius, rather than his cloak, was *providus*.

51. Creator alme siderum (R)
Revised 1632 Cf *Conditor alme siderum* (M)

Creator alme siderum,
Aeterna lux credentium,
Jesu redemptor omnium,
Intende votis supplicum.

Qui daemonis ne fraudibus
Periret orbis, impetu
Amoris actus, languidi
Mundi medela factus es.

Commune qui mundi nefas
Ut expiares, ad crucem
E virginis sacrario
Intacta prodis victima.

votum: prayer, desire
supplex, supplicis: kneeling (in prayer), begging, humble

qui: *you who, and you*
daemon, daemonis (Greek): devil, demon
fraus, fraudis: lying, dishonesty, fraud
impetus, -ūs: force, power, onrush
ago, agere, egi, actus: drive, motivate, stir
languidus a um: weak, sick, powerless
medela: remedy, medicine, cure

qui: *you who, and you*
nefas (neuter indeclinable): wickeness, wrong-doing, sin
expio, expiare: expiate, make amends for, purge by sacrifice, atone for
sacrarium: shrine, sacred place, sanctuary
prodeo, prodire, prodii: come forth, emerge
intactus a um: unblemished (*intacta victima*)

51. Creator alme siderum (R)

Cujus potestas gloriae
Nomenque cum primum sonat,
Et caelites et inferi
Tremente curvantur genu.

Te deprecamur ultimae
Magnum diei Judicem,
Armis supernae gratiae
Defende nos ab hostibus.

primum (Adv): first, for the first time
sono, sonare, sonui: sound, resound
caelites et inferi: *those in heaven and those below, heavenly and infernal beings*
curvor, curvari (effectively deponent): bow, bend, be made to bow
genu: (ablative)

Notes:

1. In grammatical structure the second, third, and fourth strophes are all relative clauses. Latin will subordinate, where English prefers to co-ordinate. This structure is familiar from the Nicene Creed: *Qui propter nos homines, Qui cum Patre et Filio.*

2. Although *sonat* is singular, it has a double subject, *potestas.... nomenque*. This is possible likewise in English: "When first the power of his glory resounds, and his name, all beings in heaven etc.". Cf also Acts 3:6— *Argentum et aurum non est mihi*, "Silver and gold I have none" (DR).

52. Custodes hominum psallimus angelos
c. 1600, attrib St Robert Bellarmine

Custodes hominum psallimus Angelos,
Naturae fragili quos Pater addidit
Caelestis comites, insidiantibus
Ne succumberet hostibus.

Nam, quod corruerit proditor angelus,
Concessis merito pulsus honoribus,
Ardens invidiā, pellere nititur
Quos caelo Deus advocat.

psallo, psallere + acc: sing *about*, sing psalms, sing hymns
addo, addere, addidi: add, send, contribute
caelestis: (Pater…. caelestis)
comes, comitis: companion, partner, helper
insidior, -ari: ambush, lie in wait for
succumbo, succumbere (+dat): surrender to, be overcome by

quod: because, since, on the grounds that
corruo, corruere, corrui: fall, sink, tumble down
proditor: betrayer, traitor
concedo, -ere: grant, bestow
merito (Adv): deservedly, rightly, justly (with *pulsus*, not with *concessis*)
pello, pellere, pepuli, pulsus: expel from, deprive of (+ abl)
invidia: envy, jealousy
nitor, niti: strive, endeavour
advoco, -are: summon, invite
caelo: (dative, = *in caelum*)

Notes:

Psallimus angelos. "We hymn the angels, guardians of men." NOT "we sing *to* the angels".

Ne succumberet. Subject of *succumberet* is "it", namely *natura fragilis*.

Quos….comites. "Whom the Father sent *as* (*to be our*) companions.

Corruerit. The subjunctive is not strictly necessary here. It connotes indirect statement. "Because (so we are told) the betrayer etc".

52. Custodes hominum psallimus angelos

Huc, custos, igitur pervigil advola,
Avertens patriā de tibi creditā
Tam morbos animi, quam requiescere
Quidquid non sinit incolas.

Sanctae sit Triadi laus pia jugiter,
Cujus perpetuo numine machina
Triplex haec regitur, cujus in omnia
Regnat gloria saecula.

pervigil, pervigilis: ever-watchful
advolo, advolare: fly (hither), hasten
de: (*de patria tibi credita*)
patria: land, homeland
tam....quam: as much X, as Y; both, and; not only....but also
morbus, morbi: ailment, malady, sickness
sino, sinere, sivi: let, allow, permit
incola, -ae: inhabitant, dweller

trias, triadis: trinity
jugiter: constantly, without cease
machina: fabric, structure, frame
numen, numinis: divinity, providence, *perh* divine guidance, godly care
rego, regere: rule, govern
regno, regnare: reign
cujus: (*cujus gloria regnat*)
in: (*in omnia saecula*)

Notes:

Avertens: The double direct object of *avertens* is *tam X....quam Y*, ie. *tam morbos....quam quidquid.* "Not only ailments etc, but also whatever prevents etc."

Machina triplex: The threefold fabric of heaven, earth, and hell.

53. <u>Decora lux aeternitatis</u> (R)
Cf *Aurea luce et decore roseo* (M)

Decora lux aeternitatis auream
Diem beatis irrigavit ignibus,
Apostolorum quae coronat principes,
Reisque in astra liberam pandit viam.

Mundi magister atque caeli janitor,
Romae parentes arbitrique gentium,
Per ensis ille, hic per crucis victor necem
Vitae senatum laureati possident.

O Roma felix, quae duorum principum
Es consecrata glorioso sanguine!
Horum cruore purpurata ceteras
Excellis orbis una pulchritudines.

decorus, -a, -um: lovely, beautiful, noble
irrigo, irrigare: flood, refresh
ignis: brilliance, glow, fire
quae: (*diem quae*)
reus, -a, -um: guilty
pando, pandere, pandi, passus: open, unfold, roll out
vitae senatum: *the senate of life, the summit of life, the assembly of heaven*
laureatus a um: crowned with laurel, as winners

magister: teacher
janitor: gate-keeper
arbiter, arbitri: judge
hic....ille: the one....the other; the former....the latter (here reversed)
ensis, ensis: sword (genitive: *per necem ensis, death by sword*)
nex, necis: death, murder

cruor, cruoris: bloodshed, gore
purpuratus a um: made purple, clad in purple, ennobled
excello, excellere: surpass, exceed
orbis, orbis: world, earth (genitive)
pulchritudo, pulchritudinis: beauty
una (adj): alone, uniquely, *by yourself*
Horum etc: *Empurpled by their bloodshed, you surpass alone the remaining beauty of the world.*

54. Deus tuorum militum
Anon, c. 500 → VR

Deus tuorum militum
Sors et corona, praemium,
Laudes canentes martyris
Absolve nexu criminis.

Hic nempe mundi gaudia,
Et blandimenta noxia — Et blanda fraudum pabula
Caduca rite deputans, — Imbuta felle deputans
Pervenit ad caelestia.

sors, sortis: lot, inheritance
praemium: reward
nexus -ūs: bond, slavery (*absolve canentes a nexu criminis*)
crimen, criminis: sin

hic: (*hic martyr*, ie "He" or "She")
nempe: assuredly, of course
blandimentum: allurement, charm
noxius, -a, -um: harmful, dangerous
blandus a um: flattering, seductive
fraus, fraudis: dishonesty, lies, fraud
pabulum: food, sustenance
caducus a um: fallen, vain, transitory
rite (Adv): justly, duly, rightly
imbuo, imbuere, imbui, imbutus: saturate, infect, taint
fel, fellis: gall, bile, poison
deputo, -are: reckon, esteem, consider

54. Deus tuorum militum

Poenas cucurrit fortiter,
Et sustulit viriliter,
Pro te effundens sanguinem, Fundensque pro te sanguinem
Aeterna dona possidet.

Ob hoc precatu supplici
Te poscimus, piissime:
In hoc triumpho martyris
Dimitte noxam servulis.

curro, currere, cucurri + acc: endure, suffer (cf Eng *run a risk, run a business*)
fortiter: bravely, with strength
suffero, sufferre, sustuli: bear, endure

ob hoc: *therefore, for this reason*
precatus, -ūs: entreaty, supplication (*with humble prayer*, *with begging entreaty*)
supplex, supplicis (Adj): begging, humble, prostrate
posco, poscere: ask, request
noxa: harm, injury, punishment
servulis (abl): *from your little slaves, from your servants*

55. Doctor egregie Paule (M)
Anon, c. 500
Cf *Beate pastor Petre* (R), and *Egregie doctor Paule* (R)

Doctor egregie Paule, mores instrue,
Et mente polum nos transferre satage,
Donec perfectum largiatur plenius
Evacuato quod ex parte gerimus.

Sit Trinitati sempiterna gloria,
Honor, potestas, atque jubilatio,
In unitate cui manet imperium,
Ex tunc, et modo, per aeterna saecula.

doctor, doctoris: teacher
egregius a um: exceptional, oustanding
mos, moris: custom, behavior, way of life (*teach us how to live*)
instruo, instruere: teach
mente: *in spirit* (*by your mind, with your genius; in our mind, inwardly*)
polus, poli: heaven, sky (*carry us across the heavens*)
satago, satagere: do enough, do what is in one's power, labor diligently (+ infin)
perfectum: *the perfect, perfection* (Dir obj of *largiatur*)
largior, largiri (Depon): lavish, bestow (This vb has no apparent subj.)
plenius (< plenus): more fully than
evacuatum: *the empty life, the void, the nullity* (Abl of comparison after *plenius*)
gero gerere: lead, conduct
ex parte: in part, incompletely, from one side

ex tunc: then, from then
modo: now

Notes

The wording of the first strophe is obscure. The VR entirely rewrites it.

Evacuare is a legal term, meaning "nullify". This sense occurs at I Cor 17: *ut non evacuetur crux Christi*. "Lest the cross of Christ should be made void."

The author of the hymn is referring to yet another passage from Saint Paul:

Caritas numquam excidit, sive prophetiae evacuabuntur, sive linguae cessabunt, sive scientia destruetur. Ex parte enim cognoscimus, et ex parte prophetamus. Cum autem venerit quod perfectum est, evacuabitur quod ex parte est. Cum essem parvulus, loquebar ut parvulus, sapiebam ut parvulus, cogitabam ut parvulus. Quando autem factus sum vir, evacuavi quae erant parvuli. (I Cor 13: 8-11)

56. <u>Domare cordis</u>
c. 1600, attrib Urban VIII

Domare cordis impetūs Elizabeth
Fortis, inopsque Deo
Servire regno praetulit.

En fulgidis recepta caeli sedibus
Sidereaeque domūs
Ditata sanctis gaudiis,

Nunc regnat inter caelites beatior,
Et premit astra, docens
Quae vera sint regni bona.

Patri potestas, Filioque gloria,
Perpetuumque decus
Tibi sit, alme Spiritus.

domo, domare: tame, control
impetus, -us: impulse
inops, inopis: poor, unwealthy
praefero, praeferre, praetuli: prefer

en: (= *ecce*)
fulgidus a um: shining, dazzling
recipio, -ere: accept, admit
sidereus a um: starry, heavenly, celestial
dito, ditare: enrich, endow

premo, premere: tread upon, dwell among, surpass

Note
decus, décoris (neuter): grace, glory, honor
decor, decōris (masc): comeliness, elegance, charm
decōrus, -a, -um: fitting, suitable, seemly, proper

All these share the root DEC as in *decet,* eg:
Te decet hymnus, Deus, in Sion.

57. Dum nocte pulsa
Attrib Giovanni Bona, ob 1674

Dum, nocte pulsā, lucifer
Diem propinquam nuntiat,
Nobis refert Venantius
Lucis beatae munera.

Nam criminum caliginem
Stygisque noctem depulit,
Veroque cives lumine
Divinitatis imbuit.

Aquis sacri baptismatis
Lustravit ille patriam;
Quos tinxit undā milites,
In astra misit martyres.

Nunc angelorum particeps,
Adesto votis supplicum;
Procul repelle crimina,
Tuumque lumen ingere.

pello, pellere, pepuli, pulsus: drive off, banish, scatter
lucifer: "light-bearer", ie the Morning Star, precursor of sun-rise.
nuntio, -are: announce, declare
refero, referre: restore, renew, remind

crimen, criminis: sin (Hymnographic word for *peccatum*)
caligo, caliginis: fog, darkness
Styx, Stygis: Styx, hell
depello, depellere: remove, expel, drive away
imbuo, imbuere, imbui, imbutus: saturate, fill, imbue

lustro, lustrare: make bright, purify
tingo, tingere, tinxi, tinctus: mosten, bathe, make wet
unda, -ae: wave, water (Hymnographic word for *aqua*)

particeps, participis: partner, fellow, comrade
ingero, ingerere: pour in, lavish

58. Ecce jam noctis (M)
Attrib Gregory the Great. Probably Alcuin, c. 800
Cf *Ecce jam noctis* (R)

Ecce jam noctis tenuatur umbra,
Lucis aurora rutilans coruscat;
Nisibus totis rogitemus omnes
Cunctipotentem:

Ut Deus, nostri miseratus, omnem
Pellat languorem, tribuat salutem,
Donet et nobis pietate patris
Regna polorum.

tenuor, tenuari: diminish, lessen
rutilo, rutilare: redden, grow red
corusco, coruscare: flash, gleam, shine
nisus (defective, abl *nisu*): effort, exertion, labor
rogito, rogitare: ask eagerly, keep asking (*Ut etc* in next strophe)
cunctipotens: (= *omnipotens*)

miseror, miserari, miseratus (+gen): pity, feel pity for
languor, languoris: weakness, apathy, sluggishness
pietate patris: *with a father's kindness, with the goodness of our father*
regna polorum: (= *regnum caelorum*)

59. Ecce jam noctis (R)
 Attrib Gregory the Great. Probably Alcuin, c. 800
 Cf *Ecce jam noctis* (M)

Ecce jam noctis tenuatur umbra,
Lux et aurorae rutilans coruscat;
Supplices rerum Dominum canorā
Voce precemur:

Ut reos culpae miseratus omnem
Pellat angorem, tribuat salutem,
Donet et nobis bona sempiternae
Munera pacis.

tenuor, tenuari: grow less, lessen, diminish
rutilo, rutilare: redden, grow red
corusco, coruscare: glitter, gleam
rerum Dominum: *the Lord of everything, the Lord of all*
canorus, -a, -um: melodious, sweet-sounding

angor, angoris: anguish, torment

60. En clara vox redarguit (R)
Attrib Saint Ambrose, c. 400
Cf *Vox clara ecce intonat* (M)

En clara vox redarguit
Obscura quaeque, personans;
Procul fugentur somnia;
Ab alto Jesus promicat.

Mens jam resurgat, torpida
Non amplius jacens humi;
Sidus refulget jam novum,
Ut tollat omne noxium.

en: = ecce
redarguo, redarguere, redargui: confute, contradict, scatter
quisque, quaeque, quodque (Indef adj): any, every, each, all
obscura (Neut plu): dark, secret, unclear (*confounds all manner of darkness*)
persono, personare: sound clear, ring through, call out
promico, promicare: shine forth, flash out

torpidus a um: sleepy, dull, unconscious
humi: (locative of *humus*): *on the ground*
sidus, sideris (Neut): star
refulgeo: shine again, flash back
noxius, -a, -um: harmful, guilty, hurtful

60. <u>En clara vox redarguit</u> (R)

En Agnus ad nos mittitur
Laxare gratis debitum;
Omnes simul cum lacrimis
Precemur indulgentiam.

Ut, cum secundo fulserit,
Metuque mundum cinxerit,
Non pro reatu puniat,
Sed nos pius tunc protegat.

laxo, laxare: release, undo, cancel
gratis (Adv): freely, without payment, for nothing
indulgentia: compassion, forgiveness, forbearance

secundo (Adv): for the second time, the next time
fulgeo, fulgēre, fulsi: flash, gleam, shine
cingo, cingere, cinxi: engird, encircle, surround
metus, -ūs: fear
reatus, -ūs: guilt
pius, -a, -um: good, kind, merciful (*of His mercy, mercifully*)
protego, -ere: shelter, enfold, defend

Note on syntax:

Cum....fulserit, cinxerit. Future-perfect indicatives. This construction remains normal in the romance languages, but not in English or German.

Eg: *Cum hostes convenerint, impetum in eos faciemus*. "When the enemy have assembled (lit. will have assembled), we shall attack them."

Wenn ich morgen Zeit habe, besuche ich dich. "If I have (present tense) time tomorrow, I (shall) visit you".

Note also *cum* + the future indicative:

Cum redibit arbiter....Christus, "When Christ the Judge returns" (Strophe 5, *Exsultet orbis gaudiis*). However, the VM has the future-perfect indicative: *Cum judex advenerit Christus.*

61. En ut superba criminum
Anon, c. 1700

En ut superba criminum
Et saeva nostrorum cohors
Cor sauciavit innocens
Merentis haud tale Dei.

Vibrantis hastam militis
Peccata nostra dirigunt,
Ferrumque dirae cuspidis
Mortale crimen acuit.

en ut: see how….!
crimen, criminis: sin, misdeed
cohors, cohortis (fem): multitude, crowd, throng
saucio, sauciare: wound, hurt
cor…. innocens: (Accusative)
mereo, merere: deserve, merit
haud: not at all
talis, tale: such, such a thing

vibro, vibrare: brandish, menace with (*his spear*)
hasta: spear
dirigo, dirigere: steady, direct, aim
ferrum, -i: iron, ie. sword
cuspis, cuspidis (Fem): point, blade, tip
dirae cuspidis: *of dreadful blade* (Gen of description, aka gen of quality)
acuo, acuere, acui: sharpen

61. <u>En ut superba criminum</u>

Ex corde scisso Ecclesia,
Christo jugata, nascitur;
Hoc ostium arcae in latere est *
Genti ad salutem positum.

Ex hoc perennis gratia,
Ceu septiformis fluvius,
Stolas ut illic sordidas
Lavemus Agni in sanguine.

Turpe est redire ad crimina,
Quae cor beatum lacerent;
Sed aemulemur cordibus
Flammas, amoris indices.

scindo, scindere, scidi, scissus: tear, wound
jugo, jugare: bind, join, marry
ostium: entry, doorway
arca: ark
latus, lateris: side
gens, gentis: mankind, the human race

gratia: (supply *est* or *fluit*)
ceu: like, resembling
septiformis, -e: seven-fold
fluvius: river
stola: robe, gown (Cf Apoc 3:4, 7:9, 7: 14, et al)
sordidus a um: unclean, filthy

turpis, -e: shameful, vile, monstrous
lacero, lacerare: distress, pain, torment (Pres subjunc)
aemulor, aemulari: emulate, vie with, strive to be like (+ acc)
cordibus: with (our) hearts
index, indicis: mark, sign
flammas, amoris indices: *the flames, the marks of love*

* This octo-syllabic line requires three elisions:
Hoc osti*um* arc*ae* in later*e* est.
Hoc osti' arc' in later' est.

62. <u>Ex more docti mystico</u>
Attrib Saint Gregory the Great, c. 600

Ex more docti mystico
Servemus hoc jejunium,
Deno dierum circulo
Ducto quater notissimo.

Lex et prophetae primitus
Hoc praetulerunt, postmodum
Christus sacravit, omnium
Rex atque factor temporum.

Utamur ergo parcius
Verbis, cibis et potibus, *
Somno, jocis, et arctius
Perstemus in custodia.

ex: *from a mystic custom learning, instructed by our mystic way*
servo, servare: keep, observe
denus, -a, -um: ten-fold
quater (Adv): four times, by four
circulus: cycle, span
duco, ducere: reckon, calculate, perh *multiply*

primitus (Adv): for the first time, at first (cf *caeli-tus, humani-tus*)
praefero, -ferre, praetuli: present, introduce
postmodum (Adv): afterwards, later
sacro, sacrare: consecrate, set apart, make holy

utor, uti, usus (+abl): use, employ, make use of
parcus, -a, -um: frugal, sparing, little
jocus, -i: joke, jest, trifle
arctus, -a, -um (= artus): narrow, close, strict
paucius....artius: (comparatives of the adverb)
persto, perstare: stand firmly, persevere, endure
custodia: watchfulness, care, restraint

* Cf Reg Ben 49: *Subtrahat corpori suo de cibo, de potu, de somno, de loquacitate, de scurrilitate.*

62. Ex more docti mystico → VR

Vitemus autem pessima, Quae subruunt mentes vagas; Nullumque demus callidi Hostis locum tyrannidi.	Vitemus autem noxia
Dicamus omnes cernui, Clamemus atque singuli, Ploremus ante Judicem, Flectamus iram vindicem.	Flectamus iram vindicem, Ploremus ante Judicem, Clamemus ore supplici, Dicamus omnes cernui:
Nostris malis offendimus Tuam, Deus, clementiam; Effunde nobis desuper, Remissor, indulgentiam.	

noxius a um: harmful, bad
subruo, subruere: undermine, break down, demolish
vagus, -a, -um: wandering, unstable
demus: (from *do, dare*)
callidus a um: crafty, cunning, shrewd
tyrannis, tyrannidis (Gk): tyranny, despotic power

dico, dicere: speak, plead (in law), say
cernuus a um: with head bowed, humble
supplex, supplicis: kneeling, begging, humble
flecto, flectere: turn aside, avert
vindex, vindicis: avenging, punishing (Noun here used as adj)

remissor, remissoris: *you who forgive, forgiving God*

62. Ex more docti mystico

Memento quod sumus tui,
Licet caduci, plasmatis;
Ne des honorem nominis
Tui, precamur, alteri.

Laxa malum, quod fecimus;
Auge bonum, quod poscimus:
Placere quo tandem tibi
Possimus hic et perpetim.

Praesta, beata Trinitas,
Concede, simplex Unitas,
Ut fructuosa sint tuis
Jejuniorum munera.

licet: albeit, even though
caducus: fallen (*tui*, gen sing; *caduci*, nom pl)
plasma, plasmatis (neut): making, formation, creation
ne des: (*noli dare*)
alter, alterius, alteri, alterum, altero: another

laxo, laxare: release, relieve, lessen, mitigate
augeo, augēre: increase, expand
posco, poscere: ask for, pray for
quo: so that, by which
tandem: finally, at the end
perpetim: forever, without cease

fructuosus a um: fruitful
tuis: (tuis *populis*, tuis *fidelibus*)
jejuniorum munera: *gifts of fasting, duty of fasting*

63. Exsultet caelum laudibus (M)
Anon, c.900 Cf *Exsultet orbis gaudiis* (R)

Exsultet caelum laudibus,
Resultet terra gaudiis;
Apostolorum gloriam
Sacra canunt solemnia.

Vos saecli justi judices,
Et vera mundi lumina,
Votis precamur cordium:
Audite preces supplicum.

Qui caelum verbo clauditis,
Serasque ejus solvitis,
Nos a peccatis omnibus
Solvite jussu, quaesumus.

Quorum praecepto subditur
Salus et languor omnium,
Sanate aegros moribus,
Nos reddentes virtutibus:

Ut, cum Judex advenerit
Christus in fine saeculi,
Nos sempiterni gaudii
Faciat esse compotes.

resulto, resultare: respond, re-echo

justi judices: (not *saecli justi*)

sera, serae: bolt, bar, lock
jussu: *by (your) command, on (your) order*

quorum praecepto subditur: *upon whose command depends*
salus et languor: *health and sickness, salvation and loss*
aegros moribus: *sick in (their)behavior, morally unwholesome*
nos reddentes: *restoring us to…* (not *redeuntes*)

compos, compotis (+gen): sharer of, sharer in, participant in

64. Exsultet orbis gaudiis (R)
Cf *Exsultet caelum laudibus* (M)

Exsultet orbis gaudiis,
Caelum resultet laudibus;
Apostolorum gloriam
Tellus et astra concinunt.

Vos, saeculorum judices
Et vera mundi lumina,
Votis precamur cordium:
Audite voces supplicum.

Qui templa caeli clauditis
Serasque verbo solvitis,
Nos a reatu noxios
Solvi jubete, quaesumus.

orbis, orbis: *the* world
resulto, resultare: echo back, resound
tellus, telluris: earth
con-cino, con-cinere (+ acc): sing about together, together praise in song
Note: cum + cano → concino

Qui: (Antecedent is *vos* in previous verse.)
sera: bolt, bar, lock
reatus, -ūs: guilt
noxius, -a, -um: offensive
nos….solvi jubete: *order us to be released*

64. <u>Exsultet orbis gaudiis</u> (R)

Praecepta quorum protinus
Languor salusque sentiunt,
Sanate mentes languidas,
Augete nos virtutibus:

Ut, cum redibit arbiter
In fine Christus saeculi,
Nos sempiterni gaudii
Concedat esse compotes.

quorum: (*vos, quorum praecepta…, sanate etc*)
praeceptum: command, order, bidding
protinus (Adv): forthwith, at once, thereafter
languor salusque: *sickness and health, loss and salvation*
sentio, sentire: be affected by, obey
languidus a um: weak, feeble, sinful

arbiter, arbitri: judge, ruler
compos, compotis: participant in, sharer of (+ gen)

Note

The word *salus* can mean "health" or "salvation". *Languor* is the opposite of *salus*, and means "loss of health", or "sickness". Thus in the vocabulary of the hymns *languor* comes to mean "loss of salvation". And *languidus* can mean both "sick" and "sinful". The metaphor cannot be rendered nicely in English.

65. Festivis resonent compita vocibus
Anon, c. 1700

Festivis resonent compita vocibus,
Cives laetitiam frontibus explicent;
Taedis flammiferis ordine prodeant
Instructi pueri et senes.

Quem dura moriens Christus in arbore
Fudit multiplici vulnere sanguinem,
Nos facti memores dum colimus, decet
Saltem fundere lacrimas.

Humano generi pernicies gravis
Adami veteris crimine contigit;
Adami integritas et pietas novi
Vitam reddidit omnibus.

festivus: happy, pleasing, joyful
compita, -orum: cross-roads, streets
frons, frontis: forehead, brow, face
explico, explicare: unfurl, display
taeda, -ae: torch, nuptial torch
flammifer, -fera, -ferum: flame-bearing, fiery
ordine instructi: *drawn up in order, marching by rank*
prodeo, prodire: go out, go forth

arbor, arboris (fem): tree
fundo, fundere, fudi: shed (*blood* or *tears*)
multiplex, multiplicis: manifold, varied (*from His numerous wounds*)
facti memores: *mindful of the Deed,* perh *mindful of His passion*
colo, colere: revere, honor, worship
dum: (*dum colimus sanguinem quem Christus fudit....*)
saltem: at the least
nos decet fundere: *it behoves us to shed*

pernicies, perniciei: calamity, death
pernicies gravis: *a grave calamity, a terrible death*
contingo, contingere, contigi (+dat): happen to, befall
integritas, -tatis: purity, innocence, wholeness
pietas: holiness, obedience

65. Festivis resonent compita vocibus

Clamorem validum summus ab aethere
Languentis Geniti si Pater audiit,
Placari potius sanguine debuit,
Et nobis veniam dare.

Hoc quicumque stolam sanguine proluit,
Abstergit maculas; et roseum decus,
Quo fiat similis protinus angelis
Et Regi placeat, capit.

A recto instabilis tramite postmodum
Se nullus retrahat, meta sed ultima
Tangatur; tribuet nobile praemium,
Qui cursum Deus adjuvat.

validus a um: mighty, strong
clamorem validum: *a loud cry, a great cry* (cf Luke 23:46)
aether, aetheris: the aether, heaven
languens (langueo, languesco): growing faint, weakening, dying
Genitus: Son
audiit: (*aúdiit* = *audívit*, but nb shortening of vowel in penult)
potius: rather, surely
placari debuit: *He (Pater) ought to be appeased*
sanguine: *by His blood*
venia, veniae: forgiveness

proluo, proluere, prolui: wash, wash clean
abstergo abstergere (= abstergeo): wipe away
protinus (Adv): at once, forthwith
roseum decus…. capit: *obtains a rose-red beauty*

trames, tramitis: way, path, road
postmodum: later, afterwards
instabilis, -e: unsteady, uncertain, wavering
(me) retraho: withdraw, retreat, turn away
meta, -ae: turning-point (of a race), goal, finish-line (nominative)
tango, tangere: touch, reach
cursus, -us: race, journey, passage

Note: *retrahat* and *tangatur*, hortatory subjunctive; *tribuet*, future indicative; *adjuvat* present indicative. Phrasing: *Deus (qui cursum adjuvat) tribuet nobile praemium*.

65. Festivis resonent compita vocibus

Nobis propitius sis, Genitor potens,
Ut quos unigenae sanguine Filii
Emisti, et placido Flamine recreas,
Caeli ad culmina transferas.

unigena, -ae: only-begotten
emo, emere, emi: buy, purchase
placidus: gentle, still, mild
flamen, flaminis: breeze, wind (*Flamen = Spiritus*)
recreo, recreare: renew, revive (nb *recreas* is indicative)
culmen, culminis: summit, top, roof
ut: (*ut transferas illos quos emisti et recreas*)

Unigena is an adjective, feminine in form but masculine in sense. Hence *Filius unigena*, "only-begotten Son".

66. <u>Fortem virili pectore</u>
Silvio Antoniano, ob. 1603 → VM

Fortem virili pectore
Laudemus omnes feminam,
Quae sanctitatis gloriā
Ubique fulget inclita.

Haec sancto amore saucia, Haec Christi amore saucia
Dum mundi amorem noxium
Horrescit, ad caelestia
Iter peregit arduum.

fortis: valiant (DR. Cf Prov 31:10)
virilis: manly (*virili pectore*, *stout of heart*)
pectus, pectoris: *lit* chest, *metaph* heart
femina, -ae: woman
fulgeo, fulgēre: shine, be eminent
inclitus, -a, -um: illustrious, glorious(ly)
Note: *Quae…inclita* seems best. Some translators read *gloriā….inclitā*

saucius, -a, -um: wounded, struck (by love)
noxius, -a, -um: harmful, sinful
horresco: spurn, recoil from, be repelled by (+ acc)
perago, paragere, peregi: complete, finish
arduus, -a, -um: steep, difficult

66. Fortem virili pectore

Carnem domans jejuniis,
Dulcique mentem pabulo
Orationis nutriens,
Caeli potitur gaudiis.

Rex Christe, virtus fortium,
Qui magna solus efficis,
Huius precatu, quaesumus,
Audi benignus supplices.

domo, domare: tame, subjugate, mortify
mens, mentis: (In the hymns this word often means "soul".)
jejunium: fast, fasting
pabulum: food
nutrio, nutrire: feed, nourish, support
potior, potiri: obtain, become partaker of (+ abl)

virtus, virtutis: strength, might, virtue
fortium: *of the brave, of valiant souls*
magna: (Neuter plural)
efficio, efficere: achieve, perform
huius: *of this (saint)*
precatus, -ūs: prayer, prayers

67. Gentis Polonae gloria
Anon, c. 1700

Gentis Polonae gloria,
Clerique splendor nobilis,
Decus Lycaei, et patriae
Pater, Joannes inclite:

Legem superni numinis
Doces magister, et facis.
Nil scire prodest; sedulo
Legem nitamur exsequi.

Apostolorum limina
Pedes viator visitas;
Ad patriam ad quam tendimus,
Gressūs viamque dirige.

Polonus, -a, -um: Polish
clerus, -i: clergy, priesthood
decus, decoris: glory, splendor
Lycaeum, Lycaei: lyceum, university, academy
patria: fatherland, homeland
inclitus a um: renowned, famous, distinguished

doceo, docere: teach
magister: master, teacher
et facis: *and you act* (ie *and you obey the law*)
prosum, prodesse, profui: be of value, be useful
nil scire prodest: *to know (the law) is worth nothing*
sedulo (Adv): zealously, diligently
nitor, niti: endeavour, strive, make the effort
exsequor, exsequi: fulfil, follow, carry out

limen, liminis: threshhold
pedes, peditis: foot-soldier, on foot (Δ *pes, pedis*)
viator, viatoris: wayfarer, traveller
pedes viator: *pilgrim, soldier pilgrim, traveller on foot*
tendo, tendere: aim, direct one's path
gressus, -ūs: step

67. Gentis Polonae gloria

Urbem petis Jerusalem;
Signata sacro sanguine
Christi colis vestigia,
Rigasque fusis fletibus.

Acerba Christi vulnera,
Haerete nostris cordibus,
Ut cogitemus consequi
Redemptionis pretium.

Te prona mundi machina,
Clemens, adoret, Trinitas;
Et nos novi per gratiam
Novum canamus canticum.

signo, signare: mark, seal
colo, colere: venerate, adore
rigo, rigare: moisten, water, make wet (supply *them* = *vestigia*)
fletus, -ūs: weeping, *metaph* tears
fundo, fundere, fudi, fusus: pour out, shed

acerbus, -a, -um: bitter, harsh
vulnera: (Vocative)
haereo, haerere: cleave to, stay close to,
cogito, cogitare: intend, think how to (+ infin)
consequor, consequi: pursue, obtain

pronus, -a, -um: abject, lowly
machina: structure, fabric
clemens….trinitas: (Vocative)
nos: (Nominative)
novus a um: renewed, afresh, *made* new

68. Haec est dies
Urban VIII, ob. 1644

Haec est dies, qua candidae
Instar columbae, caelitum
Ad sacra templa spiritus
Se transtulit Teresiae.

Sponsique voces audiit:
"Veni, soror, de vertice
Carmeli ad Agni nuptias;
Veni ad coronam gloriae."

Te, sponse Jesu, virginum,
Beati adorent ordines,
Et nuptiali cantico
Laudent per omne saeculum.

candidus: white, dazzling white
instar (indecl, + gen): likeness, in the likeness of
columba: dove
caeles, caelitis: heavenly *being*, dweller in heaven
spiritus: soul (Nominative)
se transtulit: *betook itself to, flew up to*
Teresia: Teresa

Sponsus: Bridegroom
voces: *words, voice*
vertex, verticis: peak, top
Carmelus: *Mount* Carmel
nuptiae, -arum: wedding, marriage feast

ordo, ordinis: rank, order (of angels and saints)

Note:
Cant 4: 8
Veni de Libano, sponsa, veni de Libano, veni coronaberis....de vertice Sanir et Hermon

69. Hominis superne conditor (R)
Anon c. 600, attrib Saint Gregory the Great, rev 1632
Cf *Plasmator hominis Deus* (M)

Hominis superne conditor,
Qui cuncta solus ordinans,
Humum jubes producere
Reptantis et ferae genus:

Et magna rerum corpora,
Dictu jubentis vivida,
Per temporum certas vices
Obtemperare servulis:

Repelle, quod cupidinis
Ciente vi nos impetit,
Aut moribus se suggerit,
Aut actibus se interserit,

hominis: (hypermetric. *hom'nis* phonetically = *omnis*)
humus, -i: soil, ground, land
jubeo, jubére, jussi: bid, command
repto, reptare: creep, crawl (Cf Gen 1: 24-25)
fera, -ae: wild beast, wild animal
genus, generis: variety, class, sort

dictum, dictu: (supine of *dico*. Cf *mirabile dictu*)
magna rerum corpora: (*the bodies of big creatures)*
vividus, -a, -um: alive, full of life, animated
vices, vicium: changes, alterations, cycles
certus a um: fixed, known
tempus, temporis: season
obtempero: submit to, attend to
servulis: (supply *tuis*)

quod: *that which, whatever, what*
impeto, impetere: assail, attack
cieo, ciere, civi: stir, rouse, move
vis, vis: force, power
moribus: (*our way of life, our conduct*)
suggero: propose (*se, itself*)
actibus: (*our actions*)
intersero, interserui: interfere with, intrude *itself* into

69. Hominis superne conditor (R)

Da gaudiorum praemia,
Da gratiarum munera,
Dissolve litis vincula,
Astringe pacis foedera.

Praesta, Pater piissime,
Patrique compar Unice,
Cum Spiritu Paraclito
Regnans per omne saeculum.

dissolvo, dissolvere: release, break
lis, litis: strife, contention
astringo, astringere: tighten, bind together
foedus, foederis: covenant, agreement

Note:

This doxology occurs frequently both in the Roman and in the monastic office.

The Latin verb *praesto, praestare* is normally employed with a complement, either a noun in the accusative case, or a noun clause: *praesta nobis hoc, praesta ut*, and so forth. In such cases it means "grant".

In this doxology, however, *praesta* is employed absolutely. There is no grammatical complement.

The hymns which conclude with this doxology generally display the same poetic form.

1. They begin with an apostrophe, or an address to God, in the vocative case: *superne Conditor*, here expanded with a lengthy *qui* clause.
2. They then list one or more prayers, either in the imperative or in the subjunctive mood: *repelle, da, da, dissolve, astringe*.
3. They conclude with the doxology *Praesta* etc.

The implicit object of *praesta* is exactly those prayers of the middle section. "Grant (the foregoing)", or "Grant (what we just prayed for)". We might say that *Praesta* here has rather the meaning of "Please".

For a perfect short example of this hymnographic paradigm, cf *Te lucis ante terminum*.

70. Hostis Herodes impie (M)
Sedulius, c. 450 → VR

Hostis Herodes impie,
Christum venire quid times?
Non eripit mortalia,
Qui regna dat caelestia.

Crudelis Herodes, Deum
Regem venire quid times?

Ibant Magi, quam viderant
Stellam sequentes praeviam;
Lumen requirunt lumine;
Deum fatentur munere.

Lavacra puri gurgitis
Caelestis Agnus attigit;
Peccata, quae non detulit,
Nos abluendo sustulit.

Novum genus potentiae:
Aquae rubescunt hydriae,
Vinumque jussa fundere,
Mutavit unda originem.

eripio: snatch away, steal, take away (not *rescue*)

lavacrum: cleansing, washing (of baptism)
gurges, gurgitis: stream, river (ie the River Jordan)
attingo, attingere, attigi: come to, arrive at (+ acc)
defero: bear, carry
tollo, tollere, sustuli: remove, lift away
abluo, -ere: wash, cleanse

rubesco, -ere: turn red, become red
hydria, -ae: water jar
unda: water (lit *wave*)
origo, originis: source, origin, nature
And the water, bidden to pour as wine, changed its origin.

71. Huius obtentu (M) *
Anon, c. 750 Cf *Huius oratu* (R)

Huius obtentu, Deus alme, nostris
Parce jam culpis, vitia remittens,
Quo tibi puri resonemus almum
Pectoris hymnum.

obtentus, -ūs: entreaty, intercession
almus, -a, -um: loving
parco, parcere, peperci (+dat): overlook, pardon, forgive
vitium: defect, sin
quo: by which, so that
pectoris: *of the heart, from our hearts*

72. Huius oratu (R) *

Huius oratu, Deus alme, nobis
Debitas poenas scelerum remitte;
Ut tibi puro resonemus almum
Pectore carmen.

oratus, ūs: request, entreaty, intercession
debitus (< debere): owing, owed
scelus, sceleris: crime, sin, wickedness
puro pectore: *with pure heart*

* Excerpted from *Virginis proles opifexque matris*, qv.

73. Immense caeli conditor
Anon, c. 600, attrib St Gregory the Great

Immense caeli conditor,
Qui mixta ne confunderent,
Aquae fluenta dividens,
Caelum dedisti limitem,

Firmans locum caelestibus,
Simulque terrae rivulis,
Ut unda flammas temperet,
Terrae solum ne dissipent.

immensus a um: measureless, vast, infinite
confundo, -ere: cause confusion, confound
misceo, miscēre, miscui, mixtus: mix, mingle, mix up
fluentum: stream, flow, flood
caelum: sky, firmament (cf Gen 1: 6-8)
limes, limitis: boundary, border, limit

Infinite creator of the sky,
you gave the sky as a limit,
(and you) divided the streams of water,
lest they mingle and cause confusion.

firmo, firmare: establish, fix, appoint
caelestibus: (*rivulis caelestibus*)
rivulus: stream, water-course
unda: wave, water, waters
tempero, temperare: moderate, control, lessen
flamma: flame, heat (of the sun)
dissipo, dissipare: lay waste, destroy (subj of *dissipent* is *they = flammae*)
solum, -i: ground, surface, soil
terrae: (genitive)

73. Immense caeli conditor

→ VR

Infunde nunc, piissime,
Donum perennis gratiae,
Fraudis novae ne casibus
Nos error atterat vetus.

Lucem fides inveniat; — Lucem fides adaugeat
Sic luminis jubar ferat,
Ut vana cuncta terreat, — Haec vana cuncta proterat
Hanc falsa nulla comprimant.

fraus, fraudis (fem): cheating, deception, fraud
casus, -us: occurrence, chance, misfortune (Abl of means)
vetus, veteris: old, previous, ancient
attero, atterere, attrivi: destroy, rub out, ruin

adaugeo: increase
jubar, jubaris (neut): radiance
ferat: (*fides ferat jubar*)
terreo: frighten, frighten away (subj = *fides*)
protero, proterere, protrivi: tread down, trample under foot
haec: (*haec fides*)
hanc: (*hanc fidem*)
comprimo, comprimere, compressi: oppose, suppress, defeat
nulla falsa: *no false(hoods)*, *no false teachings*, *nothing false*

74. Inclitos Christi famulos
Cf *Beata caeli gaudia*, note.

Inclitos Christi famulos canamus,
Quos fide claros nitidisque gestis,
Hac die tellus, sociata caelo,
Laudibus ornat.

Quippe qui mites, humiles, pudici,
Nesciam culpae coluēre vitam,
Donec e terris animus volavit
Liber ad astra.

Inde jam gaudent miseris adesse,
Flentium tergunt lacrimas, medentur
Mentium plagis, vitiata reddunt
Membra saluti.

nitidus a um: bright, shining
gesta (< gerere): deeds
tellus, telluris (fem): earth
socio, sociare: unite, join, associate
orno, ornare: decorate, acclaim

quippe: indeed
quippe qui: *since they, for they indeed*
nescius, -a, -um: ignorant of, innocent of (+ gen)
colo, colere, colui: pursue, lead (*vitam*)
animus: spirit, soul

gaudent: *they rejoice that they are present (here) among the wretched*
tergo, tergere: wipe away, dry
medeor, mederi (+ dat): heal, cure
plaga, -ae: affliction, wound
vitio, vitiare: damage, corrupt, injure, spoil

74. Inclitos Christi famulos

Nostra laus ergo resonet benignis
Usque patronis, referatque grates;
Qui piā pergant ope nos juvare
Rebus in arctis.

Sit salus illi, decus atque virtus,
Qui, super caeli solio coruscans,
Totius mundi seriem gubernat
Trinus et unus.

patronus: advocate, sponsor
grates, gratium: thanks, thanksgiving, gratitude
qui: *so that they, in the hope that they* (Antecedent is *patronis*)
pergo, pergere: continue
ops, opis (fem): aid, help, solace
arctus: narrow, difficult
rebus in arctis: at difficult moments, in hard times

solium: throne
series: row, extent

Note

Decus illi sit. "Honor be to him, Let the honor be his". We cannot, however, wish *salus* or *virtus* to God. In English, therefore, some expansion is necessary. For example: *Let us acclaim that salvation and honor and might belong to Him, who*….etc.

75. <u>In monte olivis consito</u>
This hymn is a continuation of *Caelestis aulae nuntius*, qv.

In monte olivis consito
Redemptor orans procidit,
Maeret, pavescit, deficit,
Sudore manans sanguinis.

A proditore traditus
Raptatur in poenas Deus,
Durisque vinctis nexibus,
Flagris cruentis caeditur.

oliva, -ae: olive, olive tree
consero, conserere, consevi, consitus: plant
procido, procidere, procidi: fall down, fall forward
maereo, -ēre: be sorrwful, grieve, be sad
pavesco -ere: become afraid, grow fearful
sudor, sudoris: sweat, perspiration
mano, manare: flow, drip, exude

trado, tradere: hand over, hand on
proditor: betrayer
rapto, raptare: drag away, drag off
vincio, vincire, vinxi, vinctus: bind, tie, fetter
nexus, -us: bond, knot, shackle
flagrum, -i: whip, scourge, lash
cruentus, -a, -um: bloody, drawing blood
caedo, caedere: beat, strike

75. In monte olivis consito

Intexta acutis sentibus,
Corona contumeliae,
Squalenti amictum purpurā,
Regem coronat gloriae.

Molis crucem ter arduae,
Sudans, anhelans, concidens,
Ad montis usque verticem
Gestare vi compellitur.

Confixus atro stipite
Inter scelestos innocens,
Orando pro tortoribus,
Exsanguis efflat spiritum.

intexo, intexere, intextus: weave in, interweave
acutus a um: sharp
sentes, sentium: thorns
contumelia: insult, outrage
amictus, -a, um: clothed, robed, wearing
purpura, ae (noun): purple (*robed in filthy purple*)
squalens, squalentis (<squaleo): filthy, vile, dirty

moles, molis (fem): weight, bulk
arduus, -a, -um: difficult, hard, perh *heavy*
ter: three times, OR very
sudo, sudare: sweat
anhelo, anhelare: pant, be breathless
concido, concidere: fall down (nb *cóncido*; Δ *concīdo*)
vertex, verticis: top, summit
gesto, gestare: carry (*crucem*)
compello, compellere: oblige, compel

configo, configere, confixi, confixus: fasten, nail
ater, atra, atrum: black, dark
stipes, stipitis: tree, stake, beam
scelestus, -a, -um: criminal, wicked
orando: *by praying, while praying* (as if *orans*)
tortor, tortoris: torturer, tormentor
exsanguis (adj): drained of blood, out of blood
efflo, efflare: breathe out, give forth

76. Ira justa conditoris
Anon c. 1700

Ira justa conditoris,
Imbre aquarum vindice,
Criminosum mersit orbem,
Noe in arcā sospite;
Mira tandem vis amoris
Lavit orbem sanguine.

Tam salubri terra felix
Irrigata pluviā,
Ante spinis quae scatebat,
Germinavit flosculos;
Inque nectaris saporem
Transiere absynthia.

imber, imbris: rain, storm
vindex, vindicis: avenger, punisher, avenging, punishing
mergo, mergere, mersi: overwhelm, submerge
Noe: (Indecl. Here ablative)
sospes, sospitis: safe, uninjured
tandem: finally, and then

pluvia, -ae: rain
saluber, salubris: wholesome, salutary, salubrious
ante (Adv): previously, earlier, before
spina, -ae: thorn (*which previously was full of thorns*)
scateo, -ēre (+abl): abound in, be covered with
germino, -are (+acc): grow, blossom with, burst out in
flosculus: little flower, blossom
nectar, nectaris: nectar
sapor, saporis: taste, flavor
trans-eo, trans-ire: pass over into, be transformed into, be changed into
absynthium (here plural): wormwood (cf Rev 8:11)

76. Ira justa conditoris

Triste protinus venenum
Dirus anguis posuit,
Et cruenta belluarum
Desiit ferocia;
Mitis Agni vulnerati
Haec fuit victoria.

O scientiae supernae
Altitudo impervia!
O suavitas benigni
Praedicanda pectoris!
Servus erat morte dignus,
Rex luit poenam optimus.

protinus (Adv): forthwith, at once
venenum: poison, venom
dirus a um: dire, dreadful, frightful
anguis, anguis: serpent, snake
pono, ponere: lay *aside*, put *down*
cruentus a um: bloody
bellua: savage beast, wild animal
desino, desinere, desii: cease, stop, come to an end
ferocia, -ae: savagery, barbarity

impervius: unreachable (height), unfathomable (depth)
praedico, praedicare: preach, declare, extol
luo, luere, lui: release, commute, expiate

76. Ira justa conditoris

Quando culpis provocamus
Ultionem judicis,
Tunc loquentis protegamur
Sanguinis praesentia;
Ingruentium malorum
Tunc recedant agmina.

Te redemptus laudet orbis
Grata servans munera,
O salutis sempiternae
Dux et auctor inclite,
Qui tenes beata regna
Cum Parente et Spiritu.

culpis: *by our sins, by our fault*
ultio, ultionis: vengeance, punishment
sanguinis loquentis: *of the blood which is our advocate*
ingruo, ingruere: assault, assail

gratus, -a, -um: pleasing, welcome, gracious
servo, -are: keep, treasure

77. Iste confessor Domini (M)
Anon, c. 800 Cf *Iste confessor Domini* (R)

Iste confessor Domini sacratus,
Festa plebs cujus celebrat per orbem,
Hodie laetus meruit secreta *or* Hac die laetus meruit supremos
Scandere caeli. Laudis honores.

Note:
In the monastic office the first version of the verse is used when the feast is on the anniversary of the saint's death. In the BR this distinction was abolished after 1960.

Qui pius, prudens, humilis, pudicus,
Sobrius, castus fuit et quietus,
Vita dum praesens vegetavit ejus
Corporis artūs.

sacratus, -a, -um: sacred, holy, hallowed
plebs, plebis: people
festum, -i: feast (pl for sing) (disting *festus, -a, -um.* NOT *festa-plebs*)

quietus: peaceful, peaceable, quiet
vegeto, vegetare: animate, stir to action
praesens, -entis: here, present, *in this world*
artus, -ūs: limb, joint

77. <u>Iste confessor Domini</u> (M)

Ad sacrum cujus tumulum frequenter,
Membra languentum modo sanitati,
Quolibet morbo fuerint gravata,
Restituuntur.

Unde nunc noster chorus in honorem
Ipsius, hymnum canit hunc libenter;
Ut piis ejus meritis juvemur
Omne per aevum.

Sit salus illi, decus atque virtus,
Qui supra caeli residens cacumen
Totius mundi machinam gubernat,
Trinus et unus.

ad: at
sacer, sacra, sacrum: holy, sacred
tumulus: grave, tomb
frequenter: often
membrum: member, limb, organ, part
languens, languentis: weak, sickly (gen pl: *–entum*)
modo: now, presently
sanitas, sanitatis: health, soundness
quilibet, quaeliber, quodlibet: whoever, whatever, whichever
morbus: disease, illness, sickness
gravatus, -a, -um: burdened, oppressed, troubled
restituo: restore (*membra sanitati restituuntur*)

libenter: gladly, willingly

cacumen, cacuminis (neut): summit, peak
resideo, residēre: remain, reside, dwell
supra (+ acc): upon, above
machina: fabric, construction, machinery

78. <u>Iste confessor Domini</u> (R)
Anon c. 800, rev 1632 Cf *Iste confessor Domini* (M)

Iste confessor Domini, colentes
Quem pie laudant populi per orbem,
Hac die laetus meruit supremos
Laudis honores.

Qui pius, prudens, humilis, pudicus,
Sobriam duxit sine labe vitam,
Donec humanos animavit aurae
Spiritus artus.

Cujus ob praestans meritum, frequenter
Aegra quae passim jacuēre membra,
Viribus morbi domitis, saluti
Restituuntur.

Noster hinc illi chorus obsequentem
Concinit laudem celebresque palmas,
Ut piis ejus precibus juvemur
Omne per aevum.

colo, colere, colui, cultus: honor, celebrate, observe the feast of

donec: as long as, while
animo, animare: quicken, give life to (+ acc)
aura, -ae: wind, air, breath
spiritus: breath, blowing (*the wind's breath)*
artus, -ūs: limb

praestans, praestantis (Adj): distinguished, evident
passim (Adv): here and there, far and wide, everywhere
jaceo, jacere, jacui: lie, lie ill, lie abed
domo, domare, domui, domitus: tame, reduce, control
vires, virium: power, force, strength
morbus: illness, disease (*the power of the disease being overcome*)

obsequens, obsequentis: dutiful, obedient
celeber, celebris: renowned, solemn
palma, -ae: hymn of victory, song of praise, paean
concino, concinere, concinui, concentus: sing of, celebrate in song

79. Iste quem laeti
Juan Escollar, ob 1700

Iste, quem laeti colimus, fideles
Cujus excelsos canimus triumphos,
Hac die Joseph meruit perennis
Gaudia vitae.

O nimis felix, nimis o beatus,
Cujus extremam vigiles ad horam
Christus et Virgo simul astiterunt,
Ore sereno.

Hinc stygis victor, laqueo solutus
Carnis, ad sedes placido sopore
Migrat aeternas, rutilisque cingit
Tempora sertis.

Ergo regnantem, flagitemus omnes,
Adsit ut nobis, veniamque nostris
Obtinens culpis, tribuat supernae
Munera pacis.

Sint tibi plausus, tibi sint honores,
Trine qui regnas, Deus, et coronas
Aureas servo tribuis fideli
Omne per aevum.

iste: (*Iste….Joseph meruit*)

vigil, vigilis (Adj): watchful, attentive
os, oris: face, countenance

sopor, soporis: sleep
rutilus, -a, -um: golden-red, shining red
tempus, temporis: brow, forehead, temple (of the head)
serta, -ae: wreath, garland

flagito, flagitare: beseech, entreat (*regnantem ut adsit nobis*)

plausus, -ūs: applause (nom pl)
Trine….Deus: (*qui regnas….et tribuis*)

80. Jam bone pastor Petre (M)
Anon, c. 500 Cf *Beate pastor petre* (R)

Jam bone pastor Petre, clemens accipe
Vota precantum, et peccati vincula
Resolve tibi potestate traditā,
Quā cunctis caelum verbo claudis, aperis.

Sit Trinitati sempiterna gloria,
Honor, potestas, atque jubilatio,
In unitate cui manet imperium,
Ex tunc et modo, per aeterna saecula.

clemens, clementis: merciful, loving
votum, voti: prayer, vow, desire
precans, precantis (< precor, precari. *precantum* is gen pl)
tibi: (ind obj of *tradita*)
qua: (antecedent is *potestate*)
cunctis: (= *omnibus*)
claudo, claudere: close
aperio, aperire: open

cui: *in which*
ex tunc: then, at the beginning
modo: now

81. Jam Christe sol justitiae (M)
Anon, c. 500 Cf *O sol salutis* (R)

Jam Christe sol justitiae,
Mentis diescant tenebrae,
Virtutum ut lux redeat,
Terris diem cum reparas.

Dans tempus acceptabile,
Et paenitens cor tribue,
Convertat ut benignitas
Quos longa suffert pietas.

sol, solis: sun, sunlight
diesco, diescere: become day, become light
reparo, reparare: restore, return

converto, convertere: (Transitive: *ut benignitas tua convertat illos quos*)
suffero, sufferre: endure, sustain

81. Jam Christe sol justitiae (M)

Quiddamque paenitentiae
Da ferre, quamvis gravium,
Majore tuo munere,
Quo demptio fit criminum.

Dies venit, dies tua,
In qua reflorent omnia;
Laetemur in hac ad tuam
Per hanc reducti gratiam.

Te rerum universitas,
Clemens adoret Trinitas,
Et nos novi per veniam
Novum canamus canticum.

quiddam + gen: something of, a measure of, a little
da: (*da nobis ferre quiddam paenitentiae*)
quamvis: although, even though (Δ *quivis, quaevis, quodvis*)
gravis, -is: serious, grave (*criminum....quamvis gravium*)
munere: (abl of means with *ferre*)
quo: (antecedent is *munere*)
demptio, demptionis: removal, cancellation

Allow us to bear a degree of penance by virtue of your greater gift, by which the removal of our sins—although grave—is accomplished.

refloreo, reflorēre: bloom again, blossom anew
in hac: *in hac (die)*
ad tuam: *ad tuam....gratiam*
per hanc: *per hanc (diem)*

universitas: totality
clemens Trinitas: (vocative)
nos novi: *we renewed, we anew, we made new*
venia: forgiveness, pardon, grace

82. Jam Christus astra ascenderat
Anon, c. 400 → VR

Jam Christus astra ascenderat,
Reversus unde venerat,
Promissum Patris munere — Patris fruendum munere
Sanctum daturus Spiritum.

Solemnis urgebat dies,
Quo mystico septemplici
Orbis volutus septies
Signat beata tempora.

jam: now, by now, at that time (nb pluperfect tense)
fruor, frui (+abl): enjoy, use, get

urgeo, urgēre: press close, draw near
septemplex, septemplicis (noun): sevenplex, seven-fold time
volvo, volvere, volutus: turn, revolve
orbis: world, universe, sky (ie the geocentric universe of Ptolemy)
septies: seven times
orbis volutus septies: *the heavens having rotated seven times*
signo, signare: signify, proclaim, announce

Notes

1. VR *patris fruendum munere*. The syntax is unclear. Britt: "to be received as the gift of the Father". Connelly: "to be received as the Father's gift". But *fruor* is deponent and not passive. It seems that VM and VR may both be textually corrupt. LH restores an older reading:

Iam Christus astra ascenderat
regressus unde venerat
promissa Patris munera
Sanctum daturus Spiritum.

2. *quo mystico septemplici*: "by which mystical sevenplex", "and by this seven-fold mystery", "when by the mystic number seven".

82. Jam Christus astra ascenderat

Dum horā cunctis tertiā	Cum lucis horā tertiā
Repente mundus intonat;	
Orantibus apostolis	Apostolis orantibus
Deum venisse nuntiat.	Deum venire nuntiat.
De Patris ergo lumine	
Decorus ignis almus est,	
Qui fida Christi pectora	
Calore Verbi compleat.	
Impleta gaudent viscera,	
Afflata Sancto Spiritu,	
Voces diversas intonant,	Vocesque diversas sonant
Fantur Dei magnalia.	

mundus: world (ie the world around the Apostles)
intono, intonare: thunder, burst into sound
cunctis: *for everyone, in the hearing of all*
nuntiat: *it announces, the sound proclaims*

est: *proceeds, comes*
decorus….almus: *beautiful and kindly*
fida Christi pectora (acc): *hearts faithful to Christ*
calor, caloris: heat, warmth
compleo, complere: fill, fulfill

impleo, implere: fill, suffuse
afflo, afflare: inspire (cf *Divino Afflante Spiritu,* DS 3825)
voces diversas: (cf Acts 2:4, *coeperunt loqui variis linguis*)
intono, -are (+acc): burst into, begin speaking in
for, fari, fatus: speak of, declare (cf Acts 2:12, *loquentes magnalia Dei*)

82. Jam Christus astra ascenderat

Ex omni gente cogniti,	Notique cunctis gentibus
Graecis, Latinis, Barbaris,	
Cunctisque admirantibus,	Simulque demirantibus
Linguis loquuntur omnium.	
Judaea tunc incredula,	
Vesana torvo spiritu,	
Ructare musti crapulam	Madere musto sobrios
Alumnos Christi concrepat.	Christi fideles increpat
Sed signis et virtutibus	Sed editis miraculis
Occurrit, et docet Petrus,	
Falsa profari perfidos,	
Joele teste comprobans.	

ex: out of, by
demiror, -ari: wonder, be astonished (= *admiror*)

Judaea: Jewry, Judaea
incredulus a um: disbelieving, unbelieving, incredulous
vesanus, a, um: unsound, mad, insane
torvus a um: fierce, wild
ructo, ructare: belch
madeo, madēre: drink too much, get drunk
mustum: new wine
crapula: drunkenness
ructare musti crapulam: *belch the drunkenness of new wine,*
belch drunkenly on new wine
alumnus: pupil, follower
concrepo, -are: accuse, crudely accuse
increpo: accuse, reproach (*Judaea....increpat*)
VR *accuses the sober faithful followers of Christ of being drunk on new wine*

occurro, -ere: counter, go to meet (their accusation), respond
profor, profari: speak out, relate, tell
edo, edere, edidi, editus: set forth, make public
Joel, Joelis: *the prophet* Joel (*calling Joel as his witness*)
comprobo, -are: prove, demonstrate, settle the issue

83. Jam lucis orto sidere
Anon, c. 500

Jam lucis orto sidere,
Deum precemur supplices,
Ut in diurnis actibus
Nos servet a nocentibus.

Linguam refraenans temperet,
Ne litis horror insonet;
Visum fovendo contegat,
Ne vanitates hauriat.

Sint pura cordis intima,
Absistat et vecordia;
Carnis terat superbiam
Potus cibique parcitas.

Ut cum dies abscesserit,
Noctemque sors reduxerit,
Mundi per abstinentiam
Ipsi canamus gloriam.

refraeno, -are: hold back, restrain, curb
tempero, -are: govern, moderate, discipline
lis, litis: strife, argument, quarrelling
insono, insonare: make itself heard, be heard
contego, contegere: cover
visus, -us: sight, the sense of sight
fovendo: *with loving care*
haurio, haurire: dredge up, drink in (subj of *hauriat* is *it*, ie *visus*)

intima, -orum: interior, the inner parts
vecordia, -ae: foolishness, irrationality
absisto, absistere: withdraw, cease, disappear
tero, terere: rub out, wear away
parcitas, parcitatis: smallness, moderation

abscedo, abscedere, abscessi: depart, retire, withdraw
sors, sortis: fate, fixed order, providence
mundus, -a, -um: clean
ipsi: to Him (not *nos ipsi*)

84. Jam morte victor obruta
Continuation of *In monte olivis consito*, qv

Jam morte victor obrutā
Ab inferis Christus redit,
Fractisque culpae vinculis,
Caeli recludit limina. Resurrection

Visus satis mortalibus
Ascendit ad caelestia,
Dextraeque Patris assidet
Consors paternae gloriae. Ascension

Quem jam suis promiserat,
Sanctum daturus Spiritum,
Linguis amoris igneis
Maestis alumnis impluit. Pentecost

Soluta carnis pondere
Ad astra Virgo tollitur,
Excepta caeli jubilo
Et angelorum canticis. Assumption

Bis sena cingunt sidera
Almae parentis verticem;
Throno propinqua Filii
Cunctis creatis imperat. Coronation of BVM

obruo, obruere, obrui, obrutus: vanquish, overwhelm
recludo, recludere: unclose, throw open

visus….mortalibus: *seen….by mortals*
assideo, assidere: sit at, be seated at (+ dat: *dextrae assidet = sedet ad dexteram*)

maestus a um: sad, sorrowful
alumnus, alumni: pupil, follower
impluo, impluere: rain upon (c dat pers, c abl rei)

soluta + abl: *released from* (*Virgo soluta pondere carnis*)
excipio, exceptus: take up, capture, receive

seni, -ae, -a: six (*bis sena sidera = twice six stars*, ie 12)

85. Jam sol recedit igneus (R)
Anon, 350-850 Rev 1632. Cf *O lux beata Trinitas* (M)

Jam sol recedit igneus;
Tu, lux perennis, Unitas,
Nostris, beata Trinitas,
Infunde lumen cordibus.

Te mane laudum carmine,
Te deprecamur vespere;
Digneris ut te supplices
Laudemus inter caelites.

igneus, -a, -um: fiery
tu: (lux, Unitas, Trinitas)
nostris: (nostris.... cordibus)

mane (Adv): in the morning
vespere (Adv): in the evening
dignor, dignari: grant, vouchsafe, deem (us) worthy, deign
caeles, caelitis: heavenly dweller, heavenly being

86. Jam toto subitus vesper
Callisto Palumbella, c. 1750

Jam toto subitus vesper eat polo,
Et sol attonitum praecipitet diem,
Dum saevae recolo ludibrium necis,
Divinamque catastrophen.

Spectatrix aderas supplicio, Parens,
Malis uda, gerens cor adamantinum,
Natus funereā pendulus in cruce
Altos dum gemitūs dabat.

subitus, -a, -um: sudden, unexpected
eat: (subjunc of *eo, ire*)
toto eat polo: *fill all the heavens, cross the whole sky*
attonitus a um: astonished, surprised
praecipito, praecipitare: cast down, throw down
dum…. recolo: *while I recount, while I contemplate*
ludibrium: mockery, derision
nex, necis (fem): death, slaughter
catastrophen: (Greek fem acc sing)

spectatrix, spectatricis: onlooker (fem), observer
supplicium: execution, torture, suffering
Parens: *a Parent, O Mother*
udus, -a, -um: tearful, wet with tears
malis: *because of the wrongs, in the face of the evils*
gerens cor: *keeping your heart, bearing a heart*
adamantinus a um: unconquered, unbroken
dum: *dum Natus, pendulus in cruce funerea, dabat gemitus altos*
funereus, -a, -um: woeful, fatal, funereal
pendulus, -a, -um: hanging
dabat: *uttered, gave voice to*
gemitus, -ūs: sigh, groan

86. <u>Jam toto subitus vesper</u>

Pendens ante oculos Natus, atrocibus
Sectus verberibus, Natus hiantibus
Fossus vulneribus, quot penetrantibus
Te confixit aculeis.

Eheu, sputa, alapae, verbera, vulnera,
Clavi, fel, aloe, spongia, lancea,
Sitis, spina, cruor, quam variā pium
Cor pressēre tyrannide.

seco, secare, secui, sectus: cut, cut up, slash
hio, hiare: stand open, gape
fodio, fodere, fodi, fossus: dig, gouge
aculeus: sting, *metaph* dagger
quot: *he transfixed you with so many deep strokes*

Eheu, Heu: alas, woe!
sputum: spitting, spittle (*sputa.....cruor:* all in nominative case)
alapa: slap, blow
clavus: nail
aloe, aloes: bitterness, aloe (for anointing, cf John 19:39)
spongia, -ae: sponge
lancea, -ae: spear, lance
spina, -ae: thorn
premo, premere, pressi: oppress, press upon (*presserunt*)
tyrannis, tyrannidis (fem): tyranny
quam varia tyrannide: *with what manifold tyranny*

86. Jam toto subitus vesper

Cunctis interea stat generosior
Virgo martyribus prodigio novo:
In tantis moriens non moreris, Parens,
Diris fixa doloribus.

Sit summae Triadi gloria, laus, honor,
A qua suppliciter, sollicitā prece,
Posco virginei roboris aemulas
Vires rebus in asperis.

interea: meanwhile, however
stat (*stas* might be expected in the context.)
generosus, -a, -um: noble, excellent
cunctis martyribus: *than all the martyrs*
prodigio novo: *by reason of a new miracle*
fixus, -a, -um: overwhelmed by, immured in

sollicitus: diligent, careful, thoughtful
posco (+acc): ask for, pray for, request
vires, virium (fem): strength, powers
robor, roboris: strength, fortitude
aemulus: rivalling, emulating (+ gen)
virgineus: of the Virgin, Virginal
rebus in asperis: *in times of hardship*

87. Jesu corona celsior
Anon, c. 900 → VR

Jesu, corona celsior,
Et veritas sublimior,
Qui confitenti servulo,
Reddis perenne praemium.

Da supplicanti coetui,
Obtentu huius optimi, Huius rogatu, noxii
Remissionem criminum, Remissionem criminis
Rumpendo nexum vinculi.

Anni recurso tempore, Anni reverso tempore
Dies illuxit lumine, Dies refulsit lumine
Quo sanctus hic de corpore
Polum migravit praepotens. Migravit inter sidera

qui: (tu qui)
confiteor, confiteri: confess, profess, *perh* believe
praemium: reward

coetus, -ūs: gathering, assembly
obtentus, -ūs: pleading, intercession
huius: *of this (holy saint)*
rogatus, -ūs: petition, request
noxius, -a, -um: harmful, sinful, evil
crimen, criminis: sin
nexus, -ūs: grip, hold

recurso: *having come back* (as if perf part of *recurro*)
illucesco, -ere, illuxi: shine, shine forth
refulgeo: shine, shine brightly
quo: *(day) on which*
hic: *hic sanctus* (not adverbial *hic*)
polum: *heavenward, to heaven*
praepotens, praepotentis: mighty, in power

87. Jesu corona celsior

Hic vana terrae gaudia,
Et luculenta praedia,
Polluta sorde deputans,
Ovans tenet caelestia.

Te, Christe rex piissime,
Hic confitendo jugiter,
Calcavit hostem fortiter, — Calcavit artes daemonum
Superbum ac satellitem. — Saevumque Averni principem

Virtute clarus et fide,
Confessionis ordine, — Confessione sedulus
Jejuna membra deferens,
Dapes supernas obtinet.

Proinde te, piissime,
Precamur omnes supplices,
Ut huius almi gratiā — Nobis ut huius gratiā
Nobis remittas debita. — Poenas remittas debitas

praedium: property, estate
luculentus a um: splendid, lustrous
sors, sordis: filth (*defiled by filth*)
deputo, deputare: reckon, account
ovo, ovare: rejoice

jugiter: constantly, consistently
calco, calcare: trample on, tread upon
satelles, satellitis: servant, companion (perh *and his proud minions*)

confessionis ordine: *of the rank of confessor*
jejunus, -a, -um: fasting, abstinent
jejuna membra: *his fasting organs, his fasting body*
defero, deferre: bring down, constrain, mortify
daps, dapis; banquet

proinde: accordingly
huius almi: (*hujus almi sancti*, ie the saint of the day)

88. Jesu corona virginum
Attrib St Ambrose, c. 400 → VR

Jesu corona virginum,
Quem mater illa concipit,
Quae sola Virgo parturit,
Haec vota clemens accipe,

Qui pascis inter lilia, | Qui pergis inter lilia
Septus choreis virginum,
Sponsus decorus gloriā
Sponsisque reddens praemia.

Quocumque pergis, virgines | Quocumque tendis, virgines
Sequuntur, atque laudibus
Post te canentes cursitant,
Hymnosque dulces personant.

Te deprecamur: largius | Te deprecamur supplices
Nostris adauge sensibus | Nostris ut addas sensibus
Nescire prorsus omnia
Corruptionis vulnera.

pasco, pascere: feed, graze, browse (here intransitive)
pergo, pergere: proceed, continue
sepio, sepire, septus: hedge, enclose, guard
chorea, -ae: chorus (of dancers)
sponsis: (< sponsa)

tendo, tendere: direct one's steps, go
cursito, cursitare: run up and down, hasten
persono, personare: proclaim, sing out

largius (< *largus*): more abundantly, more plentifully
adaugeo, adaugēre (+dat): give increase to, add to, increase
nescire: *(so as) not to know, to be innocent of*
prorsus: absolutely, utterly

89. Jesu decus angelicum
School of Saint Bernard, ob 1153
This hymn is a cento, or excerpt, from *Jesu dulcis memoria*, qv.

Jesu decus angelicum,
In aure dulce canticum,
In ore mel mirificum,
In corde nectar caelicum.

Qui te gustant, esuriunt;
Qui bibunt, adhuc sitiunt;
Desiderare nesciunt,
Nisi Jesum quem diligunt.

decus, decoris (neut): beauty
nectar, nectaris (neut): nectar
caelicus, -a, -um: heavenly

Note

Adhuc sitiunt. Cf John 4:14, *qui autem biberit ex aqua, quam ego dabo ei, non sitiet in aeternum.*

Saint Augustine declares, *Inquietum est cor nostrum, donec requiescat in te*. The Cistercian author replies that there is no rest for the lover. The soul, which has tasted the sweetness of the Lord, never ceases to desire more.

89. Jesu decus angelicum

O Jesu mi dulcissime,
Spes suspirantis animae!
Te quaerunt piae lacrimae,
Te clamor mentis intimae.

Mane nobiscum Domine,
Et nos illustra lumine;
Pulsā mentis caligine,
Mundum reple dulcedine.

Jesu flos matris Virginis,
Amor nostri dulcedinis,
Tibi laus, honor nominis,
Regnum beatitudinis.

mi: (vocative)
suspiro, suspirare: sigh, pant, long for
clamor, clamoris: cry, call (Supply a verb, eg *quaerit*)
mens, mentis: heart, soul (In the hymns *mens* rarely means "mind".)

pello, pellere, pepuli, pulsus: drive away, banish
caligo, caliginis (fem): cloud, darkness

amor nostri dulcedinis: *the sweetness of our love, our sweetness of love*
tibi et seq: *thine are the praise, the honor of (thy)name, and the kingdom of bliss*

Note

Luke 24:29— *Mane nobiscum quoniam advesperascit*. Stay with us, because it is growing dark. The cry of the innermost heart, *clamor mentis intimae*, is precisely this: *Mane nobiscum Domine*.

90. Jesu dulcis memoria
School of Saint Bernard, ob 1153

Jesu dulcis memoria,
Dans vera cordis gaudia;
Sed super mel et omnia,
Ejus dulcis praesentia.

Nil canitur suavius,
Nil auditur jucundius,
Nil cogitatur dulcius,
Quam Jesus Dei filius.

Jesu, spes paenitentibus,
Quam pius es petentibus,
Quam bonus te quaerentibus!
Sed quid invenientibus?

Nec lingua valet dicere,
Nec littera exprimere;
Expertus potest credere,
Quid sit Jesum diligere.

Sis, Jesu, nostrum gaudium,
Qui es futurus praemium;
Sit nostra in te gloria,
Per cuncta semper saecula.

Jesu: (Genitive. Vocative, however, in stanzas 3 and 5)
memoria: (Nominative. *The thought of Jesus is sweet....*)

nil suavius: *nothing sweeter, nothing lovelier*
jucundus a um: happy, joyful

valeo, valēre (+ infin): have the power to, be adequate to
experior, experiri, expertus: test, experience

qui es futurus praemium: *who are to be (our) reward*

91. Jesu nostra redemptio (M)
Anon, c. 700 — Cf *Salutis humanae sator* (R)

Jesu, nostra redemptio,
Amor et desiderium,
Deus creator omnium,
Homo in fine temporum.

Quae te vicit clementia,
Ut ferres nostra crimina,
Crudelem mortem patiens,
Ut nos a morte tolleres! [?]

Inferni claustra penetrans,
Tuos captivos redimens,
Victor triumpho nobili
Ad dextram Patris residens.

Ipsa te cogat pietas,
Ut mala nostra superes
Parcendo, et voti compotes
Nos tuo vultu saties.

claustrum: enclosure, interior
resido, residere: sit down, be enthroned

supero, -are: conquer, defeat
compos, compotis: master of, possessing, sharing (+ gen)
votum: promise, vow
satio, satiare: fill, nourish, enrich

Note

At then end of verse 2 the VR and some editions of the VM prefer a question mark after *tolleres*.

92. <u>Jesu redemptor omnium, Perpes</u>
Anon, c. 700 →VR

Jesu redemptor omnium,
Perpes corona praesulum,
In hac die clementius
Nostris faveto precibus. Indulgeas precantibus

Tui sacri qua nominis
Confessor almus claruit;
Huius celebrat annua
Devota plebs solemnia.

Qui rite mundi gaudia
Huius caduca respuens,
Cum angelis caelestibus Aeternitatis praemio
Laetus potitur praemiis. Potitur inter angelos.

Huius benignus annue
Nobis sequi vestigia;
Huius precatu servulis
Dimitte noxam criminis.

perpes, perpitis (adj): (= *perpetuus, -a, -um*)
praesul, praesulis: bishop, leader, patron

qua: (*in hac die....qua*)
claresco, clarescere, clarui: shine forth, shine out
annua: (*devota plebs....celebrat....annua solemnia*)

caducus, -a, -um: perishable, fleeting, fallen
respuo, respuere: despise, scorn, spit upon
potior, potiri (+abl): obtain, possess

huius: (*huius....vestigia*)
annuo, annuere: nod, assent, allow (+ dat, + infin)
noxa, -ae: injury, fault

93. Jesu redemptor omnium, Quem (R)
Cf *Christe redemptor omnium, Ex Patre* (M)

Jesu, redemptor omnium,
Quem lucis ante originem
Parem paternae gloriae
Pater supremus edidit.

Tu lumen et splendor Patris,
Tu spes perennis omnium,
Intende quas fundunt preces
Tui per orbem servuli.

Memento, rerum conditor,
Nostri quod olim corporis,
Sacrata ab alvo Virginis
Nascendo, formam sumpseris.

parem: (*quem....parem = whom....like unto*)
edo, edere, edidi: generate, produce, give forth

intendo, intendere: hear, hearken to (+ acc)

memento quod: *remember that* (here followed by perf subjunc)
nostri: (*nostri corporis....formam*)
olim: once, formerly
alvus, -I (fem): womb
nascor, nasci, natus: be born

Cf Phil 2: 7— *sed semetipsum exinanivit formam servi accipiens.*

93. Jesu redemptor omnium, Quem (R)

Testatur hoc praesens dies,
Currens per anni circulum,
Quod solus e sinu Patris
Mundi salus adveneris.

Hunc astra, tellus, aequora,
Hunc omne, quod caelo subest,
Salutis auctorem novae
Novo salutat cantico.

Et nos, beata quos sacri
Rigavit unda sanguinis,
Natalis ob diem tui
Hymni tributum solvimus.

testor, testari: bear witness, testify (+ acc)
hoc....quod: *to this....namely that* (+ perf subjunc)

hunc: this man, him (*omne salutat hunc*)
quod caelo subest: *quod est sub caelo*

nos: (*Et nos....solvimus*)
rigo, rigare: moisten, water, wash
natalis, -is (noun): birth
tributum, -i: tribute, offering
solvimus: *we pay (offer) the tribute of a hymn*

94. Jesu rex admirabilis
Cento from *Jesu dulcis memoria*, qv
School of Saint Bernard, ob 1153

Jesu rex admirabilis,
Et triumphator nobilis,
Dulcedo ineffabilis,
Totus desiderabilis.

Quando cor nostrum visitas,
Tunc lucet ei veritas,
Mundi vilescit vanitas,
Et intus fervet caritas.

admirabilis: wonderful, wondrous, worthy of admiration
triumphator: victor, conqueror
nobilis: high-born, renowned
ineffabilis: inexpressible, unsayable

visito, visitare: come to see, enter, visit
luceo, lucere: shine on, give light to, illumine (+ dat)
ei: (Antecedent is *cor*)
vilesco, vilescere: lose value, seem worthless
intus (adv): inwardly, within
ferveo, fervere: glow, burn

94. Jesu rex admirabilis

Jesu, dulcedo cordium,
Fons vivus, lumen mentium,
Excedens omne gaudium,
Et omne desiderium.

Jesum omnes agnoscite,
Amorem ejus poscite;
Jesum ardenter quaerite,
Quaerendo inardescite.

Te nostra, Jesu, vox sonet,
Nostri te mores exprimant;
Te corda nostra diligant,
Et nunc et in perpetuum.

dulcedo, dulcedinis: sweetness, delight
vivus, -a, -um: living
excedo, excedere: surpass, go beyond

agnosco, agnoscere: recognise, perceive (Δ the word "agnostic" of Greek origin)
posco, poscere (+acc): ask for, request
ardenter: with burning zeal, passionately
inardesco, inardescere: be enkindled, take fire

sono, sonare: sing of, resound, ring (*te* "with your name")
mores, morum (< mos, moris): action, life, way of living
exprimo, exprimere: reflect, display, express

Note

The word *mores* has a monastic over-tone, of which the writer of this hymn would certainly have been aware: *Conversatio morum*, "conversion of one's life". (Rule, Chap 58)

95. Jesu salvator saeculi (M)
Rabanus Maurus, ob 856
Cf *Salutis aeternae dator* (R)

Jesu salvator saeculi,
Redemptis ope subveni,
Et, pia Dei Genitrix,
Salutem posce miseris.

Patriarcharum cunei,
Et prophetarum merita
Coetūs omnes angelici,
Nobis precentur veniam.

Baptista Christi praevius,
Et Claviger aethereus,
Cum ceteris Apostolis,
Nos solvant nexu criminis.

Chorus sacratus martyrum,
Confessio sacerdotum,
Et virginalis castitas
Nos a peccatis abluant.

Monachorum suffragia,
Omnesque cives caelici
Annuant votis supplicum,
Et vitae poscant praemium.

ops, opis: aid, support (Here perh redundant)
subvenio (+ dat): help, come to the help of

cuneus: crowd, throng (in classical Latin = *wedge*)
coetus, -ūs (here 2 syllables): gathering, community, society
precentur: (< *precor, precari*. Not *praecino, praecinere*)

praevius: precursor, coming before
claviger, clavigeri: key-wielder, key-bearer (ie Peter)

suffragium: intercession, support
annuo, annuere: nod (ie show a sign of favor) (+ dat)

96. Lucis creator optime
Attrib St Gregory the Great, c. 600

Lucis creator optime,
Lucem dierum proferens,
Primordiis lucis novae,
Mundi parans originem:

Qui mane junctum vesperi
"Diem" vocari praecipis:
Tetrum chaos illabitur, VR Illabitur tetrum chaos
Audi preces cum fletibus:

profero, -ferre: display, produce, offer
primordium: origin, beginning

qui: (*creator optime....., tu qui praecipis*)
praecipio, -ere: prescribe, command, teach
mane junctum vesperi: *morning linked to evening*
diem vocari: be called "day" (subj of *vocari* is *mane*)
teter, tetra, tetrum: hideous, vile
chaos (neuter): darkness, chaos
illabor, illabi: descend, fall (upon us)

Notes:
This hymn is sung at Vespers. Strophe one refers not to daybreak, but to the creation of light at the beginning of time. *Dierum* is not a simple case of poetic plural-for-singular; it refers rather to all the days of the world.

96. Lucis creator optime

Ne mens gravata crimine,
Vitae sit exsul munere,
Dum nil perenne cogitat,
Seseque culpis illigat.

Caelorum pulset intimum, Caeleste pulset ostium
Vitale tollat praemium;
Vitemus omne noxium,
Purgemus omne pessimum.

gravatus, -a, -um: burdened with, weighed down by
exsul, exsulis: (be) banished from, (be) deprived of (+ abl)
munus, muneris: gift
nil perenne: *a perpetual nothing*
sese: (= *se*)
illigo, illigare: entangle, encumber

intimum: the innermost place, the interior
ostium: gate, entrance
pulso, pulsare: knock upon, seek admission to (+ acc)
tollo, tollere: take (ie *obtain*) (disting *tollo= take away*, ie *remove*)
vitale praemium: *the reward of life*
vito, vitare: avoid, shun
purgo, purgare: cleanse away, clean out

Notes;
1. The third strophe is a subordinate clause, introduced by *ne*, and dependant on the verb phrase *audi preces* of the preceding strophe.
2. The subject of *pulset* and of *tollat* in strophe 4 is *mens* in strophe 3.

97. Lustra sex qui jam peregit (R)
Venantius Fortunatus, c. 530-610
Cento from *Pange lingua gloriosi Lauream certaminis*, qv.
Cf *Lustris sex qui jam peractis* (M)

Lustra sex qui jam peregit,
Tempus implens corporis,
Sponte liberā Redemptor
Passioni deditus,
Agnus in crucis levatur
Immolandus stipite.

Felle potus, ecce languet;
Spina, clavi, lancea
Mite corpus perforarunt;
Unda manat et cruor;
Terra, pontus, astra, mundus,
Quo lavantur flumine!

lustrum: lapse of five years, five-year period (see note 2)
qui: who, and He (ie Jesus. See note 1 at end)
perago, peragere, peregi: complete, attain (*who had now completed six lustra*)
tempus corporis: *the season of His body, His bodily time*
impleo, -ēre: complete, finish, reach the end of
spons, spontis (fem): free will, will
dedo, dedere, dedidi, deditus: surrender, give up
agnus: *the Redeemer....(as) a Lamb*
stipes, stipitis: trunk, log, beam (*in stipite crucis)*

poto, potare, potavi, potus: give to drink, offer to drink (c abl rei)
fel, fellis: gall, a foul drink
felle potus: *offered gall to drink, having been given gall to drink*
langueo, languēre: sicken, grow weary
spina, -ae: thorn (nom sing)
clavus, -i: nail (nom pl)
lancea, -ae: spear (nom sing)
perforo, perforare: pierce, dig into, penetrate
perforarunt: = *perforaverunt* (syncopated alternative form)
unda: wave, water
cruor, cruoris: gore, blood
mano, manare: flow, drip (*a surge of water and gore flows out*)
pontus, -i: the sea
quo flumine: *in what a river*!

97. Lustra sex qui jam peregit (R)

Crux fidelis inter omnes
Arbor una nobilis;
Silva talem nulla profert
Fronde, flore, germine;
Dulce ferrum, dulce lignum, mss: Dulce lignum, dulce clavo
Dulce pondus sustinent. Dulce pondus sustinens.

Flecte ramos, arbor alta,
Tensa laxa viscera,
Et rigor lentescat ille,
Quem dedit nativitas;
Et superni membra Regis
Tende miti stipite.

arbor, arboris (fem): tree (see note 4)
inter omnes: (scil. *inter omnes arbores*)
talem: (scil. *talem arborem*)
frons, frondis: branch, leafy branch, foliage
flos, floris: blossom, flower
germen, germinis: bud, sprout, fruit (*in foliage, in blossom, or in fruit*)
dulce: (see note 5)
ferrum: *ferrum (et) lignum sustinent pondus*
sustineo, sustinēre: bear, carry

flecto, flectere: bend
ramus: branch (*bow down your branches, lofty tree*)
laxo, laxare: relax, loosen
tendo, tendere, tetendi, tensus: stretch, tighten
viscera: sinews, fibres (ie of the tree)
lentesco, lentescere: relax, soften, unbend (intransitive)
rigor, rigoris: stiffness, severity
nativitas, nativitatis: birth, nature
quem (antecedent = *rigor*): *which (your) birth gave (to you)*
miti stipite: *upon (your) tender beam*
tendo, tendere: stretch out, extend, *perh* hold, hold up (see note 6)

97. Lustra sex qui jam peregit (R)

Sola digna tu fuisti
Ferre mundi victimam,
Atque portum praeparare
Arca mundo naufrago,
Quam sacer cruor perunxit,
Fusus Agni corpore.

portus, -ūs: harbor, haven
arca, -ae: ark (nom sing) (see note 7)
naufragus a um: ship-wrecked (*as an ark for a shipwrecked world*)
quam: (antecedent is *arca*)
perungo, perungere, perunxi: anoint
fusus: (modifies *cruor*) (*poured from the body of the Lamb*)

Notes:

1. The first strophe of this hymn follows the fifth strophe of the longer form of *Pange lingua*, qv. The antecedent of *qui* here is *infans* in that other hymn. The splitting of the longer form into two hymns was done without rewriting the text.

2. The *lustrum* was a political and religious cycle of five years in pre-Christian Rome. After six *lustra*, therefore, the Lord is thirty years old.

3. The relation between *potus* and *languet* is temporal and not causal. Cf Matt 27:34., and B de J note h: *Jésus refuse ce stupéfiant.* The awkward line of text occurs only in VR; Venantius did not write it.

4. Throughout this hymn the cross is figured as a tree; and the tree is figured as a person. Furthermore, the cross is understood to have been fashioned from the wood of the same tree, from which Adam and Eve ate the forbidden fruit.

5. We take *ferrum* and *lignum* as the subjects of *sustinent*. In this R text, however, they might also be accusatives of explanation: *Ah, sweet steel, ah sweet wood! They hold up a sweet weight.*

The original text (mss) displays the word-play in which Venantius delighted. *Dulce lignum*, vocative; *dulce clavo*, ablative (with *dulce* as a poetic alternative form of *dulci*) ; *dulce pondus*, accusative singular. Thus *dulce* occurs three times in one sentence, and each time in a different case.

6. This strophe does not invite the tree to release the Lord and put Him down. Rather, it invites the tree to bend, to soften its harshness and to hold the Lord more gently. The cross itself must, so to speak, take up its burden.

7. The *arca* is both the Ark of the Covenant and the ark of Noah. The Ark of the Covenant is fashioned from the same tree of life as the cross. The cross, in turn, is figured as an ark that carries mankind to safety.

98. Lustris sex qui jam peractis (M)
Venantius Fortunatus, c. 530-610
Cento from *Pange lingua gloriosi*
Lauream (proelium) certaminis, qv.
Cf *Lustra sex qui jam peregit* (R), and notes at end.

The M text is also found in the Missale Romanum during the sacred liturgy for Good Friday. That is, the R text occurs only in the Breviary, and not in the Missal. This remains the case after the revision of the liturgy of Holy Week under Pope Pius XII of blessed memory.

Lustris sex qui jam peractis,
Tempus implens corporis,
Se volente natus ad hoc,
Passioni deditus,
Agnus in crucis levatur
Immolandus stipite.

Hic acetum, fel, arundo,
Sputa, clavi, lancea:
Mite corpus perforatur;
Sanguis undā profluit.
Terra, pontus, astra, mundus,
Quo lavantur flumine!

qui: *and He* (ie Jesus. See note 1 above)
lustrum: lapse of five years, five-year period (see note 2)
perago, -ere: complete
dedo, dedere, dedidi, deditus: surrender, give up
stipes, stipitis: trunk, log, beam (*in stipite crucis)*

hic: here, then, next
acetum: vinegar
fel, fellis: gall
arundo, arundinis: reed
sputum: spit, spittle, *plu* spitting
clavus: nail
perforo, perforare: pierce, pierce through
mite corpus: (nominative. in VR accusative)
unda: *in a wave, wavelike* (ablative. in VR nominative)
profluo, -ere, profluxi: flow, flow forth, flow out
pontus, -i: the sea
quo flumine: *in what a river*!

98. Lustris sex qui jam peractis (M)

Crux fidelis, inter omnes
Arbor una nobilis;
Nulla silva talem profert
Fronde, flore, germine.
Dulce lignum, dulces clavos,
Dulce pondus sustinet.

Flecte ramos, arbor alta,
Tensa laxa viscera,
Et rigor lentescat ille,
Quem dedit nativitas;
Ut superni membra Regis
Miti tendas stipite.

arbor, arboris (fem): tree (see note 4 above)
inter omnes: (scil. *inter omnes arbores*)
talem: (scil. *talem arborem*)
frons, frondis: branch, leafy branch, foliage
flos, floris: blossom, flower
germen, germinis: bud, sprout, fruit (*in foliage, in blossom, or in fruit*)

flecto, flectere: bend
ramus: branch (*bow down your branches, lofty tree*)
laxo, laxare: relax, loosen
tendo, tendere, tetendi, tensus: stretch, tighten
viscera: sinews, fibres (ie of the tree)
lentesco, lentescere: relax, soften, unbend (intransitive)
rigor, rigoris: stiffness, severity
nativitas, -tatis: birth, nature
quem: *which (your) birth gave (to you)* (antecedent = *rigor*)
miti stipite: *upon (your) tender beam*
tendo, tendere: stretch out, extend (see note 6)

98. Lustris sex qui jam peractis (M)

Sola digna tu fuisti
Ferre saecli pretium,
Atque portum praeparare
Nauta mundo naufrago,
Quem sacer cruor perunxit,
Fusus Agni corpore.

pretium: price
portus, -ūs: harbor, haven
nauta, -ae (masc): sailor (*as a sailor, like a sailor*)
naufragus, -a, -um: ship-wrecked
quem: (Antecedent is *mundo.* Δ *quam* in VR)
sacer, sacra, sacrum: sacred
cruor, cruoris: blood, bloodshed
perungo, perungere, perunxi: anoint
fundo, fundere, fusi, fusus: pour, pour out

99. Lux alma, Jesu, mentium (R)
School of Saint Bernard, ob 1153
Cento from *Jesu dulcis memoria*, qv.
Cf *Amor Jesu dulcissime* (M)

Lux alma, Jesu, mentium,
Dum corda nostra recreas,
Culpae fugas caliginem,
Et nos reples dulcedine.

Quam laetus est quem visitas!
Consors Paternae dexterae,
Tu dulce lumen patriae,
Carnis negatum sensibus.

Splendor Paternae gloriae,
Incomprehensa caritas,
Nobis amoris copiam
Largire per presentiam.

fugo, fugare: (Δ *fuga, fugae*)

patria, -ae: *our* land, home
nego, negare, negatus: deny (*lumen negatum….sensibus*)

incomprehensus, -a, -um: (cf *tenebrae eam non comprehenderunt*)
largior, largiri: bestow, grant, increase
presentiam: *per tuam praesentiam*

Note

The R and M hymns in this case are not *versiones* of each other. The R hymn is a cento of lines—not of verses—from a Cistercian original. The M hymn was composed in the 1400s, and it borrows from the Cistercian text.

100. Lux ecce surgit aurea
Prudentius, 348-410

Lux ecce surgit aurea,
Pallens fatiscat caecitas — VR Pallens facessat caecitas
Quae nosmet in praeceps diu
Errore traxit devio.

Haec lux serenum conferat,
Purosque nos praestet sibi;
Nihil loquamur subdolum;
Volvamus obscurum nihil.

palleo, pallēre: fade, wane, fade away
caecitas, caecitatis: blindness, darkness
fatisco, fatiscere: decrease, fall away
facesso, facessere: depart, withdraw
nosmet: *nos*
praeceps, praecipitis (neut): cliff, precipice, danger
devius, -a, -um: misleading, aberrant, wandering

serenus, -a, -um: clear, fair, bright
serenum: (*caelum serenum = a clear sky, fair weather, a bright day*)
praesto, praestare: keep, furnish, guarantee
subdolus, -a, -um: cunning, deceitful, tricky
volvo, volvere: turn over (in one's mind), ponder, meditate
obscurus a um: dark, secret, sinful

100. <u>Lux ecce surgit aurea</u>

Sic tota decurrat dies,
Ne lingua mendax, ne manus
Oculive peccent lubrici,
Ne noxa corpus inquinet.

Speculator astat desuper,
Qui nos diebus omnibus,
Actusque nostros prospicit
A luce prima in vesperum.

decurro, decurrere: pass, pass by, run its course
mendax, mendacis: deceitful, lying
-ve: *aut* (*oculive* = *aut oculi*) (enclitic)
lubricus, -a, -um: impure, dangerous, slippery
noxa, noxae: crime, sin, fault
inquino, inquinare: defile, pollute

speculator: watchman, examiner
asto, astare, astiti: stand by, stand near
desuper: from above, from on high
prospicio, prospicere: survey, look over
in vesperum: *until evening, until dusk*

Note

In *oculive* and in *speculator* the [u] must be elided. Hence [oclive] and [speclator].

101. Lux o decora patriae
Anon, c.1880

Lux o decora patriae
Slavisque amica gentibus,
Salvete, fratres; annuo
Vos efferemus cantico.

Quos Roma plaudens excipit,
Complexa mater filios,
Auget coronā praesulum
Novoque firmat robore.

Terras ad usque barbaras
Inferre Christum pergitis;
Quot vanus error luserat,
Almo repletis lumine.

patriae: of *your* homeland (gen or dat)
Slavus, -a, -um: Slavic
amicus, -a, -um: friendly toward, beloved among (+ dat)
effero, efferre, extuli, elatus: extol, exalt, elevate

quos: (antecedent = *vos*)
excipio: accept, acclaim, single out
complector, complecti, complexus: embrace, ie *having embraced, embracing*
augeo, augere, auxi: enlarge, enhance, distinguish (subj = *Roma*)
praesul, praesulis: bishop, patron
corona: crown, mitre (ablative)
corona praesulum: *the crown of bishops, the crown of episcopal office*
robur, roboris: strength, sturdiness

pergo, pergere, perrexi: travel, voyage, proceed
quot (indecl): however many, as many as, everyone *whom*
vanus, -a, -um: empty, meaningless, vain
ludo, ludere, lusi: mock, trick, sport with (+ acc)

101. Lux o decora patriae

Noxis soluta pectora
Ardor supernus abripit;
Mutatur horror veprium
In sanctitatis flosculos.

Et nunc serena caelitum
Locati in aula, supplici
Adeste voto: Slavicas
Servate gentes Numini.

Errore mersos unicum
Ovile Christi congreget;
Factis avitis aemula
Fides virescat pulchrior.

noxa, noxae: sin, crime
solvo, solvere, solvi: free of, release from (+ abl)
abripio: seize, carry off (*pectora, their hearts*)
vepres, vepris: briar, thornbush
horror veprium: *the nastiness of briars*
flosculus: blossom, little flower, floret
mutatur in: *is changed into* (+ acc)

serenus: bright, calm
loco, locare: place, locate
caeles, caelitis: heavenly *person*, heavenly *being*, *those in heaven*
supplici voto: *a humble prayer*
Numen, Numinis: the Holy One, the Divine

ovile, ovilis: sheepfold, flock (nominative. subj of *congreget*)
mergo, mergere, mersi, mersus: sink, overwhelm
avitus, -a, -um: ancestral, of (our) forefathers
aemulus, -a, -um: rivalling, in imitation of (+ dat)
viresco, virescere: grow, become green, become strong, flourish

101. Lux o decora patriae

Tu nos, beata Trinitas,
Caelesti amore concita,
Patrumque natos inclita
Da persequi vestigia.

concito, concitare: arouse, stir up, excite

Exercise

Disentangle this sentence without help:
Patrumque natos inclita
Da persequi vestigia.

102. Magnae Deus potentiae
Attrib St Gregory the Great, ob 604 →VR

Magnae Deus potentiae,	
Qui ex aquis ortum genus	Qui fertili natos aquā
Partim remittis gurgiti,	Partim relinquis gurgiti
Partim levas in aëra.	
Demersa lymphis imprimens,	
Subvecta caelis irrigans:	Subvecta caelis erigens
Ut stirpe unā prodita	Ut stirpe ab una prodita
Diversa rapiant loca.	Diversa repleant loca

orior, oriri, ortus: arise, emerge, rise
genus, generis: kind, sort (of creature), species
nascor, nasci, natus: be born
natos: *offspring, creatures born*
fertilis: fruitful, prolific
partim….partim: partly….partly; some….others
remitto, -ere: send back
gurges, gurgitis: *the stormy sea, the waters of the sea*
aes, aeris (masc): air (*aera*: Greek acc singular)

demergo, demergere, demersus: sink, plunge
demersa….subvecta: (scil. *genera* or *animalia*)
imprimo, imprimere: set down, mark
lymphae, -arum: *the waters, the ocean*
subveho, -vehere, -vexi, -vectus: bring up, lift up (from below)
[irrigo, irrigare: give water to, supply with water (+ acc) (mss *irrogans*!)]
irrogo, irrogare: assign, appoint, ordain
erigo, erigere: raise, lift
stirps, stirpis: origin, branch, source (ie the water. cf Gen 1:20-23)
prodo, prodere, prodidi, proditus: bring forth, produce
loca, locorum: places (neut in pl only. cf *locus, loci*)

Note

In the VM "irrigans" makes little sense. LH restores the mss reading "irrogans", which is clearly right.

102. Magnae Deus potentiae

Largire cunctis servulis,
Quos mundat unda sanguinis,
Nescire lapsūs criminum,
Nec ferre mortis taedium.

Ut culpa nullum deprimat,
Nullum levet jactantia; Nullum efferat jactantia
Elisa mens ne concidat,
Elata mens ne corruat.

largior, largiri: grant to, bestow upon
mundo, mundare: cleanse, purify
lapsus: (acc pl)
crimen, criminis: sin, wrongdoing
fero, ferre: endure, suffer
taedium: loathsomeness, oppression, enormity

nullum: (masc acc sing)
deprimo: afflict, weigh down, oppress
levo, levare: lift up, puff up
jactantia, -ae: boasting, vainglory, arrogance
effero, efferre, extuli, elatus: exalt, puff up
elido, elidere, elisus: grind down, cast down
concido, concidere: falter, fail, be disheartened
corruo, corruere: fall down, collapse, be ruined

Note

Largire servulis nescire, "Grant to (your) servants not to know", ie. "grant that they may be innocent of…."

103. Maria castis osculis (R)
Anon, c. 800

Maria castis osculis
Lambit Dei vestigia;
Fletu rigat, tergit comis,
Detersa nardo perlinit.

castus, -a, -um: pure, chaste, modest
osculum: kiss, embrace
lambo, lambere, lambi: touch, kiss
vestigium: footprint, footstep, foot
rigo, rigare: moisten, wet, bedew
tergo, tergere, tersi, tersus: wipe, wipe clean
coma, -ae: hair
detergeo, -ēre: wipe clean, wipe dry
nardum: nard balsam, nard oil, nard (also *nardus, nardi* feminine)
perlino, perlinere: anoint, besmear

103 Nardo Maria pistico (M)

Nardo Maria pistico
Unxit beatos Domini
Pedes, rigando lacrimis,
Et detergendo crinibus.

pisticus, -a, -um: genuine, pure
crinis, crinis: hair

Notes:
1. John 12;3
Maria ergo accepit libram unguenti nardi pistici pretiosi, et unxit pedes Jesu, et extersit pedes ejus capillis suis.
2. *Rigando, detergendo*: In later Latin the ablative of the gerund develops the same meaning as a present participle.

104. <u>Martinae celebri plaudite nomini</u>
Maffeo Barberini, Pope Urban VIII, 1568-1644

Martinae celebri plaudite nomini,
Cives Romulei, plaudite gloriae;
Insignem meritis dicite virginem,
Christi dicite martyrem.

Haec dum conspicuis orta parentibus
Inter delicias, inter amabiles
Luxūs illecebras, ditibus affluit
Faustae muneribus domūs....,

celeber, celebris: renowned, famous
plaudo, plaudere (+ dat): applaud, give honor to
Romuleus a um: of Romulus, Romulan (ie. *Roman*)
insignis, -e: noteworthy, eminent
dicite: *call her, say that she is*

haec: *she* (ie Martina) (*Haec....dedicat....et....quaerit*)
dum: as, since, while (*dum... affluit*)
conspicuus a um: remarkable, well-known, famous
orta: *having arisen among, (having been) born to* (as if *nata*)
delicia, -ae: delight, luxury
amabilis, -e: enjoyable, appealing, delightful
luxus, -ūs: excess, extravagance
illecebra, -ae: charm, allurement, temptation
faustus, -a, -um: prosperous, fortunate (*faustae domūs*)
dis, ditis: rich, opulent
affluo, affluere, affluxi: abound with, be rich in (+ abl)
munus, muneris: gift (*ditibus muneribus*)

104. Martinae celebri plaudite nomini

Vitae despiciens commoda, dedicat
Se rerum Domino, et munificā manu
Christi pauperibus distribuens opes,
Quaerit praemia caelitum.

Non illam crucians ungula, non ferae
Non virgae horribili vulnere commovent;
Hinc lapsi e superum sedibus angeli
Caelesti dape recreant.

Quin et depositā saevitie leo
Se rictu placido projicit ad pedes;
Te, Martina, dans gladius neci
Caeli coetibus inserit.

commodum: blessing, advantage, comfort
rerum Domino: *to the Lord of everything*
munificus a um: generous, bountiful
ops, opis (here plu): wealth, goods, assets
caeles, caelitis: heavenly *dweller* (as if *sanctorum*)

crucio, cruciare: torment, torture
ungula: torturing claw, hook
ferus a um: fierce, savage
virga: rod, club
horribili vulnere: *with their dreadful injury*
commoveo, ēre: move, discourage
hinc: hence, and so
superum: (= *superorum,* ie *illorum qui habitant in caelo*)
labor, labi, lapsus: tumble, descend
daps, dapis: banquet
recreant: (supply *illam*)

quin et: yea verily, and indeed
saevities, saevitiei: ferocity (= *saevitia, -ae*)
depositā saevitie: *(its) savagery (having been) laid down*
rictus, -ūs: mouth, open mouth, gaping jaws
placidus a um: friendly, peaceable
se…. projicit ad pedes: *throws himself at (her) feet*
nex, necis: violent death, slaughter
insero, inserere: install, enroll
coetus, -ūs: company

104. Martinae celebri plaudite nomini

Te, thuris redolens ara vaporibus,
Quae fumat, precibus jugiter invocat,
Et falsum perimens auspicium, tui
Delet nominis omine.

A nobis abigas lubrica gaudia,
Tu, qui martyribus dexter ades, Deus
Une et trine; tuis da famulis jubar,
Quo clemens animos beas.

ara, arae: altar
fumo, fumare: smoke, give off smoke
ara… quae fumat: *the smoking altar*
thus, thuris (neut): incense
redoleo, redolēre: emit an odor, be redolent of (+ abl)
vapor, vaporis: cloud (of incense)
jugiter: constantly
invoco, -are: invoke, call upon (*Te…. ara…. invocat*)
perimo, perimere: remove, destroy
auspicium: divination, prediction, idolatry
omen, ominis: token, omen (*by the token of your name*)
nominis tui: (*Martina* < *Mars, Martis* the god of war, and father of Romulus)
perimens auspicium….delet: *removing false divination….abolishes (it)*

abigo, abigere: drive away, banish (*ab* + *ago*)
lubricus a um: dangerous, misleading, sinful
dexter dextera dexterum (+ dat): to the right of, helpful to
jubar, jubaris (neut): radiance, light
be-o, be-are: bless

Note

Pope Urban VIII not only revised the Roman breviary. He also endowed it with several of his own neo-classical Latin hymns.

105. Martyr Dei qui unicum (M)
Anon, c. 500 VR

Martyr Dei, qui unicum	Invicte martyr, unicum
Patris sequendo Filium,	Patris secutus Filium
Victis triumphas hostibus,	
Victor fruens caelestibus,	
Tui precatūs munere	
Nostrum reatum dilue,	
Arcens mali contagium,	
Vitae removens taedium.	
Soluta sunt jam vincula	
Tui sacrati corporis;	
Nos solve vinclis saeculi,	
Amore Filii Dei.	Dono superni Numinis.

fruor, frui (+abl): enjoy
caelestia, caelestium: heavenly *things* (Δ *caelestes, caelestium*)

precatus, -ūs: prayer
reatus, -ūs: guilt
diluo, diluere: wash away, dissolve
arceo, arcēre: confine, shut away, prevent
contagium: (bad) influence, temptation, contagion
taedium: weariness, difficulty

sacratus, -a, -um (< sacro): dedicated, hallowed
tui: (This hymn is addressed to the *Martyr Dei,* not to the Lord.)

Note VR

The vocative form *secute* exists. However, even in classical poetry we find some use of the nominative for the vocative. In later Latin poetry the usage occurs more frequently. For an example of the almost imperceptible merger of the two cases consider this familiar text:

Domine Fili unigenite, Jesu Christe.
Domine Deus, Agnus Dei, Filius Patris.

106. Martyr Dei Venantius
Anon, c. 1650

Martyr Dei Venantius,
Lux et decus Camertium,
Tortore victo et judice,
Laetus triumphum concinit.

Annis puer, post vincula,
Post carceres, post verbera,
Longā fame frementibus
Cibus datur leonibus.

Sed ejus innocentiae
Parcit leonum immanitas;
Pedesque lambunt martyris,
Irae famisque immemores.

Verso deorsum vertice
Haurire fumum cogitur;
Costas utrimque et viscera
Succensa lampas ustulat.

Camers, Camertis: inhabitant of Camerino (in Umbria), "Camertian"
tortor, tortoris: torturer
concino, concinere: sing, sing about, celebrate (*sings his song of triumph*)

carcer, carceris: prison
fames, famis (fem): hunger

immanitas, immanitatis: brutality, savagery, cruelty
lambo, lambere: lick, kiss (implicit subj = *leones*; dir obj = *pedes*)
immemor (+ gen): unmindful of, forgetful, heedless

deorsum: downward
vertex, verticis: top, head
fumus, fumi: smoke
haurio, haurire: draw in, inhale
costa: rib
utrimque: on both sides, on each side
succensus < succendere: set alight, on fire, burning
lampas, lampadis (fem): torch, flame
ustulo, ustulare: burn, burn up

107. Matris sub almae numine
Vincentius Tarozzi, 1849-1918

Matris sub almae numine
Septena proles nascitur;
Ipsa vocante, ad arduum
Tendit Senari verticem.

Quos terra fructūs proferet,
Dum sacra proles germinat,
Uvis repente turgidis
Onusta vitis praemonet.

Virtute claros nobili
Mors sancta caelo consecrat;
Tenent olympi limina
Servi fideles Virginis.

sub numine: *under the heavenly care of, by the godly inspiration of*
septenus a um: seven-fold
Senarius: Mount Senario (*Senari* is genitive)
vertex, verticis: summit, height
tendo, tendere ad: head for, make for, go to

profero, proferre: bear, bring forth, produce (nb future tense)
proles, -is (fem): off-spring, family (ie the Servite Order)
germino, germinare: bud, sprout, expand
uva, -ae: grape, bunch of grapes
turgidus a um: ripe, swollen (miracle of the grapevine in winter)
onustus a um: laden with, heavy with (+abl)
vitis, -is: vine, grapevine
praemoneo, praemonēre: foretell, bespeak, forewarn

clarus a um: well-known, manifest, famous (supply *them*)
limen, liminis: threshhold

Verse 2
What fruits the earth will produce, while the sacred family grows,
the heavy-laden vine foretells, with suddenly ripe grapes.

107. Matris sub almae numine

Cohors beata, Numinis
Regno potita, respice
Quos hinc recedens fraudibus
Cinctos relinquis hostium.

Ergo, per almae vulnera
Matris rogamus supplices:
Mentis tenebras disice,
Cordis procellas comprime.

Tu nos, beata Trinitas,
Perfunde sancto robore,
Possimus ut feliciter
Exempla patrum subsequi.

cohors, cohortis (fem): group, band, cohort
Numen, Numinis (init cap): Divinity, God
potior, potiri, potitus: obtain, win (+ abl)
hinc recedens: *departing hence, as you withdraw from this place*
respice quos…. relinquis: *look upon (those) whom you leave behind*
fraus, fraudis: dishonesty, deceit, fraud
cinctus, -a, -um (< cingo): encircled (by), surrounded (by)

disicio, disicere: scatter, disperse
procella, -ae: storm, turbulence
comprimo, comprimere: calm down, restrain

perfundo, perfundere: endow, anoint
robor, roboris: strength

108. Memento rerum Conditor
Little Office of Our Lady.
First stanza is from
Jesu Redemptor omnium, Quem (R)
Christe Redemptor omnium, Ex Patre (M) qqv.

Memento rerum Conditor,
Nostri quod olim corporis,
Sacratā ab alvo Virginis
Nascendo, formam sumpseris.

Maria, mater gratiae,
Dulcis parens clementiae,
Tu nos ab hoste protege
Et mortis horā suscipe.

alvus, i (fem): womb
horā: *at the hour* (= *in hora*)

Versio Monastica:

Memento salutis Auctor,
Quod nostri quondam corporis,
Ex illibatā Virgine
Nascendo, formam sumpseris.

Maria, Mater gratiae,
Mater misericordiae,
Tu nos ab hoste protege
Et horā mortis suscipe

109. Miris modis repente liber (R)
Cf *Petrus beatus catenarum laqueos* (M)
Saint Paulinus, c. 730-802

This hymn belongs to the feast of Saint Peter ad Vincula, removed from the Roman calendar after 1960.

Miris modis repente liber ferrea,
Christo jubente, vincla Petrus exuit;
Ovilis ille pastor et rector gregis,
Vitae recludit pascua et fontes sacros,
Ovesque servat creditas, arcet lupos.

Patri perenne sit per aevum gloria,
Tibique laudes concinamus inclitas,
Aeterne Nate; sit, superne Spiritus,
Honor tibi decusque; sancta jugiter
Laudetur omne Trinitas per saeculum.

liber, libera, liberum: free
ferreus a um: iron, of iron
exuo, exuere, exui: take off, remove
ovile, -is: sheep-fold
grex, gregis: flock
pascuum: food, nourishment, pasture
recludo, -ere, reclusi: disclose, reveal, hold open
creditas: *entrusted (to him)*
arceo, -ēre: keep out

concino, concinere: sing, sing together
inclitus a um: renowned, noble
decus, decoris: honor, glory, praises
jugiter: forever, constantly

110. Nobiles Christi famulas diserta
Cf *Beata caeli gaudia*, note

Nobiles Christi famulas disertā
Voce cantemus, decus aemulatas
Feminae fortis, sacra cui profudit
Pagina laudes.

His fides vivax, pia spes, amorque
In Deum fervens, operum bonorum
Fertilis radix, amor unde fratrum
Nascitur ultro.

Non eas mundus laqueis revinxit,
Quas Deus jussis regit hinc volentes,
Ut bonum Christi satagant ubique
Spargere odorem.

nobilis, -is: distinguished, renowned
famula, -ae: servant (female), maidservant
disertus, -a, -um: eloquent
aemulatus (<aemulor, aemulari): desirous of, aiming for (+ acc)
decus, decoris: honor, glory, respect
profundo, profundere, profudi: pour out
Sacra Pagina: *The Sacred Page, Holy Scripture* (Prov 31: 10-31)

his (scil *est*): *Their's is*, or *They have*
vivax, vivacis: vigorous, lively
fertilis, -e: fruitful, prolific, fertile
radix, radicis: root
ultro: further, even more

revincio, revincire, revinxi: bind, capture
laqueus: snare, trap (*with its snares*)
jussum, jussi: command, decree (*by His decrees*)
hinc: here, from here
satago, satagere (+ infin): be busy, work diligently
spargo, spargere: spread, extend

110. Nobiles Christi famulas diserta

Edomant corpus, precibusque mentem
Nutriunt sanctis; peritura temnunt
Lucra, ut inquirant sibi permanentis
Praemia vitae.

Hostium probris nihil atque poenis
Territae, Christo remanent fideles;
Sanguine ac fuso fidei superna
Dogmata firmant.

Motus illarum meritis, remitte
Sontibus nobis scelus omne, Jesu,
Ut tibi puro resonemus aequas
Pectore laudes.

edomo, edomare: tame, subdue
nutrio, nutrire: feed, nourish
pereo, perire: perish, pass away
temno, temnere: reject, despise, scorn
lucrum: gain, advantage, profit
inquiro, inquirere: seek, search for
praemium: reward

probrus, -i: shame, indecency
nihil (adv): not at all
sanguine ac fuso: (ablative absolute)
firmo, firmare: affirm, confirm

moveo, movere, movi, motus: move, affect
sons, sontis: guilty (*from us though we be guilty*)
scelus, sceleris: sin, crime, wrongdoing
resono, -are: ring out, sing out
aequus a um: equal (to their merits), fitting
puro…. pectore: *with a pure heart, pure of heart*

111. <u>Nocte surgentes vigilemus omnes</u>
Attrib St Gregory the Great, 540-604 → VR

Nocte surgentes vigilemus omnes
Semper in psalmis meditemur, atque
Viribus totis Domino canamus Voce concordi…..
Dulciter hymnos.

Ut pio Regi pariter canentes
Cum suis sanctis mereamur aulam
Ingredi caeli, simul et beatam ….simul et perennem
Ducere vitam.

vigilo, vigilare: be awake, be watchful
meditor, meditari: pray *with psalms*, sing *the psalms* in prayer
concors, concordis: harmonious

pius pia pium: gracious, holy
pariter: likewise
ducere (vitam): enjoy, lead

112. Nox atra rerum contegit
Attrib Saint Gregory the Great, 540-604

Nox atra rerum contegit
Terrae colores omnium;
Nos confitentes poscimus
Te, juste judex cordium:

Ut auferas piacula,
Sordesque mentis abluas;
Donesque, Christe, gratiam,
Ut arceantur crimina.

Mens ecce torpet impia,
Quam culpa mordet noxia;
Obscura gestit tollere,
Et te, Redemptor, quaerere.

Repelle tu caliginem
Intrinsecus quam maxime,
Ut in beato gaudeat
Se collocari lumine.

ater, atra, atrum: black, dark
contego, -ere, -exi: cover, envelop

piaculum: sin, crime, guilt
sordes, sordium: filth, dirt, uncleanness
arceo, arcere: prevent, restrain

torpeo, torpēre: be sluggish, be numb
mordeo, mordēre, momordi, morsus: bite
noxius a um: harmful, damaging
obscura: *dark things,* ie *sins, darkness, the darkness of sin*
gestio, gestire: desire, long (Subj = "it", ie *mens*)
tollo, tollere: remove, take away

intrinsecus (Adv): inside, inwardly
intrinsecus, -a, -um: (If adjective, modifies *tu*)
gaudeat: (subj = *mens*.)
se collocor, -ari: find a place, be located, be settled

113. Nox et tenebrae et nubila
Prudentius, c. 348-410

Nox et tenebrae et nubila
Confusa mundi et turbida….,
Lux intrat, albescit polus,
Christus venit, discedite!

Caligo terrae scinditur
Percussa solis spiculo;
Rebusque jam color redit,
Vultu nitentis sideris.

Te, Christe, solum novimus;
Te mente purā et simplici,
Flendo et canendo quaesumus;
Intende nostris sensibus.

nubilum: cloudy sky, *plu* clouds
[*Nox, tenebrae, nubila, confusa, turbida* all vocative.]
confundo, confundere, confusus: mix together, confuse
turbidus, -a, -um: confused, chaotic
albesco, albescere: lighten up, become white, grow light
polus: sky, pole

caligo, caliginis (fem): fog, mist, darkness
scindo, scindere: split, divide, rend, separate (antonym of *confundo*)
percutio, percutere, percussus: strike, hit
spiculum: dart, ray, arrow
niteo, nitēre: shine, be bright
vultu: *at the sight of, in the face of*
sidus, sideris: star (in this case the morning star still visible in the dawn)

flendo et canendo: (as if *flentes et canentes*)
intende: *take aim at, shine upon, aim your light at*

113. Nox et tenebrae et nubila

Sunt multa fucis illita,
Quae luce purgentur tuā;
Tu, lux Eoi sideris, VR Tu vera lux caelestium
Vultu sereno illumina.

illino, illinere, illevi, illitus: smear, cover, bedaub
fucus, i: deceit, pretense (lit *red dye, rouge*)
E-ó-us: the East, the Orient (3 syllables, stress on penult)
illumina: *give (us) light, enlighten (us)*
vultu sereno: *with your serene countenance*

114. Nullis te genitor blanditiis trahit
Pope Boniface VIII, c. 1600

Nullis te genitor blanditiis trahit,
Non vitae caperis divitis otio,
Gemmarumve nitore,
Regnandive cupidine.

Diris non acies te gladii minis,
Nec terret perimens carnificis furor;
Nam mansura caducis
Praefers gaudia Caelitum.

genitor: *your* father,
blanditia, -ae: flattery, inducement
traho, trahere: draw, attract, persuade
otium: leisure, idleness
dives, divitis (adj): rich, wealthy
—ve….—ve: or….or; (after neg: nor….nor)
nitor, nitoris: glitter, brilliance

dirus a um: dire, frightening, dangerous
acies, aciei: edge, sharpness, sharp blade
minae, minarum: threats, menace
te: (*non terret) te….nec terret*
perimo, perimere: slaughter, annihilate (*bloodthirsty rage of the hangman*)
carnifex, carnificis: executioner
maneo, manere; abide, last (*mansura* is acc neut plu)
caducus, -a, -um: perishable, worthless (neut dat pl: *things*)
praefero: prefer (A to B), choose (A over B)
Caelitum: *of the Heavenly Persons* (Dessain 1910, 1960)
caelitum: *of the blessed, of them who dwell in heaven* (Benziger, Britt)

114. Nullis te genitor blanditiis trahit

Nunc nos e Superum protege sedibus
Clemens; atque preces, dum canimus tuā
Quaesitam nece palmam,
Pronis auribus excipe.

Sit rerum Domino jugis honor Patri,
Et Natum celebrent ora precantium,
Divinumque supremis
Flamen laudibus efferant.

Superum: *Superorum*
preces: (dir obj of *excipe*)
palma: palm, palm of victory, hymn of triumph
palmam: (dir obj of *canimus*)
quaesitam (< quaero): sought, desired
nex, necis: death
tuā quaesitam nece palmam; *the victory sought by your death*
pronus, -a, -um: inclined, attentive (not *flat*)
excipio: admit, accept, hear (as opposed to *ignore*)

jugis, jugis: continual, perpetual
Divinum Flamen: *the Breath of God* (=*Sanctum Spiritum*)
supremus, -a, -um: lofty, highest
effero, efferre: exalt, extol

115. Nunc Sancte nobis Spiritus
Attrib Saint Ambrose

Nunc Sancte nobis Spiritus,
Unum Patri cum Filio,
Dignare promptus ingeri,
Nostro refusus pectori.

Os lingua mens sensus vigor
Confessionem personent;
Flammescat igne caritas,
Accendat ardor proximos.

unum + dat: *as one with, together with*
dignor, dignari: grant, vouchsafe, deign
promptus, -a, -um: swift, quick, ready
ingero, ingerere: lavish on, pour into, give generously
refundo, refusus: pour again, restore, pour back
pectus, pectoris: *lit* chest, *metaph* heart

vigor, vigoris: strength, energy
confessionem: *your* praise, *song of* praise, *words of* faith
persono, personare: sound out, ring forth
flammesco, flammescere: be enflamed, burn hot
accendo, accendere: enkindle, set fire to (+ acc)
ardor, ardoris: heat, passion, enthusiasm
proximos: *our* neighbors

Note

Flammescat igne caritas, Accendat ardor proximos. Newman's translation is noteworthy:

And love light up our mortal frame
Till others catch the living flame.

116. O gente felix hospita
Pope Leo XIII, 1810-1903

O gente felix hospita,
Augusta sedes Nazarae,
Quae fovit alma Ecclesiae
Et protulit primordia.

Sol, qui pererrat aureo
Terras jacentes lumine,
Nil gratius per saecula
Hac vidit aede, aut sanctius.

Ad hanc frequentes convolant
Caelestis aulae nuntii;
Virtutis hoc sacrarium
Visunt, revisunt, excolunt.

hospita, -ae: hostess, one who welcomes, host-city (*O felix hospita*)
gens, gentis: family (ie the Holy Family)
gente felix: *happy in your family, blest by your family*
augustus, -a, -um: majestic, venerable, noble
sedes, sedis (fem): seat
Nazara, -ae: *Nazareth*
foveo, fovēre, fovi: cherish, sustain
profero, protuli: bring forth, produce
primordium: beginning, origin (*quae fovit et protulit alma primordia Ecclesiae*)

per-erro, pererrare (+acc): roam over, travel throughout
terras jacentes: *the lands below, the earth outspread*
gratus: pleasing, beloved
aedes, aedis (fem): dwelling, temple, palace, home
vidit: (subj = *sol*)

ad hanc: *ad hanc aedem (= sedem, = hospitam*)
frequens, frequentis: repeated, crowded
convolo, -are: fly together (*throng together in flight*)
sacrarium: sanctuary, holy place
viso, visere: see, behold, contemplate
excolo, -ere: venerate, worship

Note:
Notice *quae fovit et protulit,* instead of *quae fovisti et protulisti*. This is "metri gratia", for the sake of the meter.

116. O gente felix hospita

Quā mente Jesus, quā manu,
Optata patris perficit!
Quo Virgo gestit gaudio
Materna obire munera!

Adest amoris particeps
Curaeque Joseph conjugi,
Quos mille jungit nexibus
Virtutis auctor gratiā.

Hi diligentes invicem
In Jesu amorem confluunt,
Utrique Jesus mutuae
Dat caritatis praemia.

Sic fiat, ut nos caritas
Jungat perenni foedere,
Pacemque alens domesticam
Amara vitae temperet.

opto, optare: wish, choose (*optata* = *wishes*)
perficio, -ere: perform, carry out
gestio, gestire: exult, long (to do something), desire
gestit gaudio: *leaps with joy, longs joyfully*
obeo, obire: fulfill, perform

adsum, adesse: be at hand, be present, be near to (+ dat)
particeps, participis: sharer, partner
conjunx, conjugis: *his* spouse
quos: *whom* (ie Mary and Joseph)
jungo, jungere: join, link
mille….nexibus: *with a thousand links*

confluo, confluere: flow together, unite, join
uterque, *dat* utrique: each, both
mutuus, -a, -um: mutual, shared, common (*mutuae… caritatis*)

foedus, foederis: covenant, bond
alo, alere: nourish, support
amarus, -a, -um: bitter
tempero, temperare: moderate, soften, reduce

117. <u>O gloriosa Domina</u> (*O gloriosa virginum*)
Venantius Fortunatus, c. 530-610
Cento from *Quem terra pontus sidera* → VR

O gloriosa Domina,	O gloriosa virginum
Excelsa super sidera,	Sublimis inter sidera
Qui te creavit provide,	Qui te creavit, parvulum
Lactasti sacro ubere.	Lactente nutris ubere.
Quod Heva tristis abstulit,	
Tu reddis almo germine;	
Intrent ut astra flebiles,	
Caeli fenestra facta es.	Caeli recludis cardines
Tu Regis alti janua,	
Et porta lucis fulgida:	Et aula lucis fulgida
Vitam datam per Virginem,	
Gentes redemptae, plaudite.	

sublimis, -is: lofty, elevated, exalted
provide: with foresight, wisely
lacto, lactare: give suck, give milk to
lacteo, lactere: produce milk, lactate
nutrio, nutrire: nourish, suckle
uber, uberis: breast, teat

flebilis, -is: sorrowing, wretched, weeping
fenestra, -ae: window
recludo, recludere: throw open, open up

fulgidus a um: shining
plaudo, plaudere: applaud, acclaim, rejoice in

118. <u>O lux beata caelitum</u>
Pope Leo XIII

O lux beata caelitum
Et summa spes mortalium,
Jesu, o cui domestica
Arrisit orto caritas:

Maria, dives gratiā,
O sola quae casto potes
Fovere Jesum pectore,
Cum lacte donans oscula:

Tuque ex vetustis patribus
Delecte custos Virginis,
Dulci patris quem nomine
Divina Proles invocat:

caeles, caelitis: heavenly dweller, person in heaven
arrideo, arridere, arrisi: smile *on* (+ dat)
cui etc: *on whom family love smiled after your birth*

casto pectore: *with a chaste breast, with a pure heart*
foveo, fovēre: cherish, love
osculum: kiss

tuque: *And you* (ie Joseph)
vetustus a um: old, ancient
delectus < deligere: chosen, selected
custos, custodis: guardian, attendant
proles, prolis: child, offspring, son
quem: *quem puer divinus invocat dulci nomine "patris".*

118. <u>O lux beata caelitum</u>

De stirpe Jesse nobili
Nati in salutem gentium,
Audite nos, qui supplices
Vestras ad aras sistimus.

Dum sol redux ad vesperum
Rebus nitorem detrahit,
Nos hic manentes intimo
Ex corde vota fundimus.

Quā vestra sedes floruit
Virtutis omnis gratiā,
Hanc detur in domesticis
Referre posse moribus.

nati: (Masc nom sing, refers to Jesus, Mary, and Joseph)
vestras ad aras: *at your altars, at your worship*
sisto, sistere, stiti: betake *oneself*, appear, stand, assist

redux, reducis (adj): returned, returning
nitor, nitoris: brightness, brilliance
detraho, -ere: take away, remove

vestra sedes: *your home*
hanc: (sci *hanc gratiam*, dir obj of *referre*)
detur: *may it be given, grant that* (+ acc and infin)
posse: (sci *nos posse*)
refero, referre: carry over, reproduce, imitate
in domesticis....moribus: *in our own family life*

119. <u>O lux beata Trinitas</u> (M)
Anon, c. 400. Attrib Saint Ambrose
Cf *Jam sol recedit igneus* (R)

O lux beata Trinitas,
Et principalis Unitas:
Jam sol recedit igneus,
Infunde lumen cordibus.

Te mane laudum carmine,
Te deprecemur vespere;
Te nostra supplex gloria
Per cuncta laudet saecula.

principalis, -is: original, first, perfect

te mane: (supply *deprecemur*)
nostra gloria: *our (expression of your) glory, our words of praise*

120. Omnis expertem maculae Mariam
Anon, c. 1900. Attrib to Leo XIII

Omnis expertem maculae Mariam
Edocet summus fidei Magister;
Virginis gaudens celebrat fidelis
Terra triumphum.

Ipsa se praebens humili puellae
Virgo spectandam, recreat paventem,
Seque conceptam sine labe, sancto
Praedicat ore.

O specus felix, decorate divae
Matris aspectu! veneranda rupes,
Unde vitales scatuēre pleno
Gurgite lymphae!

macula, -ae: stain, spot, blemish
expers, expertis: free of, lacking in (Δ *expertus, -a, -um*)
edoceo, -ēre: teach clearly, instruct
Magister: (ie Pope Pius IX)

ipsa: *virgo ipsa praebens se*
praebeo, -ēre: show, reveal
humili puellae: (ie Bernadette) (dat of agent with *spectandam*)
recreat paventem: *calms her fears, reassures the frightened girl*
labes, labis: spot, stain, = *macula*
praedico, predicare: teach, explain, declare

specus, -ūs (masc): grotto, cave
decoro, decorare: adorn, make lovely, make beautiful
decorate: (vocative of *decoratus*) (*O specus….decorate*)
divus a um: divine, godly
aspectus, -ūs: appearance, vision
rupes, rupis (fem): cliff, rocky hill
veneranda: (supply *est*)
vitalis, -is: living, life-giving
scateo, -ēre, scatui: gush, bubble up, flow
lympha: water, pure water, (poetic word for *aqua*)
pleno gurgite: *in full spate, with surging flow*

120. Omnis expertem maculae Mariam

Huc catervatim pia turba nostris,
Huc ab externis peregrina terris
Affluit supplex, et opem potentis
Virginis orat.

Excipit Mater lacrimas precantum,
Donat optatam miseris salutem;
Compos hinc voti patrias ad oras
Turba revertit.

Supplicum, Virgo, miserata casūs,
Semper o nostros refove labores,
Impetrans maestis bona sempiternae
Gaudia vitae.

huc: hither
catervatim (adv): in throngs, in crowds
nostris: *nostris* (*a terris)*
peregrina: (*et turba) peregrina ab externis terris*
ops, opis: help, aid, succour
oro, orare (+acc): pray for

excipio, excipere: accept, receive
compos, compotis (+ gen): possessing, having, getting
opto, optare (+acc): long for, wish for, want
salus, salutis: health, well-being
compos voti: *receiving their wish, their prayer fulfilled*
ora, -ae: shore, border, country

miseror, miserari, miseratus (+acc): pity, take pity on, have compassion for
casus, casūs: case, misfortune
refoveo, -ēre: revive, refresh, reinvigorate
labor, laboris: effort, pains
impetro, -are (+acc): ask for, pray for
maestus, -a, um: sorrowful, afflicted
maestis: *for the afflicted* (ind obj of *impetrans*)

121 O nimis felix meritique celsi (M)
Cf *O nimis felix meritique celsi* (R)
Attrib Paul the Deacon c. 720- 800
Cento from *Ut queant laxis.* Cf also *Antra deserti teneris*

O nimis felix meritique celsi,
Nesciens labem nivei pudoris,
Praepotens Martyr, nemorumque cultor, Mss eremique cultor
Maxime Vatum!

Serta ter denis alios coronant
Aucta crementis, duplicata quosdam;
Trina centeno cumulata fructu
Te, sacer, ornant.

nimis (adv): very, most
meritum: merit
celsus, -a, -um: sublime, noble, high
meriti celsi: (Gen of description. cf Eng: *a man of courage*)
niveus, -a, -um: snowy, snow-white
pudor, pudoris: purity, chastity
labem pudoris: *stain (on your) purity*
praepotens: mighty
nemus, nemoris: forest, woods (image of the desert)
cultor, cultoris: dweller, *hermit of the forests*
vates, vatis: prophet (*O greatest of prophets!*)

serta, -orum: wreath(es), garland(s), *metaph* rewards
deni, -ae, -a: times ten
ter deni: thirty-fold, three times ten, thirty
crementum: growth, increase (= *incrementum*)
augeo, augēre, auctus: enlarge, increase
aucta ter denis crementis: *enlarged by thirty-fold enhancements*
duplico, duplicare, duplicatus: double
duplicata: (*ter denis duplicata*, ie *sixty-fold, sixty times*)
quidam, quaedam (pl): some (people)
alios….quosdam: *some….others*
trini, trinae, trina: three-fold, triple
trina serta: *threefold garlands, a triple crown* (ie Martyr, Hermit, Prophet)
centenus: a hundred-fold
fructus, -us (masc): fruit, gain
centeno fructu: *with fruit a hundred times over*
cumulo, cumulare: heap up, overload

Paul the Deacon was the finest Latinist of his age. He loved the syntactic complexity of Horace. However, he does not achieve the clarity of that poet, and his language is often obscure.

The meter here is the Horatian Sapphic with an Adonic final. See *Sedibus caeli nitidis receptos* infra for an illustration of the metric scansion.

Here is the second verse with a translation into simplified Latin prose.

Original

Serta ter denis alios coronant
Aucta crementis, duplicata quosdam;
Trina centeno cumulata fructu
Te, sacer, ornant.

Simplified

Serta aucta triginta incrementis coronant quosdam.
[Serta] duplicata coronant alios.
Trina [serta] cumulata centeno fructu
Ornant te, sacer.

Translated

Garlands enlarged by thirty times crown some.
Doubled, they crown others.
A triple garland bulging with fruit a hundred-fold
adorns you, Sacred Sir.

121. <u>O nimis felix meritique celsi</u>

Nunc potens nostri meritis opimis
Pectoris duros lapides repelle,
Asperum planans iter, et reflexos
Dirige calles.

Ut pius mundi Sator et Redemptor,
Mentibus pulsa livione puris,
Rite dignetur veniens sacratos
Ponere gressūs.

opimus, -a, -um: rich, abundant
duros lapides pectoris nostri: (cf English, "stony-hearted", "heart of stone")
repello, -ere: cast out, drive out, expel
plano, planare: make smooth
callis, -is: path, narrow path
dirigo, dirigere: make straight, straighten out
reflexus a um: bending, crooked

sator, satoris: *lit* sower, source, creator
livio, livionis (fem): stain, blemish
livor, livoris (not in text): stain, blemish
pulsā livione (abl absol): *the stain having been removed*
rite (adv): rightly, justly
dignor, dignari: condescend, deign
gressus, -ūs: step
mentibus….ponere: *set (his) sacred steps into (our) pure hearts*

Notes:
1. A noun *serta, sertae* in the fem sing also exists. However, it is not consistent with the pl *coronant.*

2. *Ter denis, duplicata, centeno*: Cf Matt 13: 8— *Alia autem ceciderunt in terram bonam; et dabant fructum, aliud centesimum, aliud sexagesimum, aliud trigesimum*. Hence 30, 60, 100.

3. The word *livio* is doubtful. Neither Lewis and Short nor Niermeyer admit it. The morpheme /liv/ refers to a bruise, a dark blemish. Apart from the lexicographic silence, however, the meaning seems clear. If the author did in fact write *livione*, then his word must refer to the *stain* or *blemish* of sin.

122. O nimis felix meritique celsi (R)

The following notes refer only to the Roman revisions of the original hymn. For the rest of the text cf VM supra.

Strophe one unchanged.

Serta ter denis alios coronant
Aucta crementis, duplicata quosdam;
Trina te fructu cumulata centum
Nexibus ornant.

Nunc potens nostri meritis opimis
Pectoris duros lapides revelle,
Asperum planans iter, et reflexos
Dirige calles.

Ut pius mundi Sator et Redemptor
Mentibus culpae sine labe puris
Rite dignetur veniens beatos
Ponere gressūs.

trina: *tria serta fructu cumulata ornant te*
fructu cumulata: heaped up with fruit
centum nexibus: *with a hundred loops, intertwined a hunded times*

revello, revellere: pluck out, snatch away, remove

123. Opes decusque regium reliqueras
Pope Urban VIII

Opes decusque regium reliqueras,
Elizabeth, Dei dicata numini,
Recepta nunc bearis inter angelos;
Libens ab hostium tuere nos dolis.

Praei, viamque, dux salutis, indica:
Sequemur. O sit una mens fidelium;
Odor bonus sit omnis actio. Tuis
Id innuit rosis operta caritas.

Beata caritas, in arce siderum
Potens locare nos per omne saeculum:
Patrique Filioque summa gloria,
Tibique laus perennis, alme Spiritus.

regius a um: royal, kingly, of kings
reliqueras: (Metri causa pluperfect for aorist. = *reliquisti*)
dicare, dicatus: dedicate, consecrate
beo, beare, beatus: bless
libens, libentis: free(ly), glad(ly)
tueor, tueri, tutus: guard, defend, protect
dolus: guile, deception

prae-eo, praeire: go before (us), go ahead
indico, indicare: show, mark out
dux salutis: *leader (on the path) of salvation, guide to salvation*
omnis actio: *omnis actio (fidelium)*
bonus odor: (cf *Christi bonus odor sumus*, II Cor 2:15)
innuo, innuere: intimate, signify, be an example of (+ acc)
id: *this* (ie the prayer, *Odor bonus sit etc*)
operio, operire, opertus: cover, conceal, clothe

arx, arcis: citadel, throne, stronghold
loco, locare: place, locate, establish

Note

Cf Lectio V (in BR ante 1961): *Pecunias pauperibus distribuendas, ut regem laterent, hiberno tempore in rosas convertit.*

124. <u>O prima Virgo prodita</u>
Vittorio Genovesi, SJ circa 1950

O prima, Virgo, prodita
E Conditoris Spiritu,
Predestinata Altissimi
Gestare in alvo Filium.

Tu perpes hostis femina
Praenuntiata daemonis,
Oppleris una gratiā
Intaminatā origine.

Tu ventre Vitam concipis,
Vitamque ab Adam perditam,
Diae litandae Victimae
Carnem ministrans, integras.

prodo, prodere, proditus: bring forth, produce
gesto, gestare: carry
alvus, alvi (fem): womb

perpes, perpetis: perpetual, everlasting
hostis: (nominative)
praenuntio, -are: foretell
daemon, daemonis: devil, demon
oppleo, opplere: fill
una (nominative): *you alone are filled by grace*
intaminatus, -a, -um: unspotted, unstained
intaminata origine: *of unstained origin*

dius, -a, -um: godlike, divine
lito, litare: sacrifice, offer public sacrifice
ministro, ministrare: provide, supply, serve
integro, integrare: make whole, heal, restore (dir obj = *vitamque* etc)

124. O prima Virgo prodita

Merces piaclo debita,
Devicta mors te deserit,
Almique consors Filii
Ad astra ferris corpore.

Tantā coruscans gloriā
Natura cuncta extollitur,
In te vocata verticem
Decoris omnis tangere.

Ad nos, triumphans, exsules,
Regina, verte lumina
Caeli ut beatam patriam,
Te, consequamur, auspice.

merces, mercedis: ransom, price
piac(u)lum: sin, punishment, expiation
devictus (< devincere): conquered, defeated
desero, deserere, deserui: forsake, desert, not touch, not affect
merces etc: *Death, the price owing for sin, is conquered and touches you not.*
consors, consortis: companion
ferris: (*feror, ferris, fertur* etc <*fero, ferre*)
corpore: *in your body, in bodily form, physically*

corusco, -are: glitter, shine
cunctus a um: all, as a whole, in (its) entirety
extollo, -ere: lifte up, raise up, elevate
vertex, verticis: summit, peak
decor, decoris: beauty

auspex, auspicis: protector, sponsor
te…. auspice: *under your protection, with your favor*

125. <u>O quot undis lacrimarum</u>
Callistus Palumbella, c. 1750

O quot undis lacrimarum,
Quo dolore volvitur,
Luctuosa de cruento
Dum revulsum stipite,
Cernit ulnis incubantem
Virgo Mater Filium!

Os suave, mite pectus
Et latus dulcissimum,
Dexteramque vulneratam
Et sinistram sauciam,
Et rubras cruore plantas
Aegra tingit lacrimis.

volvitur: *she is overwhelmed, she is overcome*
luctuosus, -a, -um: sorrowful, grieving
cruentus, -a, -um: bloody, bleeding
dum: *dum luctuosa Virgo Mater cernit Filium revulsum* etc
revello, revulsus: tear down, pull down, take down
stipes, stipitis (masc): trunk, log, *metaph* cross
ulna, -ae: arm
ulnis: *in her arms*
incubo, incubare: lie in

os, oris (neut): mouth (Δ *os, ossis*)
os, pectus, latus: (Acc sing. dir objects of *tingit*)
mitis, mite: meek, gentle, tender
latus, lateris: side
saucius, -a, -um: injured, hurt
ruber, rubra, rubrum: red
cruor, cruoris: gore, blood
planta, -ae: sole (of the foot), foot
aegra: sick (with grief), *in sore distress*
tingo, tingere: moisten, wet

125. <u>O quot undis lacrimarum</u>

Centiesque miliesque
Stringit arctis nexibus;
Pectus illud et lacertos,
Illa figit vulnera;
Sicque tota colliquescit
In doloris osculis.

Eja, Mater, obsecramus
Per tuas has lacrimas
Filiique triste funus,
Vulnerumque purpuram,
Hunc tui cordis dolorem
Conde nostris cordibus.

centies, milies (adv): a hundred times, a thousand times
stringo, stringere: hold tight, squeeze
arctus, -a, -um: close, tight
nexus, -us: grasp, embrace
lacertus: (upper) arm
figo, figere, fixi: fix, imprint
illa figit vulnera: *she fixes those wounds (* ie in her heart, in her mind's eye)
colliquesco, -ere: melt, dissolve (intrans)
dolor: sorrow, suffering, pain
osculum: kiss

eja: oh! please!
obsecro, obsecrare: beseech, implore
funus, funeris (neut): funeral, death
per: (per lacrimas, *per* funus, *per* purpuram)
purpura, -ae (noun): purple
vulnus, vulneris: wound (*the purple of the wounds*)
condo, condere: embed, implant

126. O sola magnarum urbium
Prudentius, 348-410

O sola magnarum urbium
Major Bethlem, cui contigit
Ducem salutis caelitus
Incorporatum gignere.

Quem stella, quae solis rotam
Vincit decore ac lumine,
Venisse terris nuntiat
Cum carne terrestri Deum.

sola magnarum urbium major: *you alone are greater than great cities*
contingo, -ere, contigi: happen, befall
caelitus (adv): divinely, from heaven
incorporatus: embodied, incarnate
gigno, gignere: bear, beget, give birth to

quem: (Antecedent is *ducem: quem stella nuntiat venisse*)
stella: (Nominative. *stella quae vincit rotam solis*)
rota, -ae: wheel, cycle
rotam solis: *the wheel of the sun, the sun in its orbit*
vinco, vincere: defeat, surpass, exceed
terris (= *in terram*): on earth

Notes:

1. *Magnarum urbium* instead of the ablative *magnis urbibus*. This is the poetic genitive of comparison, a hellenism.

2. How many syllables is *cui*? If only one, then it is a homophone of *qui*. The pronouns *tuī* and *suī* are bisyllabic. But there the final [i] is long, whereas in *cui* it is short. In the music for this hymn—Lauds on the feast of the Epiphany—the word *cui* is sung on two notes. However, if *cui* is two syllables, then the line has nine syllables. And we should then have one of the rare examples of an anapest in the third foot.

Maior Bethlem cui con tigit
— — — — ∪∪— ∪∪

3. Some publishers write "Bethlem" as "Beth*l*ehem", with the elision of [e] marked by italics. If [h] is silent, the result is the same.

126. O sola magnarum urbium

Videre postquam illum Magi,
Eoa promunt munera;
Stratique votis offerunt
Thus, myrrham, at aurum regium.

Regem Deumque annuntiant
Thesaurus et fragrans odor
Thuris Sabaei, ac myrrheus
Pulvis sepulcrum praedocet.

vidēre: (= viderunt)
videre postquam: *when they have seen him, as soon as they see him*
E-ó-us, Eóa, Eóum: Eastern, oriental, of the dawn (tri-syllabic in all forms)
promo, promere, prompsi, promptus: bring forward, produce, offer
strati (< sterno): *bending down, prostrate* (= *prostrati*)
votum: prayer, offering
votis (unclear): perh *in prayer*
thus, thuris: incense, frankincense
myrrha, -ae: (used *inter alia* for anointing the dead. Hence *sepulcrum* below)
regius, -a, -um: kingly, royal

thesaurus: treasury (ie the gift of gold)
Sabaeus, -a, -um: Sabaean, of Saba
myrrheus, -a, -um: of myrrh
pulvis, pulveris (masc): powder, grains
sepulcrum: tomb, grave
praedoceo: foretell

127. O sol salutis intimis (R)
Cf *Jam Christe sol justitiae* (M)

O sol salutis, intimis,
Jesu, refulge mentibus,
Dum, nocte pulsa, gratior
Orbi dies renascitur.

Dans tempus acceptabile,
Da lacrimarum rivulis
Lavare cordis victimam,
Quam laeta adurat caritas.

Quo fonte manavit nefas,
Fluent perennes lacrimae,
Si virga poenitentiae
Cordis rigorem conterat.

Dies venit, dies tua,
In qua reflorent omnia;
Laetemur et nos, in viam
Tuā reducti dexterā.

refulgeo, refulgēre: shine on, shine in, illuminate (+ dat)
intimis mentibus: *our innermost thoughts, our hearts within*
gratior orbi: *more pleasing to the world, more welcome to the world*

da: (da *nobis* lavare)
rivulus: stream
cordis victima: *the oblation of (our) heart, our heart in sacrifice*
aduro, adurere: enkindle, set ablaze

mano, manare: flow, arise, spread
nefas (indecl): sin, evil
fluo, fluere, fluxi: (*fluent* is future indicative)
rigor, rigoris: hardness, stiffness
contero, conterere, contrivi: crush, smash, bruise

refloreo, reflorere: bloom again, flourish anew
dies tua: (Easter Sunday)
reduco, reducere: lead, lead back, guide

128. Pange lingua gloriosi Corporis
Saint Thomas Aquinas, 1225-1274

Pange, lingua, gloriosi
Corporis mysterium,
Sanguinisque pretiosi,
Quem in mundi pretium
Fructus ventris generosi
Rex effudit gentium.

Nobis datus, nobis natus
Ex intactā Virgine,
Et in mundo conversatus,
Sparso verbi semine,
Sui moras incolatūs
Miro clausit ordine.

In supremae nocte cenae
Recumbens cum fratribus,
Observatā lege plene
Cibis in legalibus,
Cibum turbae duodenae
Se dat suis manibus.

pango, pangere (+acc): sing *about*, tell *of*, celebrate
in....pretium: *as the price, for the ransom*
fructus: (Nom sing, in apposition to *rex*)
generosus: of noble birth, noble, generous

conversor, -ari, -atus: dwell, live
spargo, spargere, sparsus: sow, scatter, spread
incolatus, -ūs (masc): sojourn, residence, habitation
mora: pause, span of time

supremus: last, highest
plene: fully
cibis in legalibus: *regarding foods according to the Law*
turba: group
duodenus: twelve-fold

128. Pange lingua gloriosi Corporis

Verbum caro, panem verum
Verbo carnem efficit;
Fitque sanguis Christi merum;
Et si sensus deficit,
Ad firmandum cor sincerum
Sola fides sufficit.

Tantum ergo sacramentum
Veneremur cernui;
Et antiquum documentum
Novo cedat ritui.
Praestet fides supplementum
Sensuum defectui.

Genitori Genitoque
Laus et jubilatio;
Salus honor virtus quoque
Sit et benedictio;
Procedenti ab utroque
Compar sit laudatio.

verbum caro: *the Word (made) flesh*
merum: wine, pure wine (*Vinum* would not rhyme here.)

vener-or, vener-ari: (*vener-e-mur* = present subjunctive)
cernuus, -a, -um: bowing, prostrate
cedo, cedere: give way to, yield to, be replaced by
ritus, -us: ceremony, liturgy
praesto, -are: supply, furnish

129. Pange lingua gloriosi Proelium
Venantius Fortunatus, c. 530-610 VR

Pange, lingua, gloriosi	
Proelium certaminis,	Lauream certaminis
Et super crucis trophaeum	Et super crucis trophaeo
Dic triumphum nobilem,	
Qualiter Redemptor orbis	
Immolatus vicerit.	
De parentis protoplasti	
Fraude Factor condolens,	
Quando pomi noxialis	
Morsu in mortem corruit;	In necem morsu ruit
Ipse lignum tunc notavit,	
Damna ligni ut solveret.	

pango, pangere (+acc): sing *about*, tell *of*, celebrate
proelium: battle, warfare
certamen, certaminis: struggle, contest
laurea: laurel, wreath, (symbol of) victory
super: over, about, concerning
dico, dicere (+acc): speak of, talk about, tell
trophaeum: trophy, victory
crucis trophaeum: *victory of the cross, trophy (relic) of the cross*
triumphum: (Noun, dir obj of *dic*)

protoplastus, -a, -um: first-made
fraus, fraudis: crime, sin
condoleo, condolēre: have compassion, sympathise
de: by reason of, on account of (with *condolens*)
pomum: apple, fruit
noxialis: harmful, sinful
morsus, -ūs: bite, biting (morsu: *with a bite, by biting*)
corruo, corruere, corrui: fall, tumble (subj = *he*, ie Adam)
nex, necis: death, ruin, disaster
ruo, ruere, rui: fall, rush
Ipse: *He himself* (ie *Factor*,"the Maker", in line 2)
noto, notare: designate, prepare, mark
damnum: injury, harm

Note: This hymn was composed to welcome a relic of the true cross.

129. Pange lingua gloriosi Proelium

Hoc opus nostrae salutis
Ordo depoposcerat:
Multiformis proditoris
Ars ut artem falleret, — MSS arte ut artem
Et medelam ferret inde,
Hostis unde laeserat.

Quando venit ergo sacri
Plenitudo temporis,
Missus est ab arce Patris
Natus, orbis Conditor;
Atque ventre virginali
Caro factus prodiit. — VR Carne amictus prodiit

ordo, ordinis: order, good order, right order
deposco, deposcere, depoposci: demand, require
multiformis, -is: manifold, devious
proditor: betrayer, traitor, deceiver
ars, artis: art, skill
fallo, fallere: foil, refute, deceive
medela: cure, healing, medicine
laedo, laedere, laesi: injure, inflict a wound
inde, unde: (cf Praef de S Cruce: *ut unde mors oriebatur, inde vita resurgeret*)

arx, arcis: citadel
prodeo, prodire: come forth
amictus a um (+abl): clothed in, wearing

Note

"Caro factus" quotes Saint John. "Carne amictus" quotes no one.

129. Pange lingua gloriosi proelium

Vagit infans inter arcta
Conditus praesepia;
Membra pannis involuta
Virgo Mater alligat;
Et manus pedesque et crura   Et Dei manus pedesque
Strictā cingit fasciā.

vagio, vagire: cry, wail
arctus, -a, -um: tight, narrow
condo, condere, conditus: confine, hide (nb: *Conditor….conditus*)
inter: within, inside
praesepium: manger, crib (plu for sing)
panni, -orum: swaddling clothes
involvo, involvere, involutus: wrap, roll up
alligo, alligare: bind, tie
crus, cruris (neut): leg
stringo, strictus: hold tight, tighten
cingo, cingere: loop around, girdle
fascia, -ae: band, ribbon, sash

Note on Meter:

Trochaic tetrameter: alternating lines of 8 and 7 syllables. The dominant foot is the trochee (long-short). The spondee (long-long) occurs almost as often. Rhyme is employed with no consistent pattern. The marching songs of the Roman army were trochaic.

Membra pannis invo luta
— ∪ — — — ∪ — ∪
Virgo Mater alli gat
— — — ∪ — ∪ ∪

When these lines are read accentually we get:

Membra pannis invo luta
— ∪ — ∪ — ∪ — ∪
Virgo Mater alli gat
— ∪ — ∪ — ∪ ∪

130. Paschale mundo gaudium (R)
Cf *Claro paschali gaudio* (M)

Paschale mundo gaudium
Sol nuntiat formosior,
Cum luce fulgentem novā
Jesum vident Apostoli.

In carne Christi vulnera
Micare tamquam sidera
Mirantur, et quidquid vident
Testes fideles praedicant.

Rex Christe clementissime,
Tu corda nostra posside,
Ut lingua grates debitas
Tuo rependat nomini.

Ut sis perenne mentibus
Paschale, Jesu, gaudium,
A morte dirā criminum
Vitae renatos libera.

formosus, -a, -um: lovely, beautiful
fulgeo, fulgēre: shine, be radiant

mico, micare: glitter, shine
miror, mirari: (+ acc and infin)
praedico, praedicare: proclaim, teach

grates, gratium: thanks (= *gratias*) (Δ adverb *gratis*)
rependo, rependere: repay, pay back
libero, -are: free, set free

131. Pater superni luminis
Saint Robert Bellarmine, 1542-1621

Pater superni luminis,
Cum Magdalenam respicis,
Flammas amoris excitas,
Geluque solvis pectoris.

Amore currit saucia
Pedes beatos ungere,
Lavare fletu, tergere
Comis, et ore lambere.

Astare non timet cruci,
Sepulcro inhaeret anxia,
Truces nec horret milites;
Pellit timorem caritas.

O vera, Christe, caritas,
Tu nostra purga crimina,
Tu corda reple gratia,
Tu redde caeli praemia.

gelu, -ūs: frost, cold, ice

saucius, -a, -um: wounded, suffering
comae, -arum: hair
ore lambere: *to kiss with her lips*

inhaereo, inhaerēre: cling to, remain near
nec horret: *she does not shrink from, she is not frightened by* (+ acc)
trux, trucis: rough, grim
caritas: (cf *Perfecta caritas foras mittit timorem*, I John 4:18)

132. Petrus beatus catenarum laqueos (M)
Saint Paulinus, c. 730-802
Cf *Miris modis repente liber* (R)

Petrus beatus catenarum laqueos,
Christo jubente, rupit mirabiliter;
Custos ovilis et Doctor Ecclesiae,
Pastorque gregis, conservator ovium,
Arcet luporum truculentam rabiem.

Gloria Patri per immensa saecula;
Sit tibi, Nate, decus et imperium;
Honor potestas Sanctoque Spiritui:
Sit Trinitati salus individua
Per infinita saeculorum saecula.

catena: chain
laqueus: bond, fetter, restraint, lock, *perh* manacle (cf Acts 3:7 *de manibus*)
rumpo, rumpere, rupi: break, smash
ovile, ovilis: sheep-fold
arceo, arcere, arcui: keep out, ward off
lupus: wolf
truculentus: fierce, savage, dangerous
rabies, rabiei: madness, rage

Sit Trinitati salus individua: *the Trinity be praised for the salvation of everyman*

Note on Meter

Iambic trimeter. As usual the foot is doubled, so that this is in effect an iambic hexameter. The spondee is permitted. Almost any line of 12 syllables will qualify.

Per in finī ta sae cu lō rum sae cula
◡ — ◡ — ◡ — ◡ — — — ◡ ◡

133. <u>Placare Christe servulis</u> (R)
Cf *Christe redemptor omnium, Conserva* (M)

Placare, Christe, servulis
Quibus Patris clementiam
Tuae ad tribunal gratiae
Patrona Virgo postulat.

Et vos, beata per novem
Distincta gyros agmina,
Antiqua cum praesentibus,
Futura damna pellite.

Apostoli cum Vatibus,
Apud severum Judicem
Veris reorum fletibus
Exposcite indulgentiam.

placor, placari (+ dat): be pleased with, be reconciled to
quibus: *for whom, on whose behalf* (ind obj of *postulat*)
ad: at,before
tribunal, tribunalis (neut): judgment seat, court
patrona: protectress, patroness

Et vos: *And you* (angels)
distinguo, distinguere, distinctus: separate, divide
gyrus, gyri: circle, order
per novem gyros: *into nine circles*
agmen, agminis (neut): rank, *perh* choir
antiqua: scil *damna*
damnum, damni: hurt, harm, injury
pello, pellere: remove

vates, vatis: prophet, seer
apud: before (a judge), in the court of
reorum fletibus: *by reason of the tears of the guilty*
exposco, exposcere: beg for
indulgentia: mercy, forgiveness

133. Placare Christe servulis

Vos, purpurati Martyres,
Vos, candidati praemio
Confessionis, exsules
Vocate nos in patriam.

Chorea casta Virginum,
Et quos eremus incolas
Transmisit astris, caelitum
Locate nos in sedibus.

Auferte gentem perfidam
Credentium de finibus,
Ut unus omnes unicum
Ovile nos Pastor regat.

purpuratus: empurpled, ennobled
candidatus: white-robed
praemium: reward
exsules (acc pl): *exsules.... nos*

chorea: chorus
eremus, -i: desert, wilderness
incola, incolae: inhabitant, dweller
transmitto, -ere: send, convey
astris: *ad astra* (poetic use of dative)
caeles, caelitis: dweller in heaven
loco, locare: locate, place
Et quos: *And you whom as hermits the desert has conveyed to the stars*

fines, finium: boundaries, borders, lands
ovile, ovilis: sheep-fold

Note

Candidati praemio confessionis: These are a second group, distinguished from the martyrs. The word *Confessor* refers the saint who suffered the torments of the martyrs, but did not die. The martyrs are *purpurati*; the confessors in this hymn are *candidati*, "white-robed". But cf *Te martyrum candidatus laudat exercitus* in the *Te Deum*.

133. <u>Placare Christe servulis</u>

(in festo Sancti Gabrielis)

Nobis adesto, Archangele,
"Robur Dei" qui denotas:
Vires adauge languidis,
Confer levamen tristibus

robur, roboris (neut): strength, power, force
denoto, denotare: signify, indicate, denote
vires, virium: vigor, strength
adaugeo, adaugere: increase
languidus: sick
levamen, levaminis: comfort, consolation
tristis: sad, unhappy

(in festo Sancti Raphaelis)

Nobis adesto, Archangele,
"Dei medelam" denotans;
Morbos repelle corporum,
Affer salutem mentibus.

medela: healing, medicine
denoto, denotare: signify, indicate, denote
morbus: disease
affero, afferre: bring

134. Plasmator hominis Deus (M)
Anon, c. 600 Cf *Hominis superne Conditor* (R)

Plasmator hominis Deus,
Qui cuncta solus ordinans,
Humum jubes producere
Reptantis et ferae genus:

Qui magna rerum corpora,
Dictu jubentis vivida,
Ut serviant per ordinem,
Subdens dedisti homini:

plasmator, -oris: maker, molder, shaper
ordino, ordinare: order, command, organise
humus, -i: soil, ground, land
jubeo, jubēre, jussi: bid, command (+ infin)
genus, generis: variety, class, sort
repto, reptare: creep, crawl (Cf Gen 1: 24-25)
fera, -ae: wild beast, wild animal

dictum, dictu: (supine of *dico*. Cf *mirabile dictu*)
magna rerum corpora: *the bodies of big creatures, large-bodied things*
corpora: (Acc, dir obj of *dedisti*)
vividus, -a, -um: alive, full of life, animated
per ordinem: *rank by rank, according to their character*
subdo, subdere: subjugate, subordinate

134. Plasmator hominis Deus (M)

Repelle a servis tuis,
Quidquid per immunditiam,
Aut moribus se suggerit,
Aut actibus se interserit.

Da gaudiorum praemia,
Da gratiarum munera;
Dissolve litis vincula,
Astringe pacis foedera.

immunditia: uncleanness
moribus (dat): *(our) way of life, (our) conduct*
suggero, suggerere: propose, suggest (*se, itself*)
actibus: *(our) actions*
se intersero, interserui: interfere with, intrude into

lis, litis: strife, contention, legal conflict
dissolvo: release, break
astringo, astringere: tighten, bind together
foedus, foederis: covenant, agreement

Note

Repelle a servis tuis. Hiatus: there is no elision of the final vowel. The revisers in 1632 will correct this: *repelle quod cupidinis*

135. <u>Plenis resultet vocibus</u>
Cf *Beata caeli gaudia*, note

Plenis resultet vocibus
Laetum diei canticum;
Ad lucis ortum concinat
Chorus beatos praesules.

En pro gregis custodia
Nullos labores neglegunt;
Tutantur illum, sanius
Impertientes pabulum.

resulto, -are: ring out, resound, be heard
laetus: happy, joyful
canticum: (nominative. subj of *resultet*)
ortus, -ūs: rising, dawn
concino, -ere (+ acc): sing about, celebrate
chorus, -i: *the* choir
praesul, praesulis: bishop, prelate

en: behold
neglego, neglegere: overlook, omit
tutor, tutari: guard, protect
illum: (ie *gregem*)
impertio, impertire: bestow, provide
pabulum: nourishment, food
sanus, -a, -um: wholesome (*sanius pabulum*)

135. Plenis resultet vocibus

Arcent lupos, e finibus
Procul latrones exigunt,
Replent oves pinguedine,
Ovile numquam deserunt.

Tot nunc potiti gaudiis,
O vos, sacrati praesules,
Nobis rogate gratiam
Apud tribunal judicis.

Perpes tibi laus, gloria
Sit, Christe Rex piissime,
Cum Patre et almo Spiritu
Regnans per omne saeculum.

arceo, arcere: ward off, keep away
lupus: wolf
fines, finium: boundaries, borders
latro, latronis: thief
exigo, exigere: drive out, expel
pinguedo, pinguedinis: rich food, fine food, fat
ovile, ovilis: sheep-fold
desero, deserere, deserui: abandon, desert

potior, potiri, potitus: obtain (+ abl)
apud: before (ie *before* a judge or a court)
tribunal, tribunalis (neut): judgement seat, court

perpes, perpitis: (= *perpetuus, -a, -um*)

136. <u>Praeclara custos virginum</u>
Anon, c. 1650

Praeclara custos virginum,
Intacta mater Numinis,
Caelestis aulae janua,
Spes nostra, caeli gaudium.

Inter rubeta lilium,
Columba formosissima,
Virga e radice germinans
Nostro medelam vulneri,

praeclarus a um: illustrious, glorious, famous
custos, custodis (here fem): guardian, protector
Numen, Numinis: Divinity, God
aula, aulae: hall, court

rubeta, -orum: thorns
lilium: lily (cf Cant 2:2)
columba: dove (cf Cant 2:10)
formosus a um: lovely, beautiful (cf Cant 4:7)
virga: rod, stem, shoot (cf Isaiah 11:1)
germino, -are: germinate, produce
medela: remedy, cure (ie the Lord, dir obj of *germinans*)
vulnus, vulneris: wound

136. Praeclara custos virginum

Turris draconi impervia,
Amica stella naufragis,
Tuere nos a fraudibus,
Tuāque luce dirige.

Erroris umbras discute,
Syrtes dolosas amove,
Fluctūs tot inter deviis
Tutam reclude semitam.

turris, -is (fem): tower
impervius, -a, -um: inaccessible, not passable (+ dat = *to* or *by*)
naufragus, -a, -um: *one who is* shipwrecked
tueor, tueri: protect, watch over
fraus, fraudis: deception, fraud

discuto, -ere: scatter, dispel
syrtis, syrtis (fem): shoal, sand-bank, reef
dolosus a um: dangerous, treacherous
amoveo, -ere: remove, move out of the way
fluctus tot inter: *amid so many waves* (lit "waves so many among")
devius: lost, off-course, off the path (*for those who are lost*)
recludo: open up, reveal (not "close again")
tutus a um: safe, secure
semita, -ae: path, way, route

137. Primo die quo Trinitas (R)
Cf *Primo dierum omnium* (M)

Primo die quo Trinitas
Beata mundum condidit,
Vel quo resurgens Conditor
Nos morte victā liberat....

Pulsis procul torporibus,
Surgamus omnes ocius,
Et nocte quaeramus Deum,
Propheta sicut praecipit....

Nostras preces ut audiat,
Suamque dextram porrigat,
Et expiatos sordibus
Reddat polorum sedibus....

Ut, quique sacratissimo
Huius diei tempore
Horis quietis psallimus,
Donis beatis muneret.

primo die quo: *on the first day when* (ie Sunday)
condo, -ere, condidi: establish, found

torpor, torporis: sluggishness, sleepiness, laziness
ocius (adv): quickly, more quickly
propheta: (David, cf Ps 133:2—*In noctibus extollite* etc)

porrigo, porrigere: offer, extend
expiatus (< expiare): cleansed *of*, having made atonement *for* (+ abl)
sordes, sordium: filth, uncleanness, sins
reddo, reddere: restore *us*
polorum sedibus: *to our heavenly seats, to our places in the heavens*

quique: = *quicumque, =nos omnes qui*
quietus: peaceful, quiet (*in the quiet hours*)
munero, munerare: endow, reward (supply *us*)
donis beatis: *with blessed gifts, with the gifts of beatitude*

137. <u>Primo die quo Trinitas</u> (R)

Jam nunc, paterna claritas,
Te postulamus affatim:
Absint faces libidinis,
Et omnis actus noxius.

Ne foeda sit vel lubrica
Compago nostri corporis,
Ob cuius ignes ignibus
Avernus urat acrius.

Mundi Redemptor, quaesumus,
Tu probra nostra diluas;
Nobisque largus commoda
Vitae perennis conferas.

claritas: glory (The glory of the Father is the Son.)
affatim: earnestly
fax, facis: torch, flame, fire
libido, libidinis: lust, desire
noxius: harmful, sinful

foedus, -a, -um: filthy, vile, ugly
lubricus: dangerous, impure
compago, compaginis (fem): structure, framework, fabric
Avernus: the underworld, hell
uro, urere: burn
acer, acrior: bitter, sharp, hot

probrum: disgrace, indecency
diluo, diluere, dilui: wash *away*, efface
largus, -a, -um: generous, giving abundantly
commodum: blessing, favor

138. Primo dierum omnium (M)
Attrib Gregory the Great, c. 600 Cf *Primo die quo Trinitas* (R)

Primo dierum omnium,
Quo mundus exstat conditus,
Vel quo resurgens Conditor
Nos morte victā liberat….

Pulsis procul torporibus,
Surgamus omnes ocius,
Et nocte quaeramus Pium
Sicut Prophetam novimus….

Nostras preces ut audiat,
Suamque dextram porrigat,
Et expiatos sordibus
Reddat polorum sedibus.

Ut, quique sacratissimo
Huius diei tempore
Horis quietis psallimus,
Donis beatis muneret.

exsto, exstare: appear, exist
condo, condere, conditus: establish, found

torpor, torporis: sluggishness, sleepiness, laziness
ocius (adv): quickly, more quickly
Pium: *the Holy One* (ie God the Father)
propheta: (David, cf Ps 133:2—*In noctibus extollite* etc)

porrigo, porrigere: offer, extend
expiatus (expiare): cleansed *of*, having atoned *for* (+ abl)
sordes, sordium: filth, uncleanness, sins
polorum sedibus: *to our heavenly seats, to our places in the heavens*

quique: = *quicumque,* = *nos omnes qui*
quietus: peaceful, quiet (*in the quiet hours*)
munero, munerare: endow, reward (perh supply *us*)
donis beatis: *with blessed gifts, with the gifts of beatitude*

138. <u>Primo dierum omnium</u> (M)

Jam nunc, paterna claritas,
Te postulamus affatim:
Absit libido sordidans
Et omnis actus noxius.

Ne foeda sit, vel lubrica
Compago nostri corporis,
Per quam averni ignibus
Ipsi crememur acrius.

Ob hoc, Redemptor, quaesumus
Ut probra nostra diluas;
Vitae perennis commoda
Nobis benigne conferas.

claritas: glory (The glory of the Father is the Son.)
affatim: earnestly
libido, libidinis: passion, lust, desire
sordido, -are: defile, pollute, soil

foedus, -a, -um: filthy, vile, ugly
lubricus: dangerous, impure
compago, compaginis (fem): joining, framework, fabric
avernus: the underworld, hell
ipsi: (*nos* ipsi)
cremo, cremare: burn
acer, acrior: sharp, hot

probrum: disgrace, indecency
diluo, diluere, dilui: wash *away*, efface
largus, -a, -um: generous, giving abundantly
commodum: blessing, favor

138. Primo dierum omnium (M)

(This penultimate strophe is omitted in the Roman Breviary. Britt and Lentini reject it as inauthentic. Connelly accepts it.)

Quo carnis actu exsules
Effecti ipsi caelibes,
Ut praestolamur cernui,
Melos canamus gloriae.

exsul, exsulis: in exile, exiled
carnis actu: *by an act of the flesh* (perh the eating of the forbidden fruit)
effecti (<efficere): *(having been) made*, *when we have been made*
ipsi: *we ourselves*
caelebs, caelibis: celibate, perh *like angels*
ut + indic: as, while
praestolor, praestolari: wait, await
cernuus: with head bowed, humbly
melos, meli (neuter): hymn, melody

Notes:

1. *Carnis actu exsules*: Connelly, "absent now from fleshly activity". Britt, "exiles by the action of the flesh".

2. The problem of *quo*:

If *quo* = *ut* + subjunc, then the phrase-structure is *quo.... canamus*, "so that we may sing". But the relative clause of purpose would normally require an antecedent, and there is none.

If *quo* = *illo*, then the phrase-structure is *quo carnis actu*, "separated by that fleshly act", or even "cut off from the fleshly act". And *canamus* is an independent subjunctive: "let us sing". And there is still no antecedent.

3. There may be a cross-reference to Matt 22:30, *In resurrectione enim neque nubent neque nubentur, sed erunt sicut angeli Dei in caelo.*

By that deed of the flesh we are in exile.
Since we have now become like angels,
While we wait with our heads bowed,
Let us sing a hymn of glory.

139. <u>Quem terra pontus aethera</u>
Venantius Fortunatus, c. 530-610

Quem terra, pontus, aethera VR sidera
Colunt, adorant, praedicant,
Trinam regentem machinam,
Claustrum Mariae bajulat.

Cui luna, sol et omnia
Deserviunt per tempora,
Perfusa caeli gratiā
Gestant puellae viscera.

quem: (dir obj of *bajulat*)
pontus: sea, ocean
aether, aetheris (neut): upper air, sky, heaven
sidus, sideris (neut): star
regentem: (*quem.... regentem*)
trinam machinam: (dir obj of *regentem*)
claustrum: enclosure
bajulo, bajulare: carry

cui: (obj of *deserviunt*)
omnia: *all things, everything* (not "omnia.... tempora")
deservio, deservire (+ dat): humbly serve, be devoted to, serve eagerly
per tempora: *throughout the seasons*
perfundo, -ere, perfusus: suffuse with, perfuse with (abl)
perfusa: *perfusa.... viscera*
gesto, gestare: carry, bear
viscera (neut plu): innards, womb

Note:

Trina machina: cf *Aeterne Rex altissime,* strophe 3, and *Custodes hominum psallimus angelos*, note. The scriptural reference is to Phil 2:10.

Cui.... gestant: The dir obj of *gestant* and antecedent of *cui* is omitted. "[Him] whom moon and sun and all things humbly serve, suffused with grace from heaven the womb of a maiden bears."

139. Quem terra pontus aethera

Beata Mater munere,
Cuius supernus artifex
Mundum pugillo continens,
Ventris sub arcā clausus est.

Beata caeli nuntio,
Fecunda Sancto Spiritu,
Desideratus gentibus
Cuius per alvum fusus est.

munus, muneris: gift, duty, office
Beata Mater munere: perh *Blessed be the Mother by (this) gift*
pugillum: fist (*in His fist, in the hollow of His hand*)
sub: hidden in, concealed by
venter, ventris: womb
arca: ark

nuntio: *by the messenger of heaven, by the message from heaven*
fecunda: *fruitful by the Holy Ghost, pregnant by the Holy Spirit*
gentibus: (dative of agent, common with gerundive, rare with participle)
desideratus: (subject of *fusus est*)
alvum: womb
fundo, fundere, fusus: bring forth, yield in abundance

Notes:
1. *Beata Mater munere*: Translators and liturgical editors are not unanimous here. The position of the comma makes a difference.
   i. *Beata Mater, munere cujus* yields "Blessed Mother, by whose gift…."
   ii. *Beata Mater munere,* yields "Mother, blessed by a gift…."

2. *Pugillum*: Cf Isaiah 40:12— *Quis mensus est pugillo aquas et caelos palmo ponderavit* ?

3. *Desideratus gentibus*: Cf Haggai 2:8—*Et veniet desideratus cunctis gentibus*.

140. Quicumque Christum quaeritis
Prudentius, 348-410

Quicumque Christum quaeritis,
Oculos in altum tollite;
Illic licebit visere
Signum perennis gloriae.

Illustre quiddam cernimus,
Quod nesciat finem pati,
Sublime, celsum, interminum,
Antiquius caelo et chao.

Hic ille rex est gentium
Populique rex Judaici,
Promissus Abrahae patri
Ejusque in aevum semini.

quicumque: (= *Vos omnes qui*, Whoever *ye be who*)
oculos: (Elide the middle vowel: oc' los)
licet (impersonal): it is permitted, it is lawful, one may
viso, visere, visi: behold, contemplate

illustris, illustre: full of light, glorious
cerno, cernere, crevi: discern, perceive
illustre quiddam cernimus: *something glorious we (can) see*
nesciat: (= *non possit* + infin. Subjunctive in indirect speech)
patior, pati: experience, suffer
finem: (dir obj of *pati*) (NOT dir obj of *nesciat*)
interminus a um: boundless
chao: (ablative of *chaos*)

Hic ille rex est: *He is the king, This is the king*
Judaicus: Jewish, Judaic
Abrahae: (dative)

140. Quicumque Christum quaeritis

Hunc, et prophetis testibus
Iisdemque signatoribus,
Testator et Pater jubet
Audire nos et credere.

hunc: (Christum)
testis, testis: witness
signator: one who attests, one who swears (to the truth)
testator, testatoris: one who makes a covenant, witness

Notes:

1. *Abrahae*. Cf *Quam olim ABRAHAE promisisti et semini ejus*, Offertory of the Requiem Mass. On the other hand: *Sicut locutus est ad patres nostros, ABRAHAM et semini ejus in saecula*, Luke 1:55. Both forms are correct.

2. *Testis* and *signator* are roughly synonymous. The *testis* sees and bears witness; the *signator* bears witness and makes a solemn, or sealed, affirmation.

> ....prophetis testibus (ablative absolute)
> iisdemque signatoribus
>
> "the prophets see
> and they bear solemn witness"

2. The *testator* is the author of a *testamentum*

> Testator et Pater jubet
> "And the Father in His covenant commands"

However, the word *testator* also means *witness*. In this sense the poet is referring to the words of the Father at the Transfiguration as a giving of testimony.

141. Quodcumque in orbe (R)
Cf *Quodcumque vinclis* (M)

Quodcumque in orbe nexibus revinxeris,
Erit revinctum, Petre, in arce siderum;
Et quod resolvit hic potestas tradita,
Erit solutum caeli in alto vertice.
In fine mundi judicabis saeculum.

nexus, -ūs: connexion. bond
revincio, revincire, revinxi: bind, tie
arx, arcis: high place, citadel
resolvo, resolvere, resolvi: unbind, loosen (*resolvit* is pres tense, as below)
hic: here
vertex, verticis: summit

nn. Quodcumque vinclis (M)
Saint Paulinus of Aquileia, c.730-802

Quodcumque vinclis super terram strinxeris,
Erit in astris religatum fortiter;
Et quod resolvis in terris arbitrio,
Erit solutum super caeli radium.
In fine mundi judex eris saeculi.

vinc[u]lum: chain
stringo, stringere, strinxi: bind, tie
religo, religare, religatus: tie, bind
arbitrio: *by (your) judgment*
radius: spoke, rod, radius

Note:

Iambic trimeter, ie hexameter.

142. Rector potens verax Deus
Attrib Saint Ambrose, c.339-397

Rector potens, verax Deus,
Qui temperas rerum vices,
Splendore mane instruis, VR Splendore mane illuminas
Et ignibus meridiem.

Exstingue flammas litium,
Aufer calorem noxium,
Confer salutem corporum,
Veramque pacem cordium.

rector, rectoris: governor, pilot
verax, veracis: true, truthful (opp = *mendax*)
tempero, temperare: moderate, regulate
(vicis) vicis: change, alteration, cycle, pattern
mane: (noun. dir obj of *instruis* or *illuminas*) (Δ *mane* = adverb)
instruo, instruere: draw up, prepare
splendor, splendoris: brilliance, glory
et ignibus: *and with a blaze of fire*
Note: *Man' illuminas.* However, *mane-instruis*, no elision.

exstinguo, -ere, exstinxi: put out (a fire), quench
lis, litis: strife, conflict, lawsuit
calor, caloris: heat, burning
noxius, -a, -um: harmful, sinful

143. <u>Regali solio fortis Iberiae</u>
Urban VIII, 1568-1644

Regali solio fortis Iberiae,
Hermenegilde, jubar, gloria martyrum,
Christi quos amor almis
Caeli coetibus inserit !

Ut perstas patiens, pollicitum Deo
Servans obsequium, quo potius tibi
Nil proponis, et arces
Cautus noxia, quae placent !

Ut motus cohibes, pabula qui parant
Surgentis vitii, non dubios agens
Per vestigia gressus,
Quo veri via dirigit !

solium: throne
regali solio: *of the royal throne*
fortis: (vocative)
iubar, iubaris: radiance, shining light
quos: (martyrum quos….)
insero, inserere: enrol, introduce

ut: how, as, when (+ indic)
persto, perstare: stand firm, persist, endure
servans: *maintaining (your) promised obedience to God*
quo: (abl of comparison with *potius*) (obsequium quo: *obedience than which*)
potius (potior): preferable, more important (Δ *potior, potiri*)
arceo, arcēre: avoid, abstain from, keep away
cautus a um: careful, safe
quae placent: *which beckon, although they are pleasing*

motus, -ūs: impulse, feeling (acc pl) (*motus….qui parant pabula*)
cohibeo, cohibēre: restrain, check
pabula, -orum (pabulum): nourishment, fuel, energy
vitium: vice, sin
agens: (modifies the implicit *tu* in *cohibes*; as if *et tu agis*)
gressūs ago: place (ones's) steps, take a step
non dubius: unhesitating, not fearful
per vestigia….quo: *on the path where, in the direction whither*

144. Regis superni nuntia
Boniface VIII

Regis superni nuntia,
Domum paternam deseris,
Terris, Teresa, barbaris
Christum datura aut sanguinem.

Note: As a child Teresa ran away to convert the Moors in Africa.

Sed te manet suavior
Mors, poena poscit dulcior;
Divini amoris cuspide
In vulnus icta concides.

O caritatis victima!
Tu corda nostra concrema,
Tibique gentes creditas
Averni ab igne libera.

nuntia, nuntiae: *female* messenger, herald
desero, -ere: desert, abandon, leave
terris barbaris: (dative)
Christum datura: *to give Christ or (to give) your blood to....*

te manet: *awaits you*
posco, poscere: claim (supply *te*)
cuspis, cuspidis: blade, tip, *perh* dart
ictus, -a, -um: smitten, struck, stabbed
cóncido, concidere: fall down, tumble, fall (as if dead) (nb tense)
vulnus, vulneris (neut): wound
in vulnus icta: perh *stabbed and wounded*

concremo, concremare: burn up, consume
Avernus: hell, underworld

145. Rerum Creator optime
Anon. Attrib both to St Ambrose and to St Gregory the Great

Rerum Creator optime,
Rectorque noster, aspice;
Nos a quiete noxia,
Mersos sopore libera.

Te, sancte Christe, poscimus,
Ignosce tu criminibus. VR Ignosce culpis omnibus
Ad confitendum surgimus,
Morasque noctis rumpimus.

Mentes manusque tollimus,
Propheta sicut noctibus
Nobis gerendum praecipit,
Paulusque gestis censuit.

Vides malum quod gessimus; VR Vides malum quod fecimus
Occulta nostra pandimus;
Preces gementes fundimus;
Dimitte quod peccavimus.

quies, quietis (fem): rest, idleness
mersus a um (mergere): overcome, deep in
noxius a um: harmful, sinful
sopor, soporis: slumber, lethargy

morasque noctis rumpimus: *we interrupt the delays of night*

propheta: (David. cf *Primo dierum omnium* supra)
nobis gerendum praecipit: *says we should*
Paulus: (cf Acts 16:25, *Media autem nocte Paulus et Silas orantes*, et seq)
gestis (gerere): *by action, by his deeds*
censeo, censēre, censui: approve, commend

pando, pandere, pandi: display, lay bare

146. <u>Rerum Deus tenax vigor</u>
Attrib Saint Ambrose

Rerum Deus tenax vigor,
Immotus in te permanens,
Lucis diurnae tempora
Successibus determinans:

Largire clarum vespere, VR Largire lumen vespere
Quo vita nusquam decidat,
Sed praemium mortis sacrae
Perennis instet gloria.

tenax, tenacis: steadfast, firm
vigor, vigoris: force, energy, strength
in te: *in Thyself* (cf *in se permanens*, Sap 7:27)
successus, -us: course (of time), interval
successibus: *by intervals, in their cycle, in sequence*

largior, largiri: grant, bestow
vespere: (VM, noun, VR, adverb)
quo: *by means of which, so that* (purpose clause)
nusquam: at no time, never
decido, decidere: fail, cease
insto, instare: ensue, follow closely
sed etc: *but may everlasting glory ensue (as) the prize of a holy death*

147. <u>Rerum supremo in vertice</u>
V. Genovesi SJ, c. 1950

Rerum supremo in vertice
Regina, Virgo, sisteris,
Exuberanter omnium
Ditata pulchritudine.

Princeps opus, formosior
Verbo creanti praenites,
Praedestinata Filium,
Qui protulit te, gignere.

Ut Christus alta ab arbore
Rex purpuratus sanguine,
Sic passionis particeps,
Tu Mater es viventium.

Tantis decora laudibus,
Ad nos ovantes respice,
Tibique sume gratulans
Quod fundimus praeconium.

vertex, verticis: summit, top, peak
sisto, sistere: put, place, stand (*As Queen, O Virgin, you are placed*)
exuberanter: abundantly, plentifully, fruitfully
dito, ditare: enrich, endow

princeps opus: (The Mother of God is the "first work" of creation.)
formosior: so lovely, very lovely (not *more lovely than*)
praeniteo, praenitēre (+dat): glitter before, shine before (here not *outshine*)
Verbo creanti: (dat with *praenites*, not abl with *formosior*)
profero, -ferre, -tuli: produce, bring forth
gigno, gignere: bear, create

ut: as, like

decorus a um: lovely, beautiful, perh *worthy of*
ovo, ovare: exult, rejoice
gratulor, gratulari: give thanks, be thankful (*gratulans praeconium*)
praeconium: proclamation, public declaration

148. Rex gloriose martyrum
Anon, c. 500

Rex gloriose martyrum, Corona confitentium, Qui respuentes terrea Perducis ad caelestia....	
Aurem benignam protinus Appone nostris vocibus; Trophaea sacra pangimus; Ignosce quod deliquimus.	 vr Intende nostris vocibus
Tu vincis in martyribus, Parcendo confessoribus; Tu vince nostra crimina, Donando indulgentiam.	Tu vincis inter martyres Parcisque confessoribus Largitor indulgentiae.

respuentes: *those who despise* (accusative. *rex qui perducis respuentes*)
terreus, -a, um: earthly, worldly

protinus (adv): immediately, constantly, further
appono, -ere: give (ear), offer (your ear)
trophaeum: trophy, *plu metaph* triumph, victory
pango, pangere: sing

Note

Parcendo, donando: In later Latin the ablative of the gerund evolves toward the meaning of a present participle. *[by] sparing, [by] giving.* Of course, *parcens* and *donans* would not fit the meter.

nn. Rex gloriose praesulum (M)

praesul, praesulis: abbot, prelate, bishop

149. Rex sempiterne caelitum (R)
Cf *Rex sempiterne Domine* (M)

Rex sempiterne caelitum,
Rerum creator omnium,
Aequalis ante saecula
Semper Parenti Filius….

Nascente qui mundo faber
Imaginem vultūs tui
Tradens Adamo, nobilem
Limo jugasti spiritum.

Cum livor et fraus daemonis
Foedasset humanum genus,
Tu carne amictus perditam
Formam reformas artifex.

Qui natus olim e Virgine,
Nunc e sepulcro nasceris,
Tecumque nos a mortuis
Jubes sepultos surgere.

caeles, caelitis: heavenly dweller, heavenly being
Filius: (Nominative, but quasi vocative)

qui: *you,* or *you who* (tu qui….jugasti)
nascente mundo: *when the world was born, at the birth of the world* (abl absol)
Adamus, -i: Adam
faber, fabri: maker, builder (*….the builder, ….as builder*)
limus, -i: slime, mud (*limo* is dative, ind obj of *jugasti*)
jugo, jugare: connect, join

livor, livoris: envy, malice, bruise (cf Isaiah 53:5— *livore ejus sanati sumus*)
fraus, fraudis: deception, fraud, swindle
foedo, foedare: pollute, defile
amictus a um (+ abl): clothed in
forma: beauty, shape, image
artifex, artificis: designer, builder

nasceris: (Present tense identified by meter)

149. <u>Rex sempiterne caelitum</u> (R)

Qui pastor aeternus gregem
Aquā lavas baptismatis:
Haec est lavacrum mentium,
Haec est sepulcrum criminum.

Nobis diu qui debitae
Redemptor affixus cruci,
Nostrae dedisti prodigus
Pretium salutis sanguinem.

Ut sis perenne mentibus
Paschale, Jesu, gaudium,
A morte dirā criminum
Vitae renatos libera.

haec: (supply *aqua*, or possibly *lavatio*)
lavacrum: washing
sepulcrum: grave, tomb, burial

nobis….debitae…. cruci: *cross due to us* or *cross owed by us*
qui: (tu) qui…. Redemptor affixus cruci (not *nobis qui*)
prodigus, -a, -um: generous, extravagant

mens, mentis: (Often used in hymns as a synonym for *anima*)
dirus a um: dire, dreadful, terrible
crimen, criminis: (Often used in hymns as a synonym for *peccatum*)
renatos…. libera: (scil *nos*)

150. Rex sempiterne Domine (M)
Anon, c. 500 Cf *Rex sempiterne caelitum* (R)

Rex sempiterne Domine,
Rerum creator omnium,
Qui eras ante saecula
Semper cum Patre Filius,

Qui mundi in primordio
Adam plasmasti hominem,
Cui tuae imagini
Vultum dedisti similem,

Quem diabolus deceperat,
Hostis humani generis,
Cujus tu formam corporis
Assumere dignatus es,

Ut hominem redimeres,
Quem ante jam plasmaveras,
Et nos Deo conjungeres
Per carnis contubernium,

qui: *tu qui*
primordium: origin, beginning
plasmo, plasmare: form, shape, fashion
cui (2 syllables): *Adam... cui dedisti vultum*
vultus, -ūs: countenance, appearance (*vultum similem imagini tuae*)

quem: *Adam* quem
hostis: (nominative)
cujus: *humani generis, cujus*

ante jam: earlier, before that time
contubernium: "tent-sharing", comradeship, intimacy

150. Rex sempiterne Domine (M)

Quem editum ex Virgine
Pavescit omnis anima,
Per quem et nos resurgere
Devotā mente credimus,

Qui nobis in baptismate
Donasti indulgentiam,
Qui tenebamur vinculis
Ligati conscientiae,

Qui crucem propter hominem
Suscipere dignatus es,
Dedisti tuum sanguinem,
Nostrae salutis pretium.

Quaesumus, Auctor omnium,
In hoc paschali gaudio,
Ab omni mortis impetu
Tuum defende populum.

quem: *tu* quem (*quem* is dir obj of *pavescit*)
edo, edere, editus: bring forth, beget
pavesco, -ere (+ acc): fear greatly, be fearful of
devota mente: *devoutly, passionately, wholeheartedly*

ligo, ligare: bind
conscientia: conscience, guilt

impetus, -ūs: onrush, force, power

151. <u>Sacra jam splendent decorata lychnis</u>
Pope Leo XIII, 1810- 1903

Sacra jam splendent decorata lychnis
Templa, jam sertis redimítur ara,
Et pio fumant redolentque acerrae
Thuris honore.

Num juvet summo Geniti Parente
Regios ortūs celebrare cantu?
Num domūs David, decora et vetustae
Nomina gentis?

Gratius nobis memorare parvum
Nazarae tectum tenuemque cultum;
Gratius Jesu tacitam referre
Carmine vitam.

splendeo, splendēre: shine, be bright
decoro, decoratus: adorn, decorate
lychnus, -i: lamp, light (Greek loan-word in Latin)
serta, -ae: garland, wreathe
redimio, redimīre: encircle, deck, crown (Δ *redimo, redimere*)
ara, arae: altar
fumo, fumare: (emit) smoke
redoleo, redolere: (emit a) smell, be redolent of
acerra, -ae: thurible, censer (*acerrae-thuris*, not *thuris-honore*)
pio honore: *in loving honor* (Britt), *pay their loving homage* (Connelly)

num juvet (juvo, juvare): *would it be agreeable, would it be pleasing* ?
summo geniti Parente: *Son from a most high Father*
ortus, -ūs: origin, birth, rising (*Geniti…regios ortus*)
num (line 3): (supply *juvet celebrare*)
domūs David: *of the house of David*
vetustus, -a, -um: ancient

> "Would it please to celebrate in song the noble names
> of the house of David and of an ancient race?"

gratius: (*it would be) more pleasing* (*gratius* answers *num juvet?*)
memoro, -are: remember, recall (Δ *memoror, -ari*)
Nazarae (<Nazara = Nazareth): (locative or genitive)
tenuis, -is: small, little, slender
cultus, -ūs: way of life, resources, family life
refero, referre: recall

151. Sacra jam splendent decorata lychnis

Nili ab extremis peregrinus oris,
Angeli ductu, propere remigrat
Multa perpessus Puer, et paterno
Limine sospes,

Arte qua Joseph humili excolendus
Abdito Jesus juvenescit aevo,
Seque fabrilis socium laboris
Adjicit ultro.

"Irriget sudor mea membra" dixit,
"Antequam sparso madeant cruore;
Haec quoque humano generi expiando
Poena luatur."

Assidet Nato pia Mater almo,
Assidet Sponso bona nupta, felix
Si potest curas relevare fessis
Munere amico.

Nilus: the Nile
ora, -ae: border, shore, edge
propere (Adv): in haste, quickly
perpetior, perpeti, perpessus: endure, undergo (dir obj = *multa*)
sospes, sospitis (Adj): safe, secure

arte qua: *in the same craft as (* or *qua Joseph = sicut Joseph*)
excolo, -ere: improve, refine (*to be educated in a humble craft, like Joseph*)
juvenesco, -ere: grow up
fabrilis, -is: of a builder, of a carpenter
adjicio, -ere: *adds himself freely as a partner in the builder's work*

irrigo, irrigāre: make wet, moisten
madeo, madēre: flow, become wet
(poenam) luo, luere: undergo (a punishment), pay (a penalty)
humano generi expiando: *in atoning for the human race* (gerundive)

assideo, -ēre: sit near, remain close
nupta, -ae: wife, bride
fessus a um: tired (*for her weary menfolk*)
amicus a um: affectionate, loving

151. Sacra jam splendent decorata lychnis

O neque expertes operae et laboris,
Nec mali ignari, miseros juvate,
Quos reluctantes per acuta rerum
Urget egestas.

Demite his fastus, quibus ampla splendet
Faustitas, mentem date rebus aequam;
Quotquot implorant columen, benigno
Cernite vultu.

Sit tibi, Jesu, decus atque virtus,
Sancta qui vitae documenta praebes,
Quique cum summo Genitore et almo
Flamine regnas.

expers, expertis: free of, unfamiliar with (+ gen) (Δ *expertus*)
opera, operae: toil, work
ignarus: unacquainted with, ignorant of (+ gen)
reluctor, reluctari: struggle against, oppose, resist
urgeo: press, push
egestas, -atis: poverty, need

demo, demere: remove, take away
fastus, -ūs (noun): contempt, arrogance (acc pl)
Faustitas, -atis: (goddess of) good omen
rebus: *in their affairs*
columen, columinis (neut): pillar, (metaph) strength, support

documentum: pattern, example, precept
quique: (et qui) (Δ *quisque* etc)

Note

This hymn has never been included in the monastic office. It was in the Roman office from 1921 to 1971. A simplified version can be found in the Liturgia Horarum.

152. Sacris solemniis juncta sint gaudia
Saint Thomas Aquinas, 1225-1274

Sacris solemniis juncta sint gaudia,
Et ex praecordiis sonent praeconia;
Recedant vetera, nova sint omnia,
Corda, voces, et opera.

Noctis recolitur cena novissima,
Qua Christus creditur agnum et azyma
Dedisse fratribus, juxta legitima
Priscis indulta patribus.

Post agnum typicum, expletis epulis,
Corpus dominicum datum discipulis,
Sic totum omnibus, quod totum singulis,
Ejus fatemur manibus.

solemnium, -ii: (or *solemnia, -ae*. not 3rd declen *solemnis*)
praecordia, praecordiorum (neut pl): heart, hearts
praeconium: praise

novissimus: last
cena: (*cena noctis qua: supper of the night on which*)
azyma, -orum (neut pl): unleavened bread
legitimus: legal, according to law, appointed by law
indultum: concession, indulgence
priscus: ancient, venerable (*priscis patribus* is dative)

typicus: figurative, symbolic
epulae, -arum: feast, banquet (fem pl with sing meaning)
expleo, expletus: finish, complete
datum: (supply *esse*)
totum: *the whole to all….the whole likewise to each*
manibus: *by His hands*

152. Sacris solemniis juncta sint gaudia

Dedit fragilibus corporis ferculum.
Dedit et tristibus sanguinis poculum,
Dicens: Accipite quod trado vasculum;
Omnes ex eo bibite.

Sic sacrificium istud instituit,
Cujus officium committi voluit
Solis presbyteris, quibus sic congruit,
Ut sumant et dent ceteris.

Panis angelicus fit panis hominum;
Dat panis caelicus figuris terminum.
O res mirabilis: manducat Dominum
Pauper, servus, et humilis.

Te, trina Deitas unaque, poscimus:
Sic nos tu visita, sicut te colimus;
Per tuas semitas duc nos quo tendimus,
Ad lucem quam inhabitas.

ferculum: dish, tray, food
poculum: cup
vasculum: (small) vessel

officium: office, service, duty
committo: assign, entrust, commit
congruo, conguere, congrui: belong to, be fitting (pres tense)

caelicus, -a, -um: heavenly, celestial
figuris terminum: *an end to symbols* (because the sacrament is real)

tendo, tendere: strive, direct one's life

Meter: This is an accentual version of the Asclepiadic, or "Choriambic" Stanza. Thomas takes liberties with vocalic length. For a more precise example of this meter, cf *Sanctorum meritis inclita gaudia*.

153. Salutis aeterne dator (R)
Cf *Jesu salvator saeculi* (M)

Salutis aeterne dator,
Jesu, redemptis subveni;
Virgo, parens clementiae,
Dona salutem servulis.

Vos Angelorum milia,
Patrumque coetus, agmina
Canora Vatum, vos, reis
Precamini indulgentiam.

Baptista Christi praevius,
Summique caeli Claviger,
Cum ceteris Apostolis,
Nexus resolvant criminum.

subvenio, subvenīre (+ dat): come to the help of, help
dono, donāre: give, grant, *obtain through thy intercession* (Britt)

milia (noun): thousands (= *millia.* always neuter)
coetus, -ūs: assembly, gathering (vocative plural)
canorus, -a, -um: melodious, harmonious
vates, vatis: = *propheta* (*vatum* = *prophetarum*)
reus, -a, -um: guilty (*reis* is dative)
precamini: (imperative)

nexūs resolvant criminum: *May they loose the bonds of sin*

153. <u>Salutis aeterne dator</u> (R)

Cohors triumphans Martyrum,
Almus Sacerdotum chorus,
Et virginalis castitas
Nostros reatus abluant.

Quicumque in altā siderum
Regnatis aulā principes,
Favete votis supplicum,
Qui dona caeli flagitant.

virginalis castitas: = *virgines castae*
reatus, -ūs: guilt (accusative plural)

aula, aulae: hall, court, temple
faveo, favēre (+dat): look with favor on, hear
votum: prayer
flagito, flagitare (+acc): beseech, beg for

154. <u>Salutis humanae sator</u> (R)
Cf *Jesu nostra redemptio* (M)

Salutis humanae sator,
Jesu, voluptas cordium,
Orbis redempti conditor,
Et casta lux amantium….

Quā victus es clementiā,
Ut nostra ferres crimina,
Mortem subires innocens,
A morte nos ut tolleres?

Perrumpis infernum chaos;
Vinctis catenas detrahis;
Victor triumpho nobili
Ad dexteram Patris sedes.

Te cogat indulgentia,
Ut damna nostra sarcias,
Tuique vultūs compotes
Dites beato lumine.

Tu, dux ad astra et semita,
Sis meta nostris cordibus….

sator, satoris: creator, source, maker (lit *sower*)
voluptas, voluptatis: pleasure, delight, joy
quā….clementiā: *by what mercy, by what pity*

perrumpo, -ere: subdue, overpower
infernus a um: infernal, of hell
chaos (Greek: Neuter accusative singular): chaos, disorder
vincio, vincīre, vinxi, vinctus: bind, put in chains
catena: chain, shackle, bond
detraho, detrahere: take away, remove (acc *from* abl)

sarcio, sarcire: make good, correct
compos, compotis: sharer, participant (+ gen)
dito, ditare: enrich (supply *nos*)

meta, metae: goal, finish-line, winning-post

155. Salvete Christi vulnera
Anon, before 1700

Salvete, Christi vulnera,
Immensi amoris pignora,
Quibus perennes rivuli,
Manant rubentis sanguinis.

Nitore stellas vincitis,
Rosas odore et balsama,
Pretio lapillos Indicos,
Mellis favos dulcedine.

Per vos patet gratissimum
Nostris asylum mentibus;
Non huc furor minantium
Unquam penetrat hostium.

pignus, pignoris: pledge, guarantor, assurance
quibus: *from which*
perennis: endless, everflowing
rivulus: stream
mano, manare: spread, flow, run down
rubeo, rubere: redden, be red, make red

vincitis: "you conquer", ie *you exceed, you surpass*
nitor, nitoris: brilliance, splendor
balsamum, -i: fragrant balm, balsam (*rosas et balsama*)
lapillus: gem, gem stone
Indicus, -a, -um: of India, Indian
favus, -i: honeycomb (*mellis favus* = *favus*. cf Luke 24:42, Vulg)

pateo, patere, patui: lie open, be exposed
gratus a um: welcome
asylum: refuge, sanctuary
minor, minari: threaten, menace (*hostium minantium*)

155. Salvete Christi vulnera

Quot Jesus in praetorio
Flagella nudus excipit!
Quot scissa pellis undique
Stillat cruoris guttulas!

Frontem venustam, proh dolor,
Corona pungit spinea;
Clavi retusā cuspide
Pedes manusque perforant.

Postquam sed ille tradidit
Amans volensque spiritum,
Pectus feritur lanceā,
Geminusque liquor exsilit.

flagellum: scourge, lash
excipio, excipere, excepi: accept, allow
pellis, -is (fem): skin
scindo, scissus: tear, cut, rend
undique: on every side, all over
stillo, stillare: drip, ooze with (+ acc)

frons, frontis (fem): brow, forehead
venustus, -a, -um: graceful, handsome
proh: alas, oh (*dolor* is vocative)
spineus, -a, -um: of thorns, thorny
pungo, pungere, pupugi, punctus: pierce, stab
clavus, -i: nail
cuspis, cuspidis (fem): point, tip
retundo, retusus: blunt, make blunt

ferio, ferire: strike, pierce
lancea, lanceae: spear
liquor, liquoris: fluid, liquid
exsilio, exsilire, exsilui: spring out

155. Salvete Christi vulnera

Ut plena sit redemptio,
Sub torculari stringitur,
Suique Jesus immemor
Sibi nil reservat sanguinis.

Venite, quotquot criminum
Funesta labes inficit;
In hoc salutis balneo
Qui se lavat, mundabitur.

Summi ad Parentis dexteram
Sedenti habenda est gratia,
Qui nos redemit sanguine,
Sanctoque firmat Spiritu.

torcular, torcularis: winepress (cf Isaiah 63:3, Lam 1:15)
stringo, stringere: crush, squeeze, press
sui: *of himself*
immemor: unmindful, heedless
sibi: *for himself, to himself*
reservo, -are: keep, reserve
nil sanguinis: *none of (his) blood, no blood*

venite quotquot: *come as many as, come all ye whom*
crimen, criminis: sin
funestus, -a, -um: deadly, fatal
labes, labis: stain, mark
inficio, -ere, infeci: stain, spoil, corrupt
balneum: bath

habere gratiam: be grateful, give thanks

Note:
Iambic dimeter. The line is octosyllabic. Three of the elisions are irregular.
Pret*io* lapillos Indicos [pre tsjo] = 2 syllables
Gem*in*usque liquor exsilit [gem nus]
Sib*i* nil reservat sanguinis [sib nil]
The other elisions are more familiar:
immens' amoris, odor' et, summ' ad, sedent' haben, habend' est

156. Salvete flores martyrum
Prudentius, 348-410

Salvete, flores martyrum,
Quos lucis ipso in limine
Christi insecutor sustulit,
Ceu turbo nascentes rosas.

Vos prima Christi victima,
Grex immolatorum tener,
Aram sub ipsam simplices VM Aram ante ipsam simplices
Palmā et coronis luditis.

limen, liminis: threshhold
insecutor, insecutoris: persecutor, opponent, enemy
tollo, tollere, sustuli, sublatus: take away, carry off
ceu: as, just as, like
turbo, turbinis: whirlwind, gale

tener, tenera, tenerum: tender, young
simplex: simple, childlike
palma et coronis: *with palm(s) and crowns*
ludo, ludere, lusi: play, frolic

Note
Apoc 6:9— *Vidi subtus altare animas interfectorum propter verbum Dei*

Examples of the iambic dimeter:

Vos pri ma Chri sti vic ti ma
— — ~ — — — ~ ~
In this case [chr] does not function as a double consonant.

Grex im mo la to rum tener
— — ~ — — — ~ ~
The [e] of *grex* is short. [x] = [ks], a double consonant.

157. <u>Sanctorum meritis inclita gaudia</u> (M)
Anon, c. 700 (Attrib Rabanus Maurus, c. 780-856)
Cf *Sanctorum meritis inclita gaudia* (R)

Sanctorum meritis inclita gaudia
Pangamus, socii, gestaque fortia;
Nam gliscit animus promere cantibus
Victorum genus optimum.

Hi sunt, quos retinens mundus inhorruit;
Ipsum nam sterili flore peraridum
Sprevēre penitus, teque secuti sunt,
Rex Christe bone caelitum.

Hi pro te furias atque ferocia
Calcarunt hominum, saevaque verbera;
Cessit his lacerans fortiter ungula,
Nec carpsit penetralia.

meritis: *by reason of their merits, for their merits*
inclita gaudia (neut acc plu): *the famous joy, the joyous renown*
pango, pangere (+ acc): sing of, sing about (*sanctorum gaudia pangamus*)
glisco, gliscere: swell, surge, rise up
animus, animi: mind, heart, spirit
promo, promere, prompsi, promptus: express, declare
genus optimum: *the best sort, the noblest race*

retineo, retinēre: restrain, hold back, cling
inhorreo, inhorrēre, inhorrui: bristle at (+ acc), repel, make to shudder
sterilis, sterilis: barren, unfruitful
peraridus, -a, -um: very dry, empty
sperno, spernere, sprevi: (*sprevēre = sprevērunt*)
penitus (adv): inwardly (Δ *penitus, -a, -um*)
caeles, caelitis: dweller in heaven, heavenly dweller

furia, furiae: rage, fury
ferocia (<ferox, ferocis): lit "fierce things", perh *barbarity, savagery,*
calco, calcare, calcavi: tread upon, trample on, belittle (syncopated form)
cessit: *the tearing hook bravely yielded to them*
lacero, lacerare: tear, rip apart
ungula, -ae: hook (tool of torture)
carpo, carpere, carpsi: seize, pluck out
penetralia (<penetralis, -is): *(their) innermost parts, (their) soul*

157. <u>Sanctorum meritis inclita gaudia</u> (M)

Caeduntur gladiis more bidentium;
Non murmur resonat, non querimonia;
Sed corde tacito mens bene conscia
Conservat patientiam.

Quae vox, quae poterit lingua retéxere,
Quae tu Martyribus munera praeparas?
Rubri nam fluido sanguine, laureis
Ditantur bene fulgidis.

Te, summa Deitas unaque, poscimus mss Te trina Deitas
Ut culpas abluas, noxia subtrahas,
Des pacem famulis, nos quoque gloriam
Per cuncta tibi saecula.

caedo, caedere: cut down, kill
more: *in the manner of, like so many, like*
bidens, bidentis: sacrificial animal (cf *Antra deserti*)
murmur, murmuris: complaint, grumble
querimonia, -ae: lamentation, complaint
conscius, -a, -um: aware, participating, bearing witness

lingua: (nominative)
retexo, retexere: unravel, repeat (Δ *retego, retexi*)
ruber, rubra, rubrum: red (*rubri* is nom masc plu)
fluidus, -a, -um: flowing, running
dito, ditare: enrich, endow
laurea: laurel, laurel wreath, perh *halo*
fulgidus: glittering, brilliant, shining

nos: (*des nos quoque gloriam tibi,* "grant also us to be thy glory")

Choriambic Meter: 3Asclepiadic lines + 1 Glyconic line.
The choriambus is — ~ ~ —

Quae tu Martyribus munera prae pa ras
— — | — ~ ~ — | — ~ ~ — | ~ —

Di tan tur bene ful gi dis
— — | — ~ ~ — | ~ —

158. <u>Sanctorum meritis inclita gaudia</u> (R)

Sanctorum meritis inclita gaudia
Pangamus, socii, gestaque fortia;
Gliscens fert animus promere cantibus
Victorum genus optimum.

Hi sunt, quos fatue mundus abhorruit;
Hunc fructu vacuum, floribus aridum
Contempsēre tui nominis asseclae,
Jesu Rex bone caelitum.

Hi pro te furias atque minas truces
Calcarunt hominum saevaque verbera;
His cessit lacerans fortiter ungula,
Nec carpsit penetralia.

meritis: *by reason of their merits*
pango, pangere (+acc): sing about, sing of (*sanctorum gaudia pangamus*)
glisco, gliscere: swell, rise, blaze up
fert: *hastens, strives* (+ infin)
promo, promere, prompsi, promptus: express, declare
victorum genus optimum: perh *the noblest race of conquerors*

fatue: foolishly
abhorreo, abhorrui: shrink from (+ acc), disdain
hunc: *this one, this world*
vacuus, -a, -um: void, empty, worthless
aridus, -a, -um: barren, parched
contemno, contempsi: condemn, reject
assecla, asseclae (masc): follower, companion
caeles, caelitis: dweller in heaven, heavenly dweller

furia, furiae: rage, fury
minae, minarum: threats, menace
trux, trucis (adj): savage, grim
calco, calcare, calcavi: tread upon, trample on, despise
cessit: *the tearing hook bravely yielded to them*
lacero, lacerare: tear, rip apart
ungula, -ae: hook
carpo, carpere, carpsi: seize, pluck out
penetralia (< penetralis, -is): *(their) innermost parts, (their) soul*

158. Sanctorum meritis inclita gaudia (R)

Caeduntur gladiis more bidentium;
Non murmur resonat, non querimonia;
Sed corde impavido mens bene conscia
Conservat patientiam.

Quae vox, quae poterit lingua retéxere,
Quae tu Martyribus munera praeparas?
Rubri nam fluido sanguine, fulgidis
Cingunt tempora laureis.

Te, summa o Deitas, unaque poscimus:
Ut culpas abigas, noxia subtrahas,
Des pacem famulis; ut tibi gloriam
Annorum in seriem canant.

caedo, caedere: cut down, kill
bidens, bidentis: sacrificial animal (cf *Antra deserti*)
murmur, murmuris: complaint, grumble
querimonia, -ae: lamentation, complaint
impavidus, -a, -um: fearless, intrepid, undaunted
conscius, -a, -um: aware, participating, bearing witness

lingua: (nominative)
retexo, retexere: unravel, repeat (Δ *retego, retegere, retexi*)
ruber, rubra, rubrum: red (*rubri* is nom masc plu)
fluidus, -a, -um: flowing, running
fulgidus a um: brilliant, shining
tempora: *their brows, their foreheads, their temples*

abigo, abigere: (*ab* + *ago*)
noxius a um: harmful, injurious, sinful

159. Sedibus caeli nitidis receptos
Anon, c.1880

Sedibus caeli nitidis receptos
Dicite athletas geminos, fideles;
Slavicae duplex columen decusque
Dicite gentis.

Hos amor fratres sociavit unus,
Unaque abduxit pietas erēmo,
Ferre quo multis celerent beatae
Pignora vitae.

nitidus: bright, shining
recipio, receptus: admit, receive
dico, dicere (+ acc): speak of, acclaim as, tell of
athleta, -ae (Greek, masc): champion, athlete
geminus: twin-born, fraternal, brother-*champions*
fideles: (vocative, = *o fideles*)
Slavicus, -a, -um: Slavic
duplex, duplicis: two-fold, double
columen, columinis: column, pillar

eremo: *from the wilderness, from their solitude*
quo: *ut* (*ut celerent ferre*, "so that they might hasten to bring")
celero, celerare: hasten, hurry (Δ *celo, celare*)
pignus, pignoris (neut): pledge, assurance

Meter: Sapphic Stanza.

The fourth, or Adonic, line is constant:
— ~ ~ | — ~

The three Sapphic lines are:
— ~ | — — | — ~ ~ | — ~ | — ~
or
— ~ | — ~ | — ~ ~ | — ~ | — ~
Caesura after the fifth syllable.

In all four lines the final syllable is *anceps*, ie long or short.

159. Sedibus caeli nitidis receptos

Luce, quae templis superis renidet,
Bulgaros complent, Moravos, Bohemos;
Mox feras turmas numerosa Petro
Agmina ducunt.

Debitam cincti meritis coronam,
Pergite o flecti lacrimis precantum;
Prisca vos Slavis opus est datores
Dona tueri.

Quaeque vos clamat generosa tellus
Servet aeternae fidei nitorem;
Quae dedit princeps, dabit ipsa semper
Roma salutem.

renideo, -ēre: shine on
compleo, -ēre: fill (*luce quae*, *with the light which*)
ferus a um: wild, savage
turma, -ae: crowd, throng, tribe
numerosa agmina: *in endless columns, in large numbers*

meritis: *rightly, by (their) merits*
cincti: *crowned with, wreathed with* (+ acc: a poetic exemption)
pergo, pergere: continue (pergite o = o pergite)
flecto, flectere, flexi, flexus: (*flecti* is pres pass infin after *pergite*)
precantum: (gen pl without -i)
opus est: *there is need* (impersonal. + acc and infin)
priscus, -a, -um: original, former, ancient
vos: *vos datores*
Slavis: *to watch over (your) ancient gifts to the Slavs*

quaeque: (*quaecumque*, or *omnis tellus quae vos clamat*)
tellus, telluris (fem): land, nation
generosus: noble, excellent, great
nitor, nitoris: radiance, splendor
Roma: *Roma, quae prima dedit salutem, ipsa dabit semper*

160. <u>Si lege prisca fortibus</u>
Cf *Beata caeli gaudia*, note

Si Lege priscā fortibus
Tributa laus est feminis,
Quae vos alumnas Foederis
Decet novelli gloria!

Arsistis igne candido,
Quem Christus e Caelestium
Invexit arce, frigidus
Ut orbis incalesceret.

Urgebat haec vos caritas
Caduca lucra spernere,
Et, quae perire nesciant,
Optare tantum praemia.

priscus, -a, -um: original, ancient, previous (cf Prov 31:10 et seq)
tribuo, tribuere, tributus: render, offer, pay
alumna, alumnae: (female) follower, pupil
novellus, -a, -um: young, new
Foedus novellum: *Novum Testamentum*

ardeo, ardēre, arsi: glow, burn
candidus,-a, -um: white
Caelestis: Dweller in Heaven, Heavenly Person
inveho, invehere, invexi: bear in, bring in, introduce
arx, arcis: citadel, summit
incalesco, incalescere: grow warm
urgeo, urgēre: urge, persuade, encourage
caducus, -a, -um: perishable, transitory
lucrum, -i: gain, profit, advantage
quae perire nesciant: *which could never perish, which know not death*
opto, optare: choose
tantum (adv): only
praemium: reward

160. Si lege prisca fortibus

Docebat et viriliter
Adversa ferre, vincere
Carnem rebellem, legibus
Servire, non arbitrio.

Donabat et saevissimas
Poenas subire ac firmiter,
Jesum sequentes, propriam
Vitam libenter ponere.

Hinc nos juvate servulos,
Quos tanta virtus excitat,
Ad sanctitatis verticem
Possimus ut contendere.

docebat: (subj = *caritas Christi* = *ignis candidus*)
adversa, -orum: hardship, difficulties, adversity
rebellis, -is: insurgent, antagonistic, rebellious
servio, servire (+dat): serve, be in service to, obey
arbitrium, arbitrii: *their* will

subeo, subire: undergo, endure
libenter: freely, willingly
pono: lay down (cf John 10:15—*animam meam pono pro ovibus meis*)

juvo, -are: help
excito, -are: encourage, motivate, stimulate
possimus ut: *ut possimus*
contendo, -ere: strive, make an effort

Note

The Latin word for *will*, as in the philosophical concept of *free will*, is *arbitrium*. Cf Augustine: *De Gratia et Libero Arbitrio*. See likewise Aquinas sv *arbitrium*.

Augustine also says, "Nihil tam in potestate quam ipsa voluntas est" (*Retrac* I:22). In this sense Pascal will receive from Augustine the idea that efficient grace is a *victrix delectatio*, "a prevailing desire", or a "winning delight".

The alternative—or "kinetic"—theory of grace, holds that grace is a force that exerts an initial push upon the soul. Without such a grace the soul is *incapax boni*, morally inert. The denial of this theorem—and its embedded defintion of grace—is the heresy of Pelagianism.

161. Sic patres vitam peragunt in umbra
Continuation of *Bella dum late furerent*.
E Poletti or V Tarozzi, c.1900

Sic patres vitam peragunt in umbra,
Lilia ut septem nivei decoris,
Virgini excelsae bene grata, Petro
Visa nitere.

Jamque divinā rapiente flammā,
Cursitant urbes, loca quaeque oberrant,
Si queant cunctis animis dolores
Figere Matris.

perago, peragere: finish, complete, spend
umbra, -ae: shadow, shade
lilium, lilii: lily
lilia ut: *like lilies, as lilies*
niveus, -a, -um: snowy, snow-white
decoris: *of snowy loveliness, of snow-white beauty*
Petro visa: *seemed to Peter, seeming to Peter* (Saint Peter of Verona)
niteo, nitēre: shine, glitter

cursito, cursitare: range through, visit every (+ acc)
quisque, quaeque, quodque: each, every, all (in pl)
oberro, oberrare: wander about, wander through (+ acc)
queant: *possint*
si queant: *just in case they might be able, hoping to*
figo, figere: fix, implant (*in all souls the sorrows of the Mother)*

161. Sic patres vitam peragunt in umbra

Hinc valent iras domuisse caecas,
Nescia et pacis fera corda jungunt,
Erigunt maestos, revocant nocentes
Dicta piorum.

At suos Virgo comitata servos
Evehit tandem superas ad oras;
Gemmeis sertis decorat per aevum
Omne beatos.

Eja nunc coetūs gemitum precantis
Audiant, duros videant labores;
Semper et nostris faveant benigno
Lumine votis.

hinc: hence, thus, for this reason
valeo, valere: have the strength to, be able to (+ infin)
domo, domare, domui: tame (as if *valebant domare)*
jungo, jungere: unite, appease
ferus, -a, -um: savage, brutal
nescia pacis: *ignorant of peace, unfamiliar with peace*
maestus, -a, -um: sorrowing, sad
nocentes: *evil-doers*
dicta piorum: *the words of the goodly men* (*dicta* is subj of *valent, jungunt* etc)

at: but
comitor, comitari, comitatus: accompany, follow, stay with (+ acc)
eveho, evehere, evexi: raise, draw up
ora, orae: shore, border
gemmeus, -a, -um: jewelled, gem-encrusted
serta, sertae: garland

eja: oh, please!, hasten!
gemitus, -ūs: groaning, moaning
coetus, -ūs: group, congregation, community

Note: The word *coetus* or *coitus* (< cum+ ire) has 3 short vowels in classical Latin. In later use—as here—the word will often have 2 syllables.

162. Solis O Virgo radiis amicta
Vittorio Genovesi SJ, c. 1950

Solis, o Virgo, radiis amicta,
Bis caput senis redimita stellis,
Luna cui praebet pedibus scabellum
Inclita fulges.

Mortis, inferni domitrixque noxae,
Assides Christo studiosa nostri,
Teque reginam celebrat potentem
Terra polusque.

seni, -ae, -a: six each, six (*bis senis = 12*)
redimio, redimīre, redimītus: encircle, wreath around (Δ *redimo, redimere*)
caput: *about your head* (Acc of respect, a hellenism)
cui: (*O Virgo, cui luna praebet scabellum pedibus*)
fulgeo, fulgēre: shine, be glorious, stand out

domitrix (domitor): tamer, subduer, vanquisher
noxa, noxae: hurt, harm, punishment
assides: *you sit near to* (+ dat)
studiosus: diligent, zealous, fond
nostri: *of us, for us*
polus: heaven, sky

Note
Cf Apoc 12:1— *Mulier amicta sole, et luna sub pedibus ejus, et in capite ejus corona stellarum duodecim.*

162. Solis O Virgo radiis amicta

Damna sed perstat soboli minari
Creditae quondam tibi dirus anguis;
Mater, huc clemens ades, et maligni
Contere collum.

Asseclas diae fidei tuere,
Transfugas adduc ad ovile sacrum, LH Dissitos adduc ad….
Quas diu gentes tegit umbra mortis
Undique coge.

Sontibus mitis veniam precare,
Adjuva flentes, inopes et aegros,
Spes mica cunctis per acuta vitae
Certa salutis.

persto, perstare: persist, continue (+ infin)
anguis, anguis (masc): serpent, snake (subject of *perstat*)
minor, minari: threaten, menace (*perstat minari*)
damnum: injury, harm (*damna* = dir obj of *minari*)
soboles, sobolis (suboles) (fem): offspring, progeny (ind obj of *minari*)
creditus a um (+dat): entrusted to
ades: (2nd pers sing pres imperative. pl = *adeste*)
collum, -i: neck

assecla, asseclae: follower
dius, dia, dium: godlike, holy, divine
transfuga, transfugae: deserter, apostate
dissitus, -a, -um: widely scattered
quas: (*coge gentes quas etc*) (not *transfugas quas*)
tego, tegere, texi: cover
cogo, cogere: collect, gather, lead in

sons, sontis: guilty (here = *peccator; sontibus = peccatoribus*)
mitis, mitis: mild, tender (*tu mitis precare*)
precor, precari: obtain, pray for (+ acc rei and dat pers)
mico, micāre: glitter, shine
certa: *esto spes certa salutis, micans etc*

163. Somno refectis artubus
Anon c. 600

Somno refectis artubus,
Spreto cubili, surgimus;
Nobis, Pater, canentibus
Adesse te deposcimus.

Te lingua primum concinat,
Te mentis ardor ambiat,
Ut actuum sequentium
Tu, Sancte, sis exordium.

somnus, somni: sleep (Δ *somnium, somnii*, "dream")
reficio, reficere, refectus: "remake", refresh, restore
artūs, artuum (plu): joints, limbs, *metaph* body (*artubus* = abl)
sperno, sperenere, spretus: reject, abandon, despise
cubile, cubilis: bed
deposco, -ere: ask, beg, pray

primum (adv): first, first of all
concino, concinere (+acc): sing *about*, celebrate in song
ambio, ambire: "go round", embrace, strive for
actuum sequentium: (ie during the coming day)
exordium, exordii: beginning, source

163. Somno refectis artubus

Cedant tenébrae lumini,
Et nox diurno sideri,
Ut culpa quam nox intulit,
Lucis labascat munere.

Precamur iidem supplices,
Noxas ut omnes amputes,
Et ore te canentium
Lauderis in perpetuum. VR Lauderis omni tempore

sidus, sideris: star
infero, inferre, intuli: inflict, bring with *it*
lucis munere: *by the gift of light*
labasco, labascere: vanish, yield

iidem: (nom masc pl. = eidem. after elision here = [idem])
noxa: harm, sin, evil
amputo, amputare: remove, take away, prune away

Note on meter:

Why *tenébrae*? The [e] is short; and [br] does not operate as a double consonant. Cf *lux in ténebris lucet et ténebrae eam non comprehenderunt.*

Connelly remarks, "The second syllable is normally long in poetry and short in prose".

The iambic dimeter demands a long syllable in that position.

ce dant te NE brae lu mi ni
— — | ~ — | — — | ~ —

This is a doubled meter; so in effect it is a tetrameter. The spondee is an optional variation in the first and third foot. The final syllable of the line is always *anceps*.

164. Splendor paternae gloriae
Saint Ambrose, c. 339-397

Splendor paternae gloriae, —— | ~ — | — — | ~ —
De luce lucem proferens,
Lux lucis et fons luminis, —— | ~ — | —— | ~ ~
Diem dies illuminans.

Verusque sol, illabere
Micans nitore perpeti; ~ — | ~ — | ~ — | ~ —
Jubarque Sancti Spiritūs
Infunde nostris sensibus.

Votis vocemus et Patrem,
Patrem perennis gloriae, vr Patrem potentis gratiae
Patrem potentis gratiae: vr Patrem perennis gloriae,
Culpam releget lubricam.

splendor, splendoris: brilliance, grandeur, Majesty (ie the Son of God)
profero, proferre: bring forth, produce, reveal
dies (nom sing): *dies illuminans diem,* "Day giving light to the day"

illabor, illabi, illapsus: descend, glide down
mico, micare: glitter, sparkle
nitor, nitoris: brilliance, brightness
perpes, perpetis (adj): unceasing, perpetual
jubar, jubaris (neut): ray, beam, light

relego, relegare: banish, remove (Δ *relego, relegere*)
lubricus, -a, -um: dangerous, impure, evil

164. Splendor paternae gloriae

Confirmet actus strenuos;
Dentes retundat invidi;
Casus secundet asperos;
Donet gerendi gratiam. vr Agenda recte dirigat

Mentem gubernet et regat,
Casto fideli corpore; vr Sit pura nobis castitas
Fides calore ferveat,
Fraudis venena nesciat.

Christusque nobis sit cibus,
Potusque noster sit fides;
Laeti bibamus sobriam
Ebrietatem Spiritūs. vr Profusionem Spiritus

confirmo, confirmare: strengthen, encourage
strenuus, -a, -um: steadfast, resolute
retundo, retundere: (make) blunt, blunten
invidus, invidi: envious, the envious one (ie the devil)
secundo, secundare: bless, assist, help, act as second for
casus asperos: "hard cases", perh *us in times of hardship*

calor, caloris: heat
ferveo, fervēre: glow, burn, be passionate
venenum, veneni: poison
fraus, fraudis: falsehood, false doctrine

bibo, bibere: drink
sobrius, -a, -um: sober
ebrietas, ebrietatis: insobriety, intoxication, drunkenness
profusio: outpouring

164. <u>Splendor paternae gloriae</u>

Laetus dies hic transeat:
Pudor sit ut diluculum,
Fides velut meridies;
Crepusculum mens nesciat.

Aurora cursūs provehit. vr Aurora lucem provehit
Aurora totus prodeat, vr Cum luce nobis prodeat
In Patre totus Filius,
Et totus in Verbo Pater.

laetus etc: *May this day pass joyfully* (Not "may this happy day pass")
pudor etc: *May (our) modesty be as the dawn*
crepusculum: dusk, twilight, coming of dark

proveho, provehere: lead forth, advance, bring forward
cursus (acc pl): *the cycle of the day, the course of the day*
prodeo, prodire: come forth, go forth
totus (line 2): *He who is All, the All*
aurora (line 2): *like dawn, as the dawn*

Note:

The vr dates from Boniface VIII and his committee of four Jesuit humanists in 1632. The version of this hymn in the *Liturgia Horarum* (2000) follows an earlier manuscript tradition, and it is almost identical to the VM. It reverses all of the "corrections" of 1632.

Saint Augustine refers to this hymn indirectly: *Veni Mediolanum ad Ambrosium episcopum....cujus tunc eloquia ministrabant adipem frumenti tui et laetitiam olei et sobriam vini ebrietatem populo suo.* (Conf V, xiii 23, cited by Connelly. See also reference there to Saint Fulgentius. For *adipem frumenti* cf Psalm 80: 17, and 147:14.)

Connelly describes *profusionem* here as "probably the most inept emendation in the whole history of literature". Technically the [i] of *ebrietatem* is short. However, when Ambrose chooses to lengthen it—and when Augustine applauds the result—we are not in a position to argue. Thus:

E bri e ta tem Spi ri tus
— — | ~ — | — — | ~ —

Instead of correcting the father of Latin hymnography, perhaps we should revise our dictionaries.

165. Summae Deus clementiae (15 September, Lauds)
Callisto Palumbella, c. 1750

Summae Deus clementiae,
Septem dolores Virginis
Plagasque Jesu Filii
Fac rite nos revolvere.

Nobis salutem conferant
Deiparae tot lacrimae,
Quibus lavare sufficis
Totius orbis crimina.

Sit quinque Jesu vulnerum
Amara contemplatio,
Sint et dolores Virginis
Aeterna cunctis gaudia.

Deus: (Vocative)
septem dolores: (Acc plu)
plaga, plagae: affliction, scourge, chastisement
rite: fitly, rightly
revolvo: ponder, contemplate, "turn over" in one's mind

deipara: *Theotokos* (*Deiparae* is gen.)
sufficis: *you begin to, you may*

quinque vulnerum: (Gen plu)
amarus a um; bitter

166. <u>Summae Deus clementiae</u> (M) (Saturday, Matins)
Anon, c. 600 Cf *Summae Parens clementiae* (R)

Summae Deus clementiae,
Mundique factor machinae,
Unus potentialiter,
Trinusque personaliter.

Nostros pius cum canticis
Fletūs benigne suscipe;
Quo corde puro sordibus
Te perfruamur largius.

machina, -ae: fabric, structure, scheme

fletus, -ūs: tears, weeping
quo: ut
puro sordibus: *cleansed of filth, purified of wickedness*
perfruor, perfrui: enjoy
largius: more abundantly

Note:

The phrase *unus potentialiter* is of interest. This hymn was written more than 500 years before the reception of Aristotle in the schools. Perhaps we see here the influence of Boethius.

The scholars of 1632 changed *Unus potentialiter* into *Unius et substantiae*. In this way they protected the standard vocabulary of *Aristoteles Latinus*; but they lost the naïve simplicity of the original hymn.

The text in the *Liturgia Horarum* is: *Qui trinus almo numine, Unusque firmas omnia*. That is a composition of the 1960s.

166. Summae Deus clementiae (M) (Saturday, Matins)

Lumbos jecurque morbidum
Adure igni congruo,
Accincti ut sint perpetim,
Luxu remoto pessimo…..

Ut quique horas noctium
Nunc concinendo rumpimus,
Donis beatae patriae
Ditemur omnes affatim.

lumbus, lumbi: loin
jecur, jecoris (neut): liver, *metaph* heart, mind
morbidus, -a, -um: diseased, depraved
aduro, adurere, adussi: burn, set on fire
congruus, -a, -um: fitting, apt, timely
accincti: *ut (lumbi) accincti sint* (cf Luke 12:35, Eph 6:14, I Pet 1:13)
perpetim: constantly, at all times
luxus, -ūs: debauchery, lust
removeo, -ēre, remotus: remove, take away

quique: *all of us who, those of us who*
concino, -ere: sing, sing together
rumpo, rumpere: interrupt
dito, ditare: enrich, endow
affatim: sufficiently, completely

Notes:

Adure igni and *accincti ut*: hiatus, ie no elision. This will be corrected in the Roman text of 1632.

Ut…. ditemur. The fourth strophe is a purpose clause dependant on *adure* in the third strophe.

167. Summae Parens clementiae (R) (Saturday, Matins)
Cf *Summae Deus clementiae* (M)

Summae Parens clementiae,
Mundi regis qui machinam,
Unius et substantiae,
Trinus personis Deus:

Nostros pius cum canticis
Fletūs benigne suscipe,
Ut corde puro sordium
Te perfruamur largius.

Lumbos jecurque morbidum
Flammis adure congruis,
Accincti ut artūs excubent,
Luxu remoto pessimo.

Quicumque ut horas noctium
Nunc concinendo rumpimus,
Ditemur omnes affatim
Donis beatae patriae.

regis qui: = qui regis
machina, -ae: fabric, structure, scheme

puro sordium: *cleansed of filth, purified of wickedness*
perfruor, perfrui: enjoy
largius: more abundantly

lumbus, lumbi: loin
jecur, jecoris (neut): liver, *metaph* heart, mind
morbidus, -a, -um: diseased, depraved
aduro, adurere, adussi: burn, set on fire
congruus, -a, -um: fitting, apt, timely
artus, -ūs: limb, plu perh *body*
excubo, excubare: keep watch, be on guard
luxūs, -us: debauchery, lust

rumpo, rumpere: interrupt
dito, ditare: enrich, endow
affatim: sufficiently, completely

168. Summae Deus clementiae (M) (Matins, Trinity Sunday)
and Summae Parens clementiae (R)

Summae Deus clementiae,	VR Summae Parens clementiae
Mundique factor machinae,	Mundi regis qui machinam
Unus potentialiter,	Unius et substantiae
Trinusque personaliter:	Trinusque personis Deus.
Da dexteram surgentibus,	
Exsurgat et mens sobria,	VR Exsurgat ut mens sobria
Flagrans et in laudem Dei	
Grates rependat debitas.	

machina, -ae: fabric, structure, scheme
regis qui: = qui regis
potentialiter: See note page 302 surpra

surgo, surgere: rise, arise, get up
exsurgo, -ere: rise, arise
mens: mind, soul
sobrius a um: sober, moderate, sensible
flagrans < flagrare: burning, passionate, ardent
grates, gratium: thanks, thanksgiving
rependo, -ere: pay, repay

169. <u>Summi Parentis Unice</u> (R)
Cf *Aeterni Patris Unice* (M)

Summi Parentis Unice,
Vultu pio nos respice,
Vocans ad arcam gloriae
Cor Magdalenae poenitens.

Amissa drachma regio
Recondita est aerario;
Et gemma deterso luto
Nitore vincit sidera.

Jesu, medela vulnerum,
Spes una poenitentium,
Per Magdalenae lacrimas
Peccata nostra diluas.

Dei Parens piissima,
Hevae nepotes flebiles
De mille vitae fluctibus
Salutis in portum vehas.

arca, arcae: ark
cor poenitens: (Accusative. *O Unice, qui vocas cor poenitens*)

amissa etc; *the drachma missing from the kingdom*
recondo, -ere, reconditus: restore, put back
aerarium: treasury
gemma: gemstone, precious stone
deterso luto (abl abs): *with grime wiped off, cleansed of dirt*
nitor, nitoris: brilliance, beauty

diluo, diluere: wash away, efface

Heva: Eve
nepos, nepotis: descendant
flebilis: weeping, sorrowing
portus, -ūs: harbor, haven
veho, vehere: bring, carry, draw

170 Surge jam terris fera bruma
Vittorio Genovesi SJ, c. 1950

Surge! Jam terris fera bruma cessit,
Ridet in pratis decus omne florum,
Alma quae Vitae Genetrix fuisti,
Surge, Maria!

Lilium fulgens velut in rubeto,
Mortis auctorem teris una, carpens
Sontibus fructum patribus negatum
Arbore vitae.

ferus a um: wild, savage, rough
bruma: winter, winter-time
rideo, ridere, risi: laugh, smile
pratum, prati: meadow
quae: *Tu quae fuisti*

rubeta, -orum: thorn-bush, brambles
tero, terere, trivi, tritus: bruise, crush
sons, sontis (Adj): guilty
carpo, carpere: pluck, gather
arbore: *from the tree*

Notes:

1. This hymn entered the BR after 1950, and the BM after 1960. It displaces a hymn in the older office by Venantius Fortunatus. The LH wisely discards it.

2. The singular *rubeto* may be a mistake. Neither Lewis and Short nor Niermeyer recognise the singular form.

170. <u>Surge jam terris fera bruma</u>

Arca non putri fabricata ligno
Manna tu servas, fluit unde virtus
Ipsa quā surgent animata rursus
Ossa sepulcris.

Praesidis mentis docilis ministra,
Haud caro tabo patitur resolvi;
Spiritūs imo sine fine consors
Tendit ad astra.

Surge! Dilecto pete nixa caelum,
Sume consertum diadema stellis,
Teque natorum recinens beatam
Excipe carmen.

arca: box, jar, container (*vas.... ad servandum*, Exod 16:33)
putris, -is: rotten
manna (here accusative): manna
servo, servare: preserve, contain
quā: *virtus ipsa qua = that very power by which*
sepulcris: *from their tombs*

praesidis mentis.... ministra: *servant of the mind that rules (you)*
tabum: corruption, sickness
caro (nom): *(your) flesh*
haud patitur resolvi: *is never subject to be unmade*
spiritūs consors: *companion of (your) heart, companion of the Spirit*
imo (immo): on the contrary
tendit: (subject is *caro*, meaning *your body*)

nixus a um + dat (< nitor, niti): leaning on, resting upon
sumo, sumere: take up, put on, receive
diadema, diadematis (neut): crown
consertus a um (< consero, -ere): entwined with, fitted with (abl)
carmen te recinens beatam: *a song repeating that you are blessed*
natorum: *of (your) sons*
excipio, -ere: accept, hear, listen to

171. Te deprecante corporum
Anon, c. 1750

Te deprecante, corporum
Lues recedit, improbri
Morbi fugantur, pristina
Redeunt salutis munera.

Phthisi febrique et ulcere
Diram redactos ad necem,
Sacratas morti victimas,
Ejus rapis e faucibus.

lues, luis: disease, plague
improbrus, -a, -um: troublesome, bad
morbus, morbi: sickness, illness, disease
fugo, fugare: put to flight, rout, scatter
pristinus, -a, -um: original, earlier, former
salus, salutis: health

phthisis, phthisis: consumption (*phthisi*, pronounced [ftisi], ablative case)
febris, febris: fever
ulcus, ulceris: ulcer, sore, boil
dirus a um: dire, fearful, dreadful
nex, necis: slaughter, death, mortality
redago, redagere, redactus: lead off, lead away, take down
fauces, faucium: jaw, throat, clutches

Note 2nd Stanza

Main verb is *rapis.* Dir obj is (*homines) redactos*. *Victimas* is in apposition to dir obj. *Sacratas* modifies *victimas*. Antecedent of *ejus* is *morti*. It is impossible to preserve this sentence structure in English translation.

By consumption, by fever, and by sores,
Men led off to dreadful slaughter,
Victims consecrated to death,
You snatch them from its jaws.

171. <u>Te deprecante corporum</u>

Te deprecante, tumido
Merces abactae flumine,
Tractae Dei potentiā,
Sursum fluunt retrogradae.

Cum tanta possis, sedibus
Caeli locatus, poscimus:
Responde votis supplicum,
Et invocatus subveni.

tumidus, -a, um: swollen, fast-moving
merx, mercis (fem): goods, stock (Δ *merces, mercedis*)
abago, abagere, abactus: carry away, carry off
traho, trahere, tractus: pull *up*, pull *back*
sursum: upwards, upstream, to the surface
retrogradus, -a, -um: backwards, in the other direction

cum tanta possis: *since you can do such things*
locor, locari, locatus: be located on, be placed upon (dat)

172. Te dicimus praeconio
Anon.

Te dicimus praeconio,
Intacta Mater Numinis,
Nostris benigna laudibus
Tuam repende gratiam.

Sontes Adami posteri,
Infecta proles gignimur;
Labis paternae nescia
Tu sola, Virgo, crederis.

te dicimus: *we speak of you*
praeconium, praeconii: words of celebration, public praise
intactus, -a, -um: unsullied, inviolate, untouched
rependo, rependere: reward, requite, give in return

sons, sontis (adj): guilty, sinful
posteri, posterorum: descendants, offspring
Adamus, Adami: (= *Adam, Adae*)
inficio, inficere, infectus: pollute, stain
proles, prolis: offspring, child
gigno, gignere, genui, genitus: beget, bring forth
labes, labis (fem): stain, blemish, defect
paternus, -a, -um: ancestral, of our fathers
nescius, -a, -um: unaware of, innocent of (+ gen)

172. Te dicimus praeconio

Caput draconis invidi
Tu conteris vestigio,
Et sola gloriam refers
Intaminatae originis.

O gentis humanae decus,
Quae tollis Hevae opprobrium,,
Tu nos tuere supplices,
Tu nos labantes erige.

Serpentis antiqui potens
Astūs retunde et impetūs,
Ut caelitum perennibus
Per te fruamur gaudiis.

draco, draconis: snake, dragon
vestigium, vestigii: footprint, step, foot
refero, referre: restore, bring back, reflect, bear
intaminatus, -a, -um: undefiled, unspotted

Heva: Eve
tueor, tueri: watch over, protect
labo, labare: fall, stumble (= *labor, labi, lapsus*)

potens: (modifies implicit *Tu*)
astus, -ūs: cunning, cleverness (*astus* and *impetus* are acc pl)
retundo, retundere: blunt, make blunt
caelitum: (gen pl)
fruor, frui: (+ abl)

173. Te gestientem gaudiis
Eustachius Sirena OP, ob 1769

Te gestientem gaudiis,
Te sauciam doloribus,
Te jugi amictam gloriā,
O Virgo Mater, pangimus.

Ave, redundans gaudio
Dum concipis, dum visitas;
Et edis, offers, invenis,
Mater beata, Filium.

gestio, gestire: exult, leap with joy
saucius, -a, -um: wounded
jugis, juge (adj): perpetual, continuous (cf adv *jugiter*)
pango, pangere: sing

redundo, redundare: overflow
edo, edere, edidi, editus: produce, beget, give birth to
offero: (*tulerunt illum in Jerusalem ut sisterent eum Domino*, Luke 2:22)

Note:

First strophe: Summary of the Mysteries of the Rosary. *Gaudiis,* the Joyful Mysteries; *doloribus,* the Sorrowful Mysteries; *gloria*, the Glorious Mysteries.

Second strophe: the Five Joyful Mysteries—

Concipis, the Annunciation; *Visitas*, the Visitation; *Edis*, The Nativity of the Lord; *Offers*, the Presentation; *Invenis*, the Finding of Jesus in the Temple.

173 Te gestientem gaudiis

Ave, dolens et intimo
In corde agonem, verbera,
Spinas crucemque Filii
Perpessa, princeps Martyrum.

Ave, in triumphis Filii,
In ignibus Paracliti,
In regni honore et lumine,
Regina fulgens gloriā.

Venite, gentes, carpite
Ex his rosas mysteriis;
Et pulchri amoris inclitae
Matri coronas nectite.

intimus, -a, -um: innermost, interior (adj)
intimo in corde: *in the interior of your heart*
agon, agonis (Greek): agony
verber, verberis: lash, blow, stroke
perpetior, perpeti, perpessus: endure, undergo, suffer
princeps martyrum: *first among martyrs, first of the martyrs*

regina: (vocative)

amor, amoris: (masculine)
necto, nectere: weave, wreathe

Note:

Perpetior is a synonym of *patior, pati, passus*. The perfect participle of a deponent verb is active in meaning, and can therefore govern a direct object in the accusative case. Thus *agonem perpessa,* "having endured the agony". Recall the line of Vergil (Aeneid I, 199) :

O passi graviora, dabit deus his quoque finem

O pas si gravi o ra da bit deus his quoque finem

— — | — ~ ~ | — ~ ~ | — ~ ~ | — ~ ~ | — ~

174. Te Joseph celebrent
Juan de la Concepcion, ob. 1700

Te, Joseph, celebrent agmina caelitum,
Te cuncti resonent christiadum chori,
Qui clarus meritis junctus es inclitae
Casto foedere Virgini.

Almo cum tumidam germine conjugem
Admirans, dubio tangeris anxius,
Afflatu superi Flaminis angelus
Conceptum Puerum docet.

agmen, agminis: column (of soldiers), battalion, multitude
caeles,caelitis: heavenly dweller, one in heaven
christiades, -um: Christians
foedus, foederis: covenant, bond

tumidus a um: swollen
conjunx, conjugis: spouse, wife
germen, germinis: bud, sprout
almo germine: *with loving new life*
admiror, admirari: wonder *at*, be astonished *by* (+ acc)
dubium, dubii: doubt
flamen, flaminis: breath, wind, spirit
superi Flaminis: (= *Sancti Spiritūs*)
docet: *angelus te docet puerum conceptum esse*
afflatus, -ūs: blowing, inspiration

Meter

This meter is called "the Asclepiadic strophe" or the "Lesser Asclepiad". The fourth line is called "Glyconic".

— — | — ~ ~ — | — ~ ~ — | ~ — (lines 1-3, dodeca-syllabic)
— — | — ~ ~ — | ~ — (line 4, octo-syllabic)

174. Te Joseph celebrent

Tu natum Dominum stringis; ad exteras
Aegypti profugum tu sequeris plagas;
Amissum Solymis quaeris et invenis,
Miscens gaudia fletibus.

Post mortem reliquos sors pia consecrat,
Palmamque emeritos gloria suscipit;
Tu vivens, superis par, frueris Deo,
Mirā sorte beatior.

Nobis, summa Trias, parce precantibus;
Da Joseph meritis sidera scandere,
Ut tandem liceat nos tibi perpetim
Gratum promere canticum.

stringo, stringere: hold tight, hug
profugum: *Him in flight, Him fleeing* (Cf Capitulum ad Nonam, Sap 10:10)
exterus, -a, -um: outer, remote, foreign
plaga, plagae: region, district, reach (*to the outer reaches*)
Solyma, -orum (Solymae, Solymarum): Jerusalem *

post mortem: *after (their) death* (not *after His death*)
reliqui: *other men, those who remain*
sors, sortis: fate, lot, destiny
sors pia: (as if *mors pia.* ie: *sors pia consecrat alios homines post vitam eorum)*
emereo, emereri, emeritus: deserve, earn
gloria: (nominative, subject of *suscipit*)
palmam: (direct object of *emeritos*)
emeritos: (perfect participle, direct object of *suscipit*)
superis par: *equal to the angels*

da (+ infin): *grant (us) by the merits of Joseph*
perpetim (adv): forever
promo, promere, prompsi, promptus: utter, express

Note: *Solymis* is in the locative case. Cf *omnibus sanctis in Christo Jesu qui sunt Philippis*, "to all the saints in Christ Jesus who are in Philippi" (Phil 1:1).

175. Telluris ingens conditor (M)
Telluris alme conditor (R)
Attrib Saint Gregory the Great, 540-604

Telluris ingens conditor,
Mundi solum qui eruens,
Pulsis aquae molestiis,
Terram dedisti immobilem:

VR Telluris alme conditor
Mundi solum qui separans

Ut germen aptum proferens,
Fulvis decora floribus,
Fecunda fructu sisteret,
Pastumque gratum redderet.

tellus, telluris: earth, land
ingens, ingentis: great, mighty
solum, soli: ground, soil
eruo, eruere: draw out, lift out, raise (ie land from the water)
pello, pellere, pulsus: remove, expel, eliminate
molestia, molestiae: trouble, harm, threat, danger (plu in Latin, singular in Eng)
do, dare: produce, make, cause

germen, germinis: bud, sprout. new growth
aptus, -a, um: suitable, convenient
profero, proferre: yield, produce, offer
decorus, -a, -m: comely, beauteous
fulvus, -a, -um: golden, gold-colored
fecundus, -a, -um: fertile, prolific
fructus, -ūs: (masculine)
sisto, sistere: exist, be, rise, grow
pastus, -ūs: food, sustenance

Note: The subject of *sisteret* and of *redderet* is "it" or "she", ie. *terra* from the preceding strophe. The same implicit *terra* is modified by *proferens, decora,* and *fecunda.*

175. Telluris ingens conditor

Mentis perustae vulnera
Munda virore gratiae,
Ut facta fletu diluat,
Motūsque pravos atterat.

Jussis tuis obtemperet;
Nullis malis approximet;
Bonis repleri gaudeat,
Et mortis actum nesciat. VR Et mortis ictum nesciat

mens, mentis: mind, soul, heart
perustus < peruro: parched (for lack of grace)
mundo, mundare: cleanse, clean
viror, viroris: freshness, verdure (= *viriditas, green-ness*)
facta: *deeds, actions, our misdeeds*
diluo, diluere: wash away, efface
attero, atterere: suppress, rub out, remove
motūs pravos: *wicked stirrings, evil temptations*

obtempero, obtemperare: obey, comply with (+ dat)
approximo, approximare: draw near to
mortis actum: *the deadly act* (ie mortal sin)
ictus, -ūs: stab, stroke

Note: The subject of all the verbs in the *ut* clause (*diluat, atterat,* as well as *obtemperet, approximet, gaudeat,* and *nesciat*) is "the parched soul", *mens perusta*.

176. Te lucis ante terminum
Anon, c. 600

Te lucis ante terminum,		
Rerum Creator, poscimus:		
Ut solitā clementiā	VR	Ut pro tuā clementiā
Sis praesul ad custodiam.		Sis praesul et custodia

Procul recedant somnia,
Et noctium phantasmata;
Hostemque nostrum comprime,
Ne polluantur corpora.

solitus, -a, -um: customary, usual
praesul, praesulis: leader, protector, patron
ad custodiam (M): *on guard, on the watch, to guard us*
custodia, -ae (R): protection, safety

somnium, somnii: dream, bad dream
phantasma, phantasmatis (neut): image, figure, fantasy
noctium: *of the night, of night-time*
comprimo, comprimere, compressi: restrain, crush
polluo, polluere, pollui, pollutus: defile, befoul

177. <u>Te Mater alma Numinis</u>
Anon, c. 1750

Te, Mater alma Numinis,
Oramus omnes supplices,
A fraude nos ut daemonis
Tuā sub umbrā protegas.

Ob perditum nostrum genus
Primi parentis crimine,
Ad inclitum Matris decus
Te rex supremus extulit.

Clementer ergo prospice
Lapsis Adami posteris;
A te rogatus Filius
Deponat iram vindicem.

daemon, daemonis: demon, devil

ob (+acc): because of, on account of, by reason of
ad Matris decus: *to the dignity of Mother, to the glory of Motherhood*
inclitus, -a, um: sublime, glorious
effero, efferre, extuli, elatus: raise, elevate, exalt

prospicio, -ere (+ dat): look upon, gaze down on
posterus: descendant, child, son
a te rogatus: *by your intercession, at your request*
depono, deponere: lay down, put aside
vindex, vindicis (adj): avenging

178. Te pater Joseph opifex colende
Evaristo D' Anversa, c. 1950

Te, pater Joseph, opifex colende,
Nazarae felix latitans in umbrā,
Vocibus magnis animisque plenis
Nocte canemus.

Regiam stirpem tenuemque victum
Mente fers aequā tacitusque portas,
Sacra dum multo manuum labore
Pignora nutris.

O Faber, sanctum speculum fabrorum,
Quanta das plebi documenta vitae,
Ut labor sudans, ut et officina
Sanctificetur.

opifex, opificis: worker
colo, colere: venerate, worship (in a liturgical sense)
Nazara, Nazarae: Nazareth
latito, latitare: be concealed, lie hidden

stirps, stirpis (fem): lineage, family
tenuis (adj): modest, plain
victus, -ūs: way of life, standard of living
tacitus a um (< tacēre): in silence, silently
Your royal origin and modest life you bear with an even mind and silently endure.
nutrio, nutrire: feed, support, rear, foster
pignus, pignoris: pledge (ie something committed to the care of another)
sacra pignora: the Sacred Trust (ie the child Jesus) (plu for sing)

speculum: mirror, image
documentum: example
ut: (result clause)
sudo, sudare: sweat
labor sudans: *sweated labor, sweaty work, manual labor, hard work*
officina, officinae: workshop

178. Te pater Joseph opifex colende

Qui carent escis, miseros foveto;
Tempera effrenos perimasque lites;
Mysticus Christus patriae sub umbrae
Tegmine crescat.

Tu Deus trinus pariterque et unus,
Qui pater cunctis opifexque rerum,
Fac patrem Joseph imitemur actu,
Morte imitemur.

careo, carēre, carui (+abl): lack, want, be without
esca, escae: food
foveo, fovere: help, support, cherish (fut imperative metri causa)
tempero, temperare: control, govern, moderate
effrenus, -a, -um: unbridled, unrestrained
perimo, perimere, peremi: put an end to, put a stop to
lis, litis: strife, conflict
patrius a um: fatherly, paternal
tegmen, tegminis: protection, shelter

qui: (*tu qui es*)
pater cunctis: *father for all, father of all*
rerum: *of things, of the world*
imitor, imitari: imitate, copy
patrem: (dir obj of *imitemur*)
fac imitemur: *make us copy, help us to imitate*

Note on meter: Sapphic stanza, with "Adonic" last line. Caesura (word end) after the 5th syllable. 2nd foot may be trochaic.

mysti cus chris tus patri ae sub umbrae
— ∪ | — — | — ∪∪ | — ∪ | — —

tegmine crescat
— ∪ ∪ | — ∪

179. <u>Te saeculorum Principem</u>
V. Genovesi SJ, 1925

Te saeculorum Principem,
Te Christe, regem gentium,
Te mentium, te cordium
Unum fatemur arbitrum.

Scelesta turba clamitat:
"Regnare Christum nolumus."
Te nos ovantes omnium
Regem supremum dicimus.

O Christe Princeps Pacifer,
Mentes rebelles subice;
Tuoque amore devios
Ovile in unum congrega.

Ad hoc cruenta ab arbore
Pendes apertis bracchiis;
Dirāque fossum cuspide
Cor igne flagrans exhibes.

fateor, fateri: confess, avow (= *confiteor*)
arbiter, arbitri: judge, witness, arbiter

scelestus, -a, um: infamous, shameless, wicked
clamito, clamitare: shout loudly, roar
ovo, ovare: rejoice

rebellis, -is, -e: rebellious, insurgent
subicio, subicere: put down, suppress
devius, -a, um: lost, straying
ovile, ovilis (neut): sheep-fold

cruentus, -a, -um: bloody
pendeo, pendére, pependi: hang (intrans) (Δ *pendo, péndere, pependi*)
fodio, fodere, fodi, fossus: wound, stab, dig
cuspis, cuspidis (fem): spear-tip, blade
flagro, flagrare: burn, blaze
exhibeo, exhibere: display, show

179. <u>Te saeculorum Principem</u>

Ad hoc in aris abderis
Vini dapisque imagine,
Fundens salutem filiis
Transverberato pectore.

Te nationum praesides
Honore tollant publico,
Colant magistri, judices,
Leges et artes exprimant.

Submissa regum fulgeant
Tibi dicata insignia;
Mitique sceptro patriam
Domosque subde civium.

Jesu, tibi sit gloria, — Gloria tibi Domine
Qui sceptra mundi temperas,
Cum Patre et almo Spiritu, — Cum Patre et Sancto Spiritu
In sempiterna saecula.

ad hoc: *for this (reason), to this end*
in aris: *upon altars*
abdo, abdere, abdidi, abditus: hide, conceal
daps, dapis: food
imagine: *under the appearance (of), in the form (of)*

praeses, praesidis: ruler, leader, president
tollo, tollere: lift up, extol
exprimo, exprimere: express, make known

submissus (< submitto): submissive, obedient
fulgeo, fulgēre: shine, be resplendent
insigne, insignis (noun, neut): standard, insignia (pl)
dico, dicare: dedicate, devote
mitis, mitis: gentle, mild
sceptrum, sceptri: sceptre, sway, rule
subdo, subdere: subdue, subject

tempero, temperare: rule, govern, regulate

180. Te splendor et virtus Patris (R)
Attrib Boniface VIII. Excluded from LH.
Cf *Tibi Christe splendor Patris* (M)
Attrib Rabanus Maurus, c. 800

Te, splendor et virtus Patris,
Te vita, Jesu, cordium
Ab ore qui pendent tuo
Laudamus inter angelos.

Tibi mille densa millium
Ducum corona militat;
Sed explicat victor crucem
Michael salutis signifer.

Draconis hic dirum caput
In ima pellit tartara,
Ducemque cum rebellibus
Caelesti ab arce fulminat.

Contra ducem superbiae
Sequamur hunc nos principem,
Ut detur ex Agni throno
Nobis corona gloriae.

ab ore pendent: *hang upon (the words of) your mouth, await your command*

corona, -ae: circle, ring (ie of defenders arrayed upon the ramparts)
densus, -a, um: numberless, dense
mille millia ducum: *of a thousand thousands of princes*
milito, -are (+ dat): fight in the service of, serve as a soldier for, fight for
explico, explicare: unfurl, display, wave
crucem: *(the standard of) the cross, (a banner showing) the cross*

hic: *he (Michael)*
imus a um: lowest, deep, bottom of
tartara, -orum: Tartarus, hell
rebellis, -is: rebel, rebellious, insurgent, mutinous, mutineer
arx, arcis: citadel
fulmino, fulminare: *hit with lightning, hurl like lightning* (dir obj = *ducem*)

181. <u>Tibi Christe splendor Patris</u> (M)
Anon, c. 800-900. Attrib Rabanus Maurus
Cf *Te splendor et virtus Patris* (R)

Tibi, Christe, splendor Patris,
Vita, virtus cordium,
In conspectu angelorum,
Votis, voce psallimus;.
Alternantes concrepando
Melos damus vocibus.

— ~ | — ~ | — ~ | — ~
— ~ | — ~ | — ~ | —

Collaudamus venerantes
Omnes caeli milites,
Sed praecipue Primatem
Caelestis exercitūs:
Michaelem in virtute
Conterentem zabulum.

Trochaic tetrameter, catalectic.
Not strictly quantitative, but roughly accentual.

votis (< votum): *in (our) prayers, with prayer, prayerfully*
concrepo, concrepare: sound, resound, sing out
alternantes concrepando: *alternating in chant, singing out in alternation*
melos, meli (Gk neuter): song, hymn, melody

venerantes: (nominative)
omnes milites: (accusative)
praecipue (adv): above all, especially
primas, primatis: primate, principal, leader
in virtute: *with power*
contero, -ere: crush
zabulus, zabuli: (= diabolus) (Δ *Zabulon, Zabulonis,* a son of Jacob)

Note:

This meter is familiar from the work of one of the masters of Latin hymnography, Venantius Fortunatus:

Pange lingua glori osi proeli um cer tami nis

— ~ | — ~ | — ~ | — ~ || — ~ | — ~ | — ~ | ~

Marching songs for the Roman army were written in trochaic meter. The VR of this hymn is in iambic dimeter.

181. Tibi Christe splendor Patris (M)

Quo custode procul pelle,
Rex Christe piissime,
Omne nefas inimici;
Mundo corde et corpore,
Paradiso redde tuo
Nos solā clementiā.

Gloriam Patri melodis
Personemus vocibus,
Gloriam Christo canamus,
Gloriam Paraclito,
Qui trinus et unus Deus
Exstat ante saecula.

quo custode: *with him as guardian, with Michael as our guard*
nefas: wickedness (Indeclinable. Dir obj of *pelle*)
paradiso: (= *in paradisum*)

melodus, -a, -um: melodious, harmonious
persono, personare: sing out, declaim
exsto, exstare: exist

182. Tristes erant Apostoli (M)
Anon, c.400
Cento from *Aurora lucis rutilat* and *Claro paschali gaudio*

Tristes erant Apostoli
De nece sui Domini,
Quem morte crudelissimā
Servi damnarant impii.

Sermone blando Angelus
Praedixit mulieribus:
"In Galilaea Dominus
Videndus est quantocius."

Illae dum pergunt concitae
Apostolis hoc dicere,
Videntes eum vivere,
Christi tenent vestigia.

Quo agnito, discipuli
In Galilaeam propere
Pergunt videre faciem
Desideratam Domini.

nex, necis: slaughter
servi: slaves, perh *his servants, his slaves*
damno, damnare: condemn (*damnarant* = *damnaverant*)

sermo, sermonis: word, words
blandus, -a, -um: soothing, reassuring
quantocius (comparative adv): in a short while, very soon

pergo, pergere, perrexi: go on their way, proceed
concitus (< concio, concīre): aroused, excited
vestigia: *feet* (cf Matt 28:9, *tenuerunt pedes ejus*)

propere: quickly, with haste

183. Tristes erant Apostoli (R)

Tristes erant Apostoli
De Christi acerbo funere,
Quem morte crudelissimā
Servi necarant impii.

Sermone verax Angelus
Mulieribus praedixerat:
"Mox ore Christus gaudium
Gregi feret fidelium."

Ad anxios Apostolos
Currunt statim dum nuntiae,
Illae micantis obvia
Christi tenent vestigia.

Galilaeae ad alta montium
Se conferunt Apostoli,
Jesuque voti compotes
Almo beantur lumine.

acerbus a um: bitter, harsh, cruel
funus, funeris: funeral, death
neco, necare: kill, slay (*necarant = necaverant*)

sermone verax: *true to his word, truthful in speech*
ore: *by speaking,* perh *in His own words, in person*

anxius a um: fearful, worried
statim: at once, immediately
dum: (*dum currunt,* not *dum tenent*)
obvia vestigia: *the feet coming to meet them, the steps drawn close*
micantis Christi: *of the radiant Christ, of the glorified Christ*

alta montium: *heights of mountains, high hills, mountain-tops*
compos, compotis (+gen): in possession of
voti compotes: *having obtained (their) prayer*
Jesu: (genitive, *almo lumine Jesu beantur*)
beo, beare: bless, make happy

184. <u>Tu Trinitatis Unitas</u> (Feria sexta ad Matutinum)
Anon, c. 500. Attrib Saint Ambrose and Saint Gregory

	VR
Tu, Trinitatis Unitas,	
Orbem potenter qui regis,	Orbem potenter quae regis
Attende laudum cantica,	Attende laudis canticum
Quae excubantes psallimus.	Quod excubantes psallimus
Nam lectulo consurgimus	
Noctis quieto tempore,	
Ut flagitemus vulnerum	Ut flagitemus omnium
A te medelam omnium.	A te medelam vulnerum

Quo fraude quidquid daemonum
In noctibus deliquimus,
Abstergat illud caelitus
Tuae potestas gloriae.

attendo, attendere: hearken to, listen to (+ acc)
excubo, excubare: be watchful, be awake, be alert

lectulo (< lectulum): *from bed, from our beds*
consurgo, consurgere, consurrexi: rise, get up
flagito, flagitare: beseech, entreat

quo (= *ut*): so that
fraus, fraudis (fem): deceit, deception
daemon, daemonis: demon, devil (*by the deception of demons*)
delinquo, delinquere, deliqui: do wrong, fail, sin (nb transitive, ie + acc)
illud: *it* (ie, *quidquid diliquimus*)
abstergo, abstergere: wash away, blot out (= *abstergeo*)
caelitus (adv): *by divine power, from heaven*

184. Tu Trinitatis Unitas (Feria sexta ad Matutinum)

Ne corpus adsit sordidum, Ne corpus astet sordidum
Nec torpor instet cordium,
Nec criminis contagio
Tepescat ardor spiritūs.

Ob hoc, Redemptor, quaesumus:
Reple tuo nos lumine,
Per quod dierum circulis
Nullis ruamus actibus.

adsit: (= *sit,* or *fiat*)
astet: (= *sit,* or *fiat*)
sordidus, -a, um: unclean, defiled
torpor, torporis: dullness, sloth, inactivity
insto, instare: threaten, follow after, ensue
contagium: infection, bad influence
tepesco, tepescere: grow weak, grow faint

dierum circulis: *during the daily round, through the cycles of the day*
ruo, ruere, rui: fall down, be ruined
nullis actibus: *by any of our actions, by no (sinful) acts*

185. Tu Trinitatis Unitas (in festo sanctissimae Trinitatis)
Cf *Aeterna caeli gloria*, strophe 3

	VR
Tu, Trinitatis Unitas,	
Orbem potenter qui regis,	Orbem potenter quae regis
Attende laudum cantica,	Attende laudis canticum
Quae excubantes psallimus.	Quod excubantes psallimus

Ortus refulget lucifer,	
Praeitque solem nuntius,	Sparsamque lucem nuntiat
Cadunt tenebrae noctium:	Cadit caligo noctium
Lux sancta nos illuminet.	

attendo, attendere: hearken to, listen to (+ acc)
excubo, excubare: be watchful, be awake

orior, oriri, ortus: rise (Δ *ortus, -ūs*)
refulgeo, -ēre: shine again
lucifer: light-bearer, morning star
prae-eo: precede, go before (+ acc)
spargo, spargere, sparsus: scatter, spread

Note:

Refulget, praeit, nuntiat, cadunt, and *cadit* are all in the indicative. However, *illuminet* is in the subjunctive.

186. <u>Urbs Jerusalem beata</u> (M)
Anon, c. 600
Cf *Caelestis urbs Jerusalem* (R)
Meter: cf *Tibi Christe splendor patris*

Urbs Jerusalem beata,
    Dicta pacis visio,
Quae construitur in caelis
    Vivis ex lapidibus,
Et angelis coronata,
    Ut sponsata comite.

Nova veniens e caelo,
    Nuptiali thalamo
Praeparata, ut sponsata
    Copuletur Domino;
Plateae et muri ejus
    Ex auro purissimo.

coronata: *crowned, ringed, thronged*
sponso, sponsare: betroth, affiance, espouse
comes, comitis: companion, retinue
ut sponsata comite: *like a bride by her companions*

thalamus: chamber
nuptiali thalamo: (Not ablative. Dative, with *praeparata*)
copulo, copulare: join, unite, wed
ut etc: *so that as bride she may be wedded to the Lord*
platea, plateae: avenue, roadway

Note
Dicta pacis visio: This is the traditional etymology. Cf also Heb 7:2, *Rex Salem quod est rex pacis*.

186. Urbs Jerusalem beata (M)

Portae nitent margaritis,
        Adytis patentibus;
Et virtute meritorum
        Illuc introducitur
Omnis qui ob Christi nomen
        Hic in mundo premitur.

Tunsionibus, pressuris
        Expoliti lapides,
Suis coaptantur locis
        Per manūs artificis,
Disponuntur permansuri
        Sacris aedificiis.

niteo, nitēre: shine, glitter
margarita, margaritae: pearl
adytum, adyti: innermost room, forbidden place, sanctuary
virtute meritorum: perh *by virtue of (His) merits*
premo, premere: oppress, persecute

tunsio, tunsionis: hitting, striking, hammering
pressura, pressurae: affliction, distress, oppression
expolio, expolīre, expolītus: polish, rub smooth
co-opto, cooptare: fit, form, join together
dispono, disponere: arrange, set in place
sacris aedificiis: *in the sacred buildings* (dat after *permansuri*)

Notes

The *Antiphonale Monasticum* prints a stress marker on the [y] of *adytis*. It is an erratum. The vowel is short, and the meter requires no adjustment here. The word *adytum* is stressed on the antepenult, ie the first syllable. This will hold true, whether we scan the line quantitatively or accentually.

Adytis patentibus. This is perhaps dative: "The doors to the inner sanctuary are shining with pearls". The phrase can also be parsed as an ablative absolute: "The doors shine with pearls, and the chambers of the interior now lie open."

187. Ut queant laxis resonare fibris
Attrib Paul the Deacon c. 720- 800
Cf *Antra deserti* and *O nimis felix*

Ut queant laxis resonare fibris
Mira gestorum famuli tuorum,
Solve polluti labii reatum,
Sancte Ioannes.

Nuntius celso veniens Olympo,
Te patri magnum fore nasciturum,
Nomen, et vitae seriem gerendae
Ordine promit.

queant: *possint* (nb Zachary, who lost his voice)
laxus, -a, -um: relaxed, loose, ready
resono, resonare: give sound to, re-echo, sing about (+ acc)
fibra, fibrae: voice, vocal chord
famuli: *(your) servants* (nom pl. subj of *queant*)
mira gestorum: *the wonders of your deeds, your wondrous deeds*
polluo, polluere, pollutus: defile, profane
labium, labii: lip
reatus, -ūs: guilt

Olympo: (abl of place from which, without a preposition)
nuntius: messenger, angel (Luke 1:11-17)
patri: *to your father* (ind obj of *promit*)
fore: (= *futurum esse*)
nasciturum fore: (= *nasciturum esse*)
nomen: *(and your) name* (Luke: *vocabis nomen ejus Joannem*)
promo, promere: express, reveal, set forth
series, seriei: sequence, events, course
ordine: *in order*
vitae gerendae: *of the life that you would lead, of your life-work*

Note

The verb *promit* has three direct objects:
te fore nasciturum, " that you would be born"
nomen, "your name", and
vitae seriem gerendae, "the course of your life's work".

187. Ut queant laxis resonare fibris

Ille promissi dubius superni,
Perdidit promptae modulos loquelae;
Sed reformasti genitus peremptae
Organa vocis.

Ventris obstruso recubans cubili
Senseras Regem thalamo manentem;
Hinc parens nati meritis uterque
Abdita pandit.

ille: he (ie *pater tuus, Zacharias*)
dubius, -a, -um: doubting, skeptical about (+ gen)
promo, promere, promptus: utter, speak
loquela, loquelae: speeking, speech, language
modulus, moduli: measure, rhythm, sound
promptae modulos loquelae: *the measures of the spoken word*
sed genitus: *but (you when) born*
perimo, peremptus: remove
organum, organi: organ (of the body), musical instrument
peremptae vocis: *of his lost voice*

venter, ventris: belly, womb
recubo, recubare: lie, rest
cubile, cubilis: den, abode
obstrusus, -a, -um: hidden, secret (= *abstrusus*)
cubili, thalamo: (poetic datives of place where, without a preposition)
hinc: *and so, hence, in this way*
nati meritis: *by the merits of (their) son*
parens uterque: *each parent, both parents*
pando, pandere, pandi: disclose, reveal
abdita, abditorum: *hidden things, what is concealed*

Parens uterque pandit: Zachary (*Benedictus Dominus)* and Elizabeth (*Benedicta tu*). Some commentators have interpreted the phrase *parens uterque* as referring to Elizabeth and Mary.

188. Veni Creator Spiritus
Anon, c. 850. Attrib Rabanus Maurus, ob 856

Veni, Creator Spiritus,
Mentes tuorum visita,
Imple supernā gratiā,
Quae tu creasti pectora.

Qui Paraclítus díceris,	VR Qui diceris Paráclitus
Donum Dei altissimi,	VR Altissimi donum Dei
Fons vivus, ignis, caritas,	
Et spiritalis unctio.	

pectora: (Dir obj of *imple*)
quae: *pectora quae*

spiritalis, -is: spiritual, of the spirit (= *spiritualis*)
Dei altissimi: (Hiatus, no elision. Corrected in VR.)
unctio, unctionis: anointing, unction

Note:

How should *paraclitus* be accented in Latin?

The meter calls for a long syllable, and the Greek vowel [i] is here long. We might therefore expect *qui paraclítus diceris* in the monastic text. On the other hand, that would make the line *surréxit ac Paráclito* more difficult to scan.

The liturgical publishers generally write *paráclitus* and *paráclito*. See Britt for further discussion and references.

188. Veni Creator Spiritus

Tu septiformis munere,
Dextrae Dei tu digitus, VR Dig *i* tus Paternae dexterae
Tu rite promissum Patris,
Sermone ditans guttura.

Accende lumen sensibus;
Infund*e* amorem cordibus,
Infirma nostri corporis
Virtute firmans perpeti.

tu: (*diceris* is perhaps still understood)
septiformis, -is: seven-fold
munere: (Ablative of respect)
digitus, digiti: finger (Cf Luke 11:20 *si in digito Dei ejicio daemonia.*)
promissum, promissi: promise
rite: rightly, properly, according to religion
dito, ditare: enrich, endow
guttur, gutturis (Neut): throat, *metaph* tongue
guttura: (ie of the Apostles)
sermone: *with speech, by your words, with your Word*

accendo, accendere: light, kindle, set fire to
accende lumen sensibus: *kindle a light in our senses, open our senses to the light*
cordibus: *into (our) hearts*
infirmus, -a, -um: weak, sickly
infirma: *weakness, weaknesses*
firmo, firmare: strengthen, heal
perpes, perpitis (Adj): *virtute perpetua* (Δ *perpetior, perpeti*)

Note

Perhaps *Tu rite "promissum Patris" diceris*, in which case *rite* modifies the implicit *diceris.* More commonly, however, *rite* is parsed as a quasi-adjective modifying *promissum.*

188. Veni Creator Spiritus

Hostem repellas longius,
Pacemque dones protinus;
Ductore sic te praevio
Vitemus omne noxium.

Per te sciamus da Patrem,
Noscamus atque Filium;
Te utriusque Spiritum   vr Teque*e* utriusque Spiritum
Credamus omni tempore.

Gloria Patri Domino,   vr Deo Patri sit gloria,
Natoque, qui a mortuis   Et Filio, qui a mortuis
Surrexit, ac Paráclito,
In saeculorum saecula.

longius (< longus): *far away*
dono, donare: grant, give
protinus (Adv): immediately, without cease
ductor, ductoris: leader, commander
praevius, -a, -um: in front, leading
noxius: sin, harm, sinful, harmful

sciamus da: *grant that we may know*
te Spiritum: (Supply *esse*)
te utriusque: (No elision)

> Through You let us know the Father,
> Let us also know the Son;
> You the Spirit of them both,
> Let us believe (in) for all time.

189. Verbum supernum prodiens, A Patre (M)
Anon, c. 600
Cf *Verbum supernum prodiens, E Patris* (R)

Verbum supernum prodiens,
A Patre olim exiens,
Qui natus orbi subvenis
Cursu declivi temporis….

Illumina nunc pectora,
Tuoque amore concrema,
Audito ut praeconio
Sint pulsa tandem lubrica.

prodeo, prodire: come forth
olim: once, previously
subvenio, -īre (+ dat): come to help, come to the aid of
declivis, -is: descending, falling
cursu declivi temporis: *when the time had come around, at the appointed time*

pectus, pectoris: chest, *metaph* heart, mind
concremo, concremare: burn up, consume
praeconium: public praise, declaration (perh this very hymn)
pello, pellere, pulsus: drive away, expel
lubricus a um: bad, sinful (thoughts)

189. Verbum supernum prodiens, A Patre (M)

Judexque cum post aderis *Cum clause….*
Rimari facta pectoris,
Reddens vicem pro abditis,
Justisque regnum pro bonis….

Non demum arctemur malis *Main clause*
Pro qualitate criminis;
Sed cum beatis compotes
Simus perennes caelibes.

post (Adv): afterwards
adsum, adesse: come, be present
rimor, rimari: rhyme off, recite (Infin to express purpose)
vicem: *turnabout, a fitting penalty*
pro abditis: *for hidden (faults)*
justisque regnum: *and a kingdom for the just*
pro bonis: *because of good deeds*

demum; finally, at length, in the end
arcto, arctare: diminish, confine, shrink (*non arctemur* = *ne arctemur*)
(cum) malis: perh *with bad men*
crimen, criminis: crime, wrongdoing, sin
compos, compotis (*cum* + *possum*): sharer, companion
caelebs, caelibis: celibate, heavenly, pure

Note
Caelebs, caelibis: The poet here associates *cael*-ebs with *cael*-um. In fact the morphemes are not related.

190. Verbum supernum prodiens, E Patris (R)
Cf *Verbum supernum prodiens, A Patre* (M)

Verbum supernum prodiens,
E Patris aeterni sinu,
Qui natus orbi subvenis,
Labente cursu temporis,

Illumina nunc pectora,
Tuoque amore concrema,
Ut cor caduca deserens
Caeli voluptas impleat:

Ut, cum tribunal Judicis
Damnabit igni noxios,
Et vox amica debitum
Vocabit ad caelum pios,

Non esca flammarum nigros
Volvamur inter turbines,
Vultu Dei sed compotes
Caeli fruamur gaudiis.

prodeo, prodire: come forth. proceed
labor, labi: move along, pass (of time)

concremo, concremare: burn up, consume
cor..deserens: (Acc. dir obj of *impleat*)
desero, deserere, deserui: abandon, forsake
caducus, -a, -um: transitory, perishable
voluptas, voluptatis: pleasure, delight

noxius a um; sinful, bad (opposite of *pios*)

non volvamur: = *ne volvamur*
volvo, volvere: toss around, whirl about
esca (Nominative): *(us) as food for the flames*
turbo, turbinis (Masc): whirlwind, storm
vultu: (Ablative with *compotes,* = *compotes* + *gen*, eg *compos mentis*)
gaudiis: (Ablative with *fruamur*)

191. Verbum supernum prodiens, Nec patris
Thomas Aquinas, c. 1264

Verbum supernum prodiens,
Nec Patris linquens dexteram,
Ad opus suum exiens,
Venit ad vitae vesperam.

In mortem a discipulo
Suis tradendus aemulis,
Prius in vitae ferculo
Se tradidit discipulis.

Quibus sub binā specie
Carnem dedit et sanguinem,
Ut duplicis substantiae
Totum cibaret hominem.

linquo, linquere: (= *relinquo*)

aemulus, aemuli: enemy, opponent, rival
ferculum, ferculi: plate, carrier (ie the plate of eucharistic bread)

binus, bina, binum: dual, in two elements
cibo, cibare: feed, give to eat (Transitive. Dir obj = *hominem*)
duplex, duplicis: double, in two parts
hominem duplicis substantiae: (ie body and soul)

191. Verbum supernum prodiens, Nec patris

Se nascens dedit socium,
Convescens in edulium,
Se moriens in pretium,
Se regnans dat in praemium.

O salutaris hostia,
Quae caeli pandis ostium.
Bella premunt hostilia:
Da robur, fer auxilium.

Uni Trinoque Domino
Sit sempiterna gloria,
Qui vitam sine termino
Nobis donet in patria.

se: (*ipse nascens dedit se socium*)
nascor, nasci, natus: *In birth he gave himself as a companion*
convescor, convesci: eat with, join in a meal
edulium, edulii: food (*se dedit in edulium*)
se: (*moriens se dat in pretium, regnans se dat in praemium*)

pando, pandere: open, lay open
ostium: entrance, door, gate
premo, premere: press close, press *us*
robur, roburis (neut): strength

dono, donare: (nb subjunctive)

192. Vexilla Christus inclita
Anonymous c. 1925

Vexilla Christus inclita
Late triumphans explicat:
Gentes, adeste supplices,
Regique regum plaudite.

Non ille regna cladibus,
Non vi metuque subdidit;
Alto levatus stipite,
Amore traxit omnia.

O ter beata civitas,
Cui rite Christus imperat,
Quae jussa pergit exsequi
Edicta mundo caelitus.

vexillum, vexilli: banner
explico, explicare: unfurl

clades, cladis: defeat, rout, battle (lost)
stipes, stipitis: beam, cross, wood
traxi: (*si exaltatus fuero a terra, omnia traham ad me ipsum*, John 12:32)

quae: (fem nom sing. antecedent = *civitas*)
pergo, pergere: continue, proceed
jussa: (neut acc pl. dir obj of *exsequi*)
exsequor, exsequi: carry out, perform, fulfill
edico, edicere, edictus: publish, promulgate
caelitus (adv): from on high, by heaven

192. Vexilla Christus inclita

Non arma flagrant impia,
Pax usque firmat foedera,
Arridet et concordia,
Tutus stat ordo civicus.

Servat fides connubia,
Juventa pubet integra,
Pudica florent limina
Domesticis virtutibus.

Optata nobis splendeat
Lux ista, Rex dulcissime:
Te, pace adeptā candidā,
Adoret orbis subditus.

flagro, flagrare: blaze up, endanger, threaten
usque (adv): continuously, permanently
foedus, foederis; treaty, pact, agreement
arrideo, arridere: smile
tutus, -a, -um: safe, secure

connubium, connubii: matrimony, marriage
juventa, juventae: (= *juventus, juventutis*)
pubeo, pubere: grow up, mature
integer, integra, integrum: unblemished, wholesome
pudicus a um: modest, chaste, pure
floreo, florere: flourish, prosper
limen, liminis: threshhold, home, household

opto, optare: choose, desire, select
adipiscor, adipisci, adeptus: obtain, achieve
candidus a um: ?white-robed, brilliant, dazzling

Notes;
1. *Pubet*: instead of *pubescit*. The verb *pubeo* is unattested.
2. *Domesticis virtutibus.* Connelly cites Ronald Knox's judgment: "easily the worst line in Latin poetry". This hymn is omitted by LH.
3. *Adepta*: although *adipiscor* is deponent, the perfect participle can be used with a passive sense.

193. <u>Vexilla regis prodeunt</u> (M)
Venantius Fortunatus, c. 530-610

Vexilla regis prodeunt:
Fulget crucis mysterium,
Quo carne carnis conditor
Suspensus est patibulo.

(The following second strophe is original. However, it is not included in the liturgical text.)

Confixa clavis viscera;
Tendens manūs, vestigia,
Redemptionis gratia
Hic immolata est hostia.

vexillum, vexilli: banner, standard, flag
prodeo, prodīre: go forth, come forward, advance
fulgeo, fulgēre: shine, shine brightly
mysterium quo: *mystery in which, mystery whereby*
carne: *in the flesh*, or *by flesh* (ie *ab hominibus*)
patibulum: lit "yoke", beam, gibbet, cross

configo, confixus: pierce, fasten, nail (supply *sunt*)
clavus, clavi: nail
tendo, tendere: hold out, stretch forth
viscera: *His guts, His body*
vestigia: = *pedes*
gratia: (if ablative, *for the sake of redemption*)
gratia: (if nominative, *the very grace of redemption*)
hic: here (ie on the cross)

Meter: Ambrosian, ie. Iambic Dimeter, or Modern Iambic Tetrameter

~ — | ~ — | ~ — | ~ — final *syllaba anceps*

Spondee permitted in first or third foot, eg;

— — | ~ — | — — | ~ —

193. <u>Vexilla regis prodeunt</u> (M)

Quo vulneratus insuper
Mucrone diro lanceae,
Ut nos lavaret crimine,
Manavit undā et sanguine.

Impleta sunt quae concinit
David fideli carmine,
Dicens in nationibus
Regnavit a ligno Deus.

insuper (postpositive prep + abl): on, upon
quo…. insuper: *on which, upon which, whereon*
vulnero, vulneratus: wound
mucro, mucronis: point, tip, blade
dirus a um: fearful, terrible, awful
lancea, lanceae: spear, lance
crimen, criminis: crime, sin, sins
mano, manavi: exude, flow, drip
unda (lit "wave"): water

concino, concinere, concinui (+ acc): sing of, sing about
fideli carmine: *with faithful chant, in (the words of) the faithful song*

Notes:

1. *Insuper*. This word can be read as an adverb meaning "moreover". On that analysis *quo* means "on which", or "where".

2. *David*: This is a reference to the *Vetus Latina* reading of Psalm 95:10, *Dicite in gentibus quia Dominus regnavit a ligno*. The Vulgate omits the phrase, *a ligno*.

193. <u>Vexilla regis prodeunt</u> (M)

Arbor decora et fulgida,
Ornata regis purpurā,
Electa digno stipite
Tam sancta membra tangere.

Beata, cujus brachiis
Saecli pependit pretium,
Statera facta est corporis
Praedamque tulit tartari.

arbor, arboris (fem): (Nominative or vocative.)
decorus a um: lovely, beautiful
fulgidus a um: shining, glittering, luminous
orno, ornare, ornatus: adorn, decorate
purpura, purpurae (noun): purple
eligo, eligere, electus: choose, select
stipes, stipitis: trunk (of a tree), stem, branch
electa digno stipite: *chosen from a worthy stock* (ie family of trees)

beata: (scil. *beata arbor*)
statera, staterae: balance, scales
praeda, praedae: booty, prey
fero, ferre, tuli: bear (away), carry (off), lift (up)
tartarus: tartarus, hell

Notes:

The *statera* was a beam or bar, used for measuring weight. The metaphor is difficult to render in English. (*Arbor beata*)....*statera facta est corporis*: "The blessed tree became the beam to weigh his body".

Digno stipite can also be read as an ablative with *tangere*: "chosen to touch such holy members with a worthy beam".

Blest Tree, whose happy branches bore
The wealth that did the world restore;
The beam that did that Body weigh
Which raised up hell's expected prey.

(WK Blount 1670, cited by Britt)

193. Vexilla regis prodeunt (M)

(This is the original seventh strophe. As in the case of the second, it is not part of the liturgical text.)

Fundis aroma cortice,
Vincis sapore nectare,
Jucunda fructu fertili
Plaudis triumpho nobili.

(This is the original eighth strophe. It has been restored in the *Liturgia Horarum.*)

Salve ara, salve victima,
De passionis gloria,
Qua vita mortem pertulit
Et morte vitam reddidit. *

fundis: (*tu* = *arbor* = *crux*)
aroma, aromatis (neut): fragrant spice, perfume
cortex, corticis: bark (*you pour perfume from your bark*)
nectar, nectaris: nectar
sapor, saporis: flavor, taste (ablative of respect)
nectare: (abl used as acc, *metri gratia*: Connelly)
vincis sapore nectare: *in taste you are finer than nectar*
jucunda: (nominative)
fertilis, fertilis: prolific, full of promise
plaudis: *you clap (your hands) in triumph glorious*

de: because of, for
(passionis gloria) qua: *in which, by which* (not *qua vita*)
vita: (nominative)
perfero, pertuli: endure, suffer
reddo, reddere, reddidi: restore

*These lines are the basis of the 1632 Roman revision of strophe one:

Qua vita mortem pertulit,
Et morte vitam protulit.

profero protuli: produce, bring forth

193. Vexilla regis prodeunt (M)

The next two strophes conclude the *versio monastica*. They are an early addition to the text, and they are not from the pen of Venantius.

O crux ave, spes unica,
Hoc passionis tempore
Auge piis justitiam,
Reisque dona veniam.

Te, summa Deus Trinitas,
Collaudet omnis spiritus;
Quos per crucis mysterium
Salvas, rege per saecula.

augeo, augere: increase, enlarge, make to grow

te: (acc. dir obj of *collaudet*)
summa Deus Trinitas: (vocative. *deus* + *summa trinitas*)
collaudo, collaudare: praise, praise together, praise with one voice
omnis spiritus: *every soul, every spirit* (not *Spiritus Sanctus*)
quos: (*rege illos quos salvas*) (not *spiritus quos*)

Notes:
Cf Psalm 150: 6, *Omnis spiritus laudet Dominum.*

Variae:

In Inventione S. Crucis
O crux ave spes unica
In hoc Paschali gaudio

In Exaltatatione S. Crucis
O crux ave spes unica
In hac triumphi gloria

194. Vexilla regis prodeunt (R)

Vexilla regis prodeunt;
Fulget crucis mysterium,
Quā Vita mortem pertulit
Et morte vitam protulit.

Quae, vulnerata lanceae
Mucrone diro, criminum
Ut nos lavaret sordibus,
Manavit undā et sanguine.

Impleta sunt quae concinit
David fideli carmine,
Dicendo nationibus: VM Dicens: In nationibus
Regnavit a ligno Deus.

vexillum: banner, flag, standard
prodeo, prodīre: go forth
fulgeo, fulgēre: shine out
crucis....quā: *cross on which, cross whereon*
perfero: endure, suffer (*Life endured death*)
profero: produce, yield (*and yielded life from death*)

Vita....quae: *who, which* (*Vita* is here personified as the Lord.)
mucro, mucronis: blade, tip
dirus a um: dire, terrible
sordes, sordium: filth, stain
criminum (gen plu): *of sin, of our sins*
mano, manare (+ abl): flow with, ooze
unda: metaph *water*

concino, concinere, concinui (+ acc): sing of, sing about
fideli carmine: *with faithful chant, in (the words of) the faithful song*

Note:

1. The ablative of the late Latin gerund can have the meaning of a participle. Thus *dicendo* here may be translated as "by saying" or simply as "saying".

2. *David*: This is a reference to the *Vetus Latina* reading of Psalm 95:10, *Dicite in gentibus quia Dominus regnavit a ligno*. The Vulgate omits the phrase, *a ligno*.

194. Vexilla regis prodeunt (R)

Arbor decora et fulgida,
Ornata regis purpurā,
Electa digno stipite
Tam sancta membra tangere.

Beata, cujus brachiis
Pretium pependit saeculi,
Statera facta corporis,
Tulitque praedam tartari.

arbor, arboris (fem): (Nominative or vocative.)
decorus a um: lovely, beautiful
fulgidus a um: shining, glittering, luminous
orno, ornare, ornatus: adorn, decorate
purpura, purpurae (noun): purple
eligo, eligere, electus: choose, select
stipes, stipitis: trunk (of a tree), stem, branch
electa digno stipite: *chosen from a worthy stock* (ie family of trees)

beata: (scil. *beata arbor*)
statera, staterae: balance, scales
praeda, praedae: booty, prey
fero, ferre, tuli: bear (away), carry (off), lift (up)
tartarus: tartarus, hell

Notes:

The *statera* was a beam or bar, used for measuring weight. The metaphor is difficult to render in English. (*Arbor beata*)....*statera facta est corporis*: "The blessed tree became the beam to weigh his body".

Digno stipite can also be read as an ablative with *tangere*: "chosen to touch such holy members with (your) noble trunk".

194. Vexilla regis prodeunt (R)

O crux ave, spes unica,
Hoc passionis tempore
Piis adauge gratiam,
Reisque dele crimina.

Te, fons salutis Trinitas,
Collaudet omnis spiritus;
Quibus crucis victoriam
Largiris, adde praemium.

adaugeo, adaugere: increase

quibus: (Starts a new sentence, no antecedent.)
largior, largiri: bestow, grant, generously give (Δ *largus, largior*)

O Trinity, fount of salvation, let every spirit join to praise you. To those upon whom you bestow the victory of the cross, add the reward.

Cf Psalm 150: 6, *Omnis spiritus laudet Dominum.*

Variae:

In Inventione S. Crucis
O crux ave spes unica
Paschale quae fers gaudium

In Exaltatatione S. Crucis
O crux ave spes unica
In hac triumphi gloria

195. <u>Virginis proles opifexque matris</u> (M)
Anon, c. 700

Virginis Proles Opifexque Matris,
Virgo quem gessit, peperitque Virgo:
Virginis festum canimus trophaeum,
Accipe votum.

(Pro Virgine non Martyre)
Virginis festum canimus beatae,
Accipe votum.

proles opifexque: (Vocative. The implicit *tu* is the Lord.)
gero, gerere, gessi: carry (in the womb)
pario, parere, peperi: bear, give birth to (+ acc)
festus a um: festal, of a feast, hallowed
festum, festi: feast
trophaeum: trophy, prize, crown (ie of martyrdom)

Notes —

Chiasmus: *Virgo quem gessit peperitque Virgo,* "Whom a Virgin carried and gave birth to while a Virgin".

Festum…. trophaeum: if *festum* is a noun, this is an example of asyndeton. The conjunction *et* is omitted. "We sing of a Virgin's festival, a martyr's crown".

Sapphic meter:

— ~ | — — | — ~ ~ | — ~ | — ~
— ~ ~ | — ~

Note:
1. The Sapphic stanza is trochaic. An iambus never occurs. The second foot may be either a trochee or a spondee.
2. The mid-line dactyl at syllables 5-6-7 is constant, and there is aways a caesura after syllable 5.
3. The short "Adonic" line is constant, allowing only a final *syllaba anceps*.

195. Virginis proles opifexque matris (M)

Haec tua Virgo duplici beata
Sorte, dum gestit fragilem domare
Corporis sexum, domuit cruentum
Corpore saeclum.

Unde nec mortem, nec amica mortis
Saeva poenarum genera pavescens,
Sanguine fuso meruit sacratum
Scandere caelum.

Huius obtentu, Deus alme, nostris
Parce jam culpis, vitia remittens,
Quo tibi puri resonemus almum
Pectoris hymnum.

sors, sortis (fem): fate, lot, destiny, perh *dowry*
duplex, duplicis: double
beata: (*virgo beata* or *beatā sorte*. Perhaps "blest with a double destiny")
gestio, gestire: desire, long to
domo, domare, domui: tame, discipline, control
fragilis: weak, frail
sexus, -us: sex, gender
cruentus, -a, -um: bloody

unde: whence, therefore, and so
pavesco, -ere (+ acc): fear, be afraid of
amicus, -a, um: allied, associated, friendly, amiable
amica (neut pl): *the friends of death, the trappings of death*
scando, scandere (+ acc): ascend (to), rise up to, mount

obtentus, -ūs: pleading, intercession
quo + subjunc: by which, so that
resono, -are: ring out, sing out
almus a um: loving
puri…. pectoris (formulaic singular): *of pure heart, pure of heart*

196. Virginis proles opifexque matris (R)

Virginis Proles Opifexque Matris,
Virgo quem gessit, peperitque Virgo….
Virginis partos canimus decorā
Morte triumphos.

Pro virgine non martyre
Virginis festum canimus beatae,
Accipe votum.

Haec enim palmae duplicis beatā
Sorte, dum gestit fragilem domare
Corporis sexum, domuit cruentum
Caede tyrannum.

proles opifexque: (Vocative. the implicit *tu* is the Lord)
gero, gerere, gessi: carry (in the womb)
pario, parere, peperi: bear, give birth to (+ acc)
partus, -a, um (< pario): born, gained, acquired, achieved
decorus a um: beautiful, admirable, noble, glorious
triumphos: (plu for sing. *triumph born of a noble death*)

sors, sortis (fem): fate, lot, destiny
duplex, duplicis: double
palma, palmae: palm, prize
gestio, gestire: desire, long to
domo, domare, domui: tame, discipline, control
fragilis: weak, frail
sexus, -ūs: sex, gender
cruentus, -a, -um: bloody
tyrannus, tyranni: tyrant
caedes, caedis: massacre, slaughter
domuit caede: *she overcame by her murder*
(tyrannum) cruentum caede: *bloody from slaughter* (both are possible)

Note—

Chiasmus: *Virgo quem gessit peperitque Virgo,* "Whom a Virgin carried and gave birth to while a Virgin".

196. Virginis proles opifexque matris (R)

Unde nec mortem nec amica mortis
Mille poenarum genera expavescens,
Sanguine effuso meruit serenum
Scandere caelum.

Huius oratu, Deus alme, nobis
Debitas poenas scelerum remitte,
Ut tibi puro resonemus almum
Pectore carmen.

unde: whence, therefore, and so
amicus, -a, um: allied, associated, friendly, amiable
amica (neut pl): *the friends of death, the trappings of death*
mille: *mille genera*
expavesco, expavescere: be terrified by, dread (+ acc)
serenus, -a, um: clear, fair, untroubled

huius: *her*
oratus, -ūs: request, entreaty, prayer
resono, -are: ring out, make resound, sing out
almum carmen: *a loving song, a song of love*
puro pectore: *with a pure heart* (formulaic singular)

197. Vox clara ecce intonat (M)
Anon, c. 400
Cf *En clara vox redarguit* (R)

Vox clara ecce intonat;
Obscura quaeque increpat.
Pellantur em'nus somnia;
Ab aethre Christus promicat.

Mens jam resurgat torpida,
Quae sorde exstat sauciā;
Sidus refulget jam novum,
Ut tollat omne noxium.

intono, intonare: ring out, sing out
obscurus, -a, um: dark, shameful, sinful
quaeque: *everything, anything* (neut plu, = *omnia*)
increpo, -are: rebuke
pello, pellere: drive away, drive off, scatter
eminus (Adv): beyond reach, far away (*e* + *manus*)
somnium: dream
aether, aetheris: "ether", sky, heaven
promico, promicare: shine forth

torpidus, -a ,-um: dull, numb, lazy
sordes, sordis: filth, defilement, impurity
saucius, -a, -um: wounded
exsto, exstare: be, continue to be, continue
sidus, sideris (Neut): star
refulget: (Indicative. By contrast *resurgat* is subjunctive)
noxius a um: harmful, bad, sinful

197. <u>Vox clara ecce intonat</u> (M)

E sursum Agnus mittitur
Laxare gratis debitum;
Omnes pro indulgentia
Vocem demus cum lacrimis.

Secundo ut cum fulserit,
Mundumque horror cinxerit,
Non pro reatu puniat,
Sed nos pius tunc protegat.

laxo, laxare: release, discharge
gratis (Adv): freely
debitum, debiti (<debeo): debt, what is owing

secundo: the second time, a second time
fulgeo, fulgere, fulsi: flash, shine, appear (in glory)
cingo, cingere, cinxi: encircle, bind
reatus, -ūs: guilt
protego, protegere: defend, shelter, cover, protect

198. <u>Vox sonat Sponsi</u>
Cf *Beata caeli gaudia*, note

Vox sonat Sponsi: Diuturna cessit
Nunc hiems, tristes abiere nimbi,
Ver adest, flores redolent; paratae
Surgite, Sponsae.

Obviam Jesu properate ovantes,
Virgines; vestrum caput ipse cinget
Liliis; secum thalamo receptas
Ipse beabit.

Vos enim nullus labor hoc in orbe
Terruit, Sponsi memores amantis;
Huius et causā tolerastis ultro
Aspera quaeque.

sono, sonare: be heard, make a sound
sponsus: bridegroom
diuturnus a um: lasting for a day, ie *brief, short*
nimbus: cloud
abeo, abire, abivi: go away
ver, veris: spring
redoleo, redolere: smell lovely, emit a scent
sponsa: bride

obviam (prep): before, to meet
propero, -are: hasten
ovo, ovare: rejoice
thalamo: *in the wedding chamber*
recipio, recipere, receptus: admit, welcome, receive

huius et causa: *and for his sake*
ultro: besides, further, freely
quaeque (neut plu): *some, all*

198. Vox sonat Sponsi

Ipse, qui vobis moriens supernas
Addidit vires, simul edomare
Corporis sexum dedit, et cruentas
Vincere pugnas.

Hinc fidem Christo, semel obligatam,
Usque servastis; rutilatque vestra
Impigre lampas, nihil imbre et atris
Victa procellis.

Terra nunc vobis patet, unde curae
Exsulant omnes, ubi nil opacat
Limpidi caeli faciem, perennis
Sol ubi fulget.

vires, virium: powers, strength
edomo, edomare: subdue, vanquish
sexus, -ūs: *female* sex
dedit vobis + infin: *gave you (the grace) to, allowed you to*
cruentus a um: bloody, sanguinary
vinco, vincere, victus (+ acc): overcome, conquer, prevail in

semel: once, a single time
obligatam: *undertaken, agreed, bound*
usque: all the way, without fail
rutilo, rutilare: glow, glow red
impigre (adv): promptly
lampas, lampadis (fem): lamp
nihil (adv): not at all, in no way
imber, imbris: storm, rain, rainstorm
procella: tempest, gale

exsulo, exsulare: be banished
opaco, opacare: darken, obscure
limpidus, -a, um: clear, bright
fulgeo, fulgere: shine

Supplementum Monasticum

1. Adeste sancti plurimo
2. Ad sacros Virgo thalamos
3. Anglorum jam apostolus
4. Aurora surgit aurea
5. Avete solitudinis
6. Fortis en praesul
7. Gaude mater Anna
8. Gemma caelestis pretiosa Regis
9. Gertrudis arca numinis
10. Hymnis angelicis ora resolvimus

11. Inter aeternas superum coronas
12. Jam noctis umbrae concidunt
13. Jam regina discubuit
14. Jesu corona caelitum
15. Jesu salvator saeculi
16. Jucunda patrum rediit
17. Lacte quondam profluentes
18. Laudibus cives resonent canoris
19. Mella cor obdulcantia
20. Mira nocturnis modulante lingua

21. Omnis sanctorum concio
22. O vos unanimes Christiadum chori
23. Puellus Placidus quem pater obtulit
24. Quiquid antiqui cecinere vates
25. Qui te posthabitis omnibus
26. Sacrata nobis gaudia
27. Salvete, cedri Libani
28. Signifer Invictissime
29. Succedit nocti lucifer
30. Te beata Sponsa Christi

    Note on Meter: Trochaic tetrameter catalectic.

1. Adeste sancti plurimo
   Anon c 1650

Adeste sancti, plurimo
Dum thure, vestra dum piis
Coluntur ossa ritibus,
Votis favete supplicum.

Paraphrased in simple prose:
Adeste, vos sancti, et favete votis supplicum, dum ossa vestra coluntur multo thure et piis ritibus.

Non illa, quamquam tristibus
Imum redacta in pulverem
Dudum sepulchris squaleant,
Divina virtus deserit.

Divina virtus non deserit illa ossa, quamquam squaleant jam in tristibus sepulchris, redacta in pulverem extremum.

thus, thuris: incense
faveo, favere, favi: favor, listen to, promote (+dat) (Δ *foveo*)
colo, colere, colui, cultus: honor, revere, venerate
votum: prayer, offering, desire, vow
supplices (< supplex): those who pray, those who kneel in prayer

non illa: (ossa)
quamquam: although
imus, -a, um: lowest, last
redigo, redegi, redactus: return, reduce
dudum: recently, before, earlier
squaleo, squalere, squalui: be dirty, be neglected, be in mourning
desero, deserere, deserui, desertus: abandon, leave, desert

1. <u>Adeste sancti plurimo</u>

Sed sancta praesenti fovet
Impletque templa numine,
Sed et futurae spiritus
Post saecla servat gloriae.

Sed (divina virtus) fovet et implet sancta templa praesenti numine, et servat spiritus futurae gloriae post saecula.

Hinc ille, qui nostris latet
Cinis sub aris conditus,
Aegris medetur efficax,
Torquet fugatque daemones.

Hic ille cinis, qui latet conditus sub aris nostris, sanat aegros efficaciter etc.

sancta: (*sancta templa*)
praesens, praesentis: at hand, here present (ie not in a squalid tomb)
foveo, fovere, fovi: cherish, keep warm, caress (subj = "it", ie *divina virtus*)
numen, numinis: divine power, holiness (ie of the relics)
sed et: *and also*
futurae gloriae (Dat): *for future glory*
spiritus (Acc plu): perh *their souls* (as opposed to their bones)

lateo, latēre, latui: lie hidden, be concealed
cinis, cineris: ash, ashes
ara: altar
conditus (< condere): installed, embedded, buried
aeger, -gra, -grum: sick
medeor, mederi: be good for, heal, cure (+dat)
efficax: effective, powerful
torqueo, torquere, torsi: twist, rack, torment

2. <u>Ad sacros Virgo thalamos</u>
   Hugo Vaillant OSB, ob. 1678

Ad sacros Virgo thalamos anhelans
Nuptias caelo celebrare gestit,
Et piis votis nimium morantem
Provocat horam.

Aegra dum languet, manifestus adstat
Caelitum turmā comitante Christus,
Atque divini recreat jacentem
Lumine vultūs.

"Surge", conclamat, "soror atque sponsa,
En tibi pando penetrale cordis,
Ut triumphali reserata scandas
Sidera curru."

thalami, -orum (< thalamus): inner room, bridal chamber
anhelo, anhelare: pant for, long for (+ *ad* + acc)
nuptiae, -arum: wedding, marriage
caelo: *in Heaven*
gestio, gestire, gestivi: rejoice, delight, leap with joy (+ infin)
nimium (adv): too much, too long
moror, morari: tarry, linger, delay
provoco, provocare: summon, call for, bring forward

langueo, languēre: be weary, be weak, be sick (subj = "she")
aeger, aegra: sick, sick *with love*
caeles, caelitis: heavenly, celestial
turma, turmae: throng, host (Δ *turba*)
comitor, comitari: accompany, follow
recreo, recreare: restore, refresh
jacentem: *(her) as she lies (there), her lying there*

en: behold, lo
pando, pandere: reveal, disclose, open up
penetralis, -e: interior, inside (here used as a noun)
resero, reserare, reseratus: open, unlock, reveal
scando, scandere, scandi: ascend to, rise up toward (+ acc)
currus, -ūs: chariot

2. <u>Ad sacros Virgo thalamos</u>

Ista vox omnes penetrat medullas
Atque compages animi resolvit;
Spiritus liber volat in reclusa
Viscera Christi.

Regios Agni thalamos petentem
Jubilans stipat superum corona,
Atque complexūs et amica cantat
Oscula Sponsi.

Virginum Sponsum, superumque Regem
Virginum sanctae celebrent choreae,
Et sacram supplex Triadem per aevum
Orbis adoret.

medulla: *lit* marrow, *metaph* heart
compages, -is: joint, connection, bond (acc pl)
resolvo: release, unbind, undo, loosen
recludo, -ere, reclusus: disclose, reveal, throw open
volo, volare: fly

stipo, -are: crowd, encompass, throng around
superus, -a, -um: (*superum* is poetic gen pl, and here used as a noun.)
corona: crown, circle, ring, assembly, multitude
complexus, -ūs: embrace, hug
amicus, -a, -um: loving, sweet
osculum: kiss
canto (+ acc): sing of, extoll in song (subj = *corona*, the ring of saints and angels)

chorea: dance, *plu perh* chorus of dancers
supplex, supplicis: kneeling, bowing in prayer, adoring
trias, triadis (fem): trinity
adoro, adorare: worship, adore

Note:

Compages also means "structure". Cf (Illi) "qui ad adspectabilem non pertinent Catholicae Ecclesiae compagem". Pius XII, *Mystici Corporis* 242, DS 3821.

3. Anglorum jam apostolus
St Peter Damian, ob 1072

Anglorum jam apostolus,
Nunc angelorum socius,
Ut tunc, Gregori, gentibus
Succurre jam credentibus.

Tu largas opum copias,
Omnemque mundi gloriam
Spernis, ut inops inopem
Jesum sequaris principem.

Videtur egens naufragus,
Dum stipem petit, angelus;
Tu munus jam post geminum
Praebes et vas argenteum.

jam (apostolus): recently, ere now, already
ut tunc: as then, like then
Gregori: (vocative)
sucurro, sucurrere, succurri (+ dat): go to the aid of, help (Δ *curro, cu-curri*)
jam (succurre): now, forthwith

largus, -a, -um: abundant, plentiful
(ops) opis: wealth, riches, treasure
copia, copiae: supply, quantity, abundance
sperno, spernere, sprevi: despise, reject (*tu.....spernis*)
inops, inopis: poor *man*, destitute

naufragus, -a, um: shipwrecked
(stips) stipis: alms, donation, contribution
geminus: double, two-fold
munus, muneris (neuter): gift
munus post geminum: *after a double gift (of alms)*
praebeo, praebēre: offer, furnish, supply
et vas argenteum: *even the silver dish*

Note: According to medieval legend, an angel appeared to Gregory in the form of a poor shipwrecked merchant. Gregory gave him alms. The angel returned, and Gregory gave him alms a second time. Finally the angel returned a third time, and Gregory gave him a silver dish—a gift from his own mother—because he had no money left.

3. Anglorum jam apostolus

Ex hoc te Christus tempore
Suae praefert Ecclesiae;
Sic Petri gradum percipis,
Cuius et normam sequeris.

O pontifex egregie,
Lux et decus Ecclesiae,
Non sinas in periculis,
Quos tot mandatis instruis.

Sit Patri laus ingenito,
Sit decus Unigenito;
Sit utriusque parili
Majestas summa Flamini.

praefero, praeferre: present, put at the head of
suae praefert ecclesiae: perh *places you over His church*
percipio, percipere: receive, assume, occupy
gradus, -ūs: rank, degree
norma: example, standard, rule

pontifex, pontificis: pope, bishop
egregius: exceptional, outstanding
decus, decoris: ornament, boast, glory
sino, sinere, sivi: leave, allow, ignore
instruo, instruere, instruxi: prepare, teach, instruct

ingenitus: unborn
parilis (+ gen): equal to, like
flamen, flaminis: spirit, wind, the Holy Ghost (Δ *flamma* and *flumen*)
utriusque parili….Flamini: *the Spirit equal to each*
Sit….majestas + dat: *majesty belongs to, we must ascribe majesty to*

4. Aurora surgit aurea
   St Peter Damian, ob. 1072

Aurora surgit aurea,
Festa restaurans annua,
Cum Benedictus arduum
Caeli scandit palatium.

Quanta in summis accipit
Qui sic in imis claruit!
Cujus micant prodigia
Per ampla mundi climata.

festa, -orum: feast, festival day, celebrations
restauro, restaurare: renew, restore
annuus: yearly, annual
scando, scandere, scandi: climb, mount, ascend
palatium: palace, royal castle, the Palatine Hill
arduus: steep, difficult

accipio, accipere: receive
in summis (summus, -a, -um): *on high, in heaven* (= *in excelsis*)
ima, imorum (imus, -a, -um): lower places (ie. here on earth)
clareo, clarere, clarui: be renowned, be illustrious
mico, micare: shine, glitter
clima, climatis (neut): region, zone
amplus: vast, wide

4. Aurora surgit aurea

Ejus carentum gratiā
Tellus vomit cadavera;
Devotis unda liquida
Sicca lambit vestigia.

Totius orbis ambitum
Per solis videt radium;
Mens in Auctore posita
Subjecta cernit omnia.

careo, carēre: lack, be without (*of those who lack his grace*)
tellus, telluris: earth
vomo, vomere, vomui: spew forth, spit out
cadaver, cadaveris: body, corpse
devotis (< devoveo): *(but) for the devoted, for those who have been dedicated*
unda: billow, water, moisture
liquidus: flowing, clear
lambo, lambere, lambi: lick, barely touch, perh *kiss*
siccus: dry
vestigium: foot, foot-print, vestige

ambitus, -ūs: area, extent
videt: *one sees, one can see*
radius: ray, rays, beams, light
posita in +abl (ponere): fixed upon, directed toward, focussed on
auctor: builder, founder
subjecta (subjicio): *in subordination, subject* (to Him)
cerno, cernere: perceive, discern

Notes on the 3rd verse:

The genitive plural of the present participle normally ends in –ium, eg. *amantes, amantium.* The form *carentum* is an exception to this rule.

Vomit cadavera, lambit vestigia. A boy left the monastery without permission. He died and was buried, but the earth spat up his body. Another boy, Saint Maurus, walked on water. With poetic license Peter Damian refers to the events in the plural.

For the historical source of these stories see Book 2 of the *Dialogues* of Saint Gregory the Great.

For the scholarly debate about that source see references to F. Clark and P. Meyvaert in the bibliography of *The Emergence of Monasticism* by Marilyn Dunn.

4. Aurora surgit aurea

Te, Pater alme, petimus
Pronae mentis visceribus,
Ut caelum des ascendere
Quos terram doces spernere.

pronus: abject, falling
pronae mentis visceribus: *in the bowels of our downcast mind,*
do, dare (+ infin): grant, allow
ascendo, -ere (+ acc): climb to, rise up to, reach
quos: *whom, those whom* (antecedent omitted)
doceo, docere, docui: teach
sperno, spernere, sprevi: despise, spurn

"You, loving Father, we do pray
from deep within an abject heart:
You teach us to despise the earth,
allow us now to ascend to heaven."

The reader will note that Peter Damian employs a medieval invention, rhyme.

5. Avete solitudinis
Anon. Medieval.

Avete, solitudinis
Claustrique mites incolae,
Qui pertulistis impios
Coetūs furentis tartari.

Gemmas et auri pondera,
Et dignitatum culmina
Calcastis, et foedissima
Quae mundus offert gaudia.

Vobis olus cibaria
Fuere, vel legumina,
Potumque lympha praebuit,
Humusque dura lectulum.

avete: hail!, greetings! (plu of *ave*, addressed to 2 or more persons)
claustrum: enclosure, cloister
mitis, mitis: meek, mild
perfero, -ferre, -tuli: endure, suffer
coetus, -ūs: gathering, company, assembly
furens, furentis: mad, raging, wild

culmen, culminis: summit, high point, heap
dignitas: rank, distinction, eminence
calco, calcare, calcavi: trample on, stomp on, reject
foedus, -a, -um: foul, filthy, unseemly (Δ *foedus, foederis*)

olus, oleris: vegetables, greens
cibaria, -orum: food, fare, victuals
fuere: = *fuerunt*
legumen, leguminis: bean
potus: drink
lympha: water
praebeo, -ere, praebui: furnish, supply
humus, humi (fem): ground
lectulus: bed

5. Avete solitudinis

Vixistis inter aspides,
Saevisque cum draconibus,
Portenta nec teterrima
Vos terruere daemonum.

Rebus procul mortalibus
Mens avolabat fervida,
Divumque juncta coetui,
Haerebat inter sidera.

Summo Parenti caelitum,
Magnaeque Proli Virginis,
Sancto simul Paraclito,
Sit summa laus et gloria.

vivo, vivere, vixi: live, dwell
aspis, aspidis: asp, adder, snake
portentum: portent, omen, vision
teter (taeter), tetra, tetrum: hideous, repulsive
terreo, terrēre, terrui: frighten, terrify

procul + abl: far from
avolo, avolare: fly away, flee, hasten away
fervidus: burning, passionate
divus, -i: divine being, heavenly being, god (*divum* = *divorum* = gen pl)
junctus (< jungere): joined, close
coetus, -ūs: gathering, company, assembly
haereo: stick, cleave, persist (*stuck close to the gathering of the divine*)

caelites, caelitum: heavenly beings, those who dwell in heaven
prolis, -is (fem): off-spring, child
Magnaeque Proli Virginis: *and to the great child of the Virgin*

6. Fortis en praesul
Le Bannier OSB, ob 1867

Fortis en praesul, monachus fidelis
Laureā doctor redimitus adstat;
Festus Anselmo chorus aemuletur
Dicere carmen.

Ante maturos sapiens hic annos,
Saeculi florem pereuntis horret;
Atque Lanfranci documenta quaerens,
Intrat erēmum.

en: behold, lo
praesul, praesulis: leader, prelate
monachus: monk
laurea. –ae: laurel, wreath, degree (viz *Theologiae Doctor*)
redimio, redimīre, redimītus: wreathe, crown (Δ *redimo,redimere, redemptus*)
adsto, adstare: be present, attend, be at hand
festus, -a, -um: festal, on the occasion of the feast
chorus: choir (viz *of monks*)
aemulor, aemulari: be jealous, be eager, compete
dico carmen: recite a poem, sing a song

maturus, -a, -um: adult, mature
hic: he
pereo, perire: perish, pass away
horreo, horrēre: disdain, fear, spurn
Lanfrancus: Lanfranc (1010-1089, Prior of Bec, ArchB of Cant)
documentum: example, lesson
eremus: desert, monastery

6. Fortis en praesul

Intimum pulsans penetrale Verbi,
Fertur immotae fidei volatu.
Dogmatum puros latices an ullus
Altius hausit?

Munus abbatis, pater alme, sumens,
Te voves carae soboli; benignis
Debiles portas humeris, alacres
Praevius hortans.

intimus, -a, -um: innermost, secret, profound
pulso, pulsare: knock (on a door), seek to enter (+ acc)
penetrale, -is: inmost part, inner chamber, interior
immotus: unmoving, steady, steadfast
volatus, -ūs: flight, *perh* ascent (ie the interior ascent, the flight of contemplation)
dogma, dogmatis: dogma, teaching, *plu* doctrine
latex, laticis: water (*the pure waters of doctrine*)
an (solitarium): (Expects emphatic answer *No*)
altus: deep
haurio, haurire, hausi: draw (*water from a well*), *metaph* study

munus, muneris: duty, office
abbas, abbatis: abbot (of Bec)
pater alme: (The hymn now addresses St Anselm directly)
voveo, vovēre: vow, dedicate, consecrate
carus, -a, -um: dear, beloved
soboles, -is: off-spring, family (ie spiritual children)
debilis: weak, feeble, infirm (*debiles* is acc plu)
portas (< portare): *you carry, you bear*
humerus: shoulder
benignus: kindly, loving, generous
alacer, alacris: quick, able, cheerful (*alacres* is acc plu)
praevius, -a, -um: leading, preceding, going ahead

6. Fortis en praesul

Praesulum defert tibi rex cathedram;
Quid times luctam? properant triumphi;
Exteras gentes, generosus exsul
Lumine reples.

Sacra libertas, ovibus redemptis
Parta, cui Christus nihil anteponit,
Urget Anselmum. Studio quis aequo
Vindicat ipsam?

praesules, -um: prelates, bishops (rex = William II of England)
cathedra: throne, primacy (ie as ArchB of Canterbury)
defero, deferre: offer, appoint (*cathedram tibi*, ie. *you to the throne*)
quid: why
lucta, -ae: struggle (Gregorian Reform and Investiture Crisis)
propero, -are: hasten (*victories come swiftly*)
exterus, -a, -um: outside, foreign, alien
generosus: noble, of noble birth
exsul, exsulis: exile, refugee (Anselm, like Lanfranc, was from Italy)
repleo, replēre; fill

partus, -a, -um (< pario): gained, acquired
antepono: set before, prefer
urgeo, urgere: drive, impel
studium: zeal, diligence
vindico, -are: defend, support (*ipsam* ie *sacram libertatem*)

Note:

Sacra libertas cui Christus nihil anteponit. " (Holy liberty) than which more highly Christ esteemeth nothing". This rhetorical claim should perhaps be understood in the historical context of the Gregorian Reform. Dom Le Bannier was a French monk. The hymn was written after the French revolution, but before the anti-clerical legislation of the Third Republic. It is one of very few post-medieval hymns included in the Monastic Breviary.

6. <u>Fortis en praesul</u>

Clara fit Romae tua fama, praesul;
Pontifex summus tibi fert honores:
Te fides poscit; siluere patres;
Dogma tuere!

Sis memor sancti gregis, et patronus
Sis ad aeternam Triadem, precamur,
Cuncta cui dignas resonent per orbem
Saecula laudes.

Romae (loc): *at Rome*
fama, -ae: fame, reputation
Te….tuere: (as if the Pope were speaking to Anselm)
posco, poscere: demand, require (*The faith needs you*)
sileo, silere, silui: not speak, be silent (*siluere* = *siluerunt*)
dogma, dogmatis (neuter): teaching, doctrine
tueor, tueri: uphold, guard, defend (*tuere* = imperative)

patronus: advocate, sponsor (ie *our* advocate *with* the Trinity)
trias, triadis: trinity
Triadem…. cui: *Trinity to whom*
resono, -are (+ acc): express, convey, ring out, sing
cuncta saecula: (Subject of *resonent*)
dignas laudes: (Direct object of *resonent*)

7. Gaude mater Anna
Anon, c. 1500

Gaude mater Anna,
Gaude mater sancta,
Cum sis parens facta
Genitricis Dei.

Plaude tali natae,
Virgini Mariae;
Ejus genitori
Joachim congaude.

In hac nostrā terrā
Primo benedictā,
Quae fuit in Evā
Quondam maledicta.

Ergo sume laudes,
Quas damus ovantes,
Nos sub omni sorde
Tuā prece terge.

cum (+ subjunc): because, since

plaudo, plaudere, plausi: clap for, applaud (+ dat)
Joachim: (Dative: *rejoice alike with Joachim, her father*)

primo (Adv): at first, at the start
quondam: once, at one time, in the past

sumo, sumere: accept
ovo, ovare: rejoice
sub omni sorde: *from every defilement, 'neath every sort of filth*
tergeo, tergere: cleanse, wipe clean

8. <u>Gemma caelestis pretiosa Regis</u>
St Peter Damian, 1007-1072

Gemma caelestis pretiosa regis,
Norma justorum, via monachorum,
Nos ab immundi, Benedicte, mundi
Subtrahe caeno.

Tu solum spernens, cor in astra figens,
Cogis heredes fieri parentes;
Vas Deo plenum reparare fractum
Promeruisti.

gemma: jewel
norma, -ae: rule, standard
immundus, -a, -um: unclean
subtraho: pull out, free, withdraw
caenum: dirt, filth (*of an unclean world*)

solum, -i: earth
figo, figere: fix, direct
cogo, cogere: gather, lead, compel, oblige
heres, heredis: heir, beneficiary
vas, vasis: vessel, bowl, sieve
reparo, reparare: restore, renew, reform
frango, frangere, fregi, fractus: break
promereo, promerēre: be worthy, merit, be able

Notes

Vas….reparare fractum promeruisti. "You were found worthy to restore a broken vessel." The story of the broken bowl (or sieve) is in Cap 1 of Book II of the *Dialogues* of Saint Gregory the Great. In this hymn the word *vas* might also refer to the monastic order in Italy before the reforms of Saint Benedict.

Cogis heredes fieri parentes. "You oblige you parents to become your heirs" ie by running away. Perh "You oblige your (monastic) heirs to become (spiritual) parents".

8. <u>Gemma caelestis pretiosa Regis</u>

Magnus in parvis eremita membris,
Vincis aetatem, superas laborem;
Arcta districtae rudimenta vitae
Fervidus imples.

Strage saxorum puerum sepultum,
Mox ut orasti, prece suscitasti;
Sensus hinc carni, caro sanitati,
Redditur aeque.

eremita, -ae (Masc): hermit
membra, -orum: components (Perhaps the *parts* or *buildings* of an abbey)
aetas, aetatis: age, perh *youth* (*you triumph over your youth*)
superas laborem: perh *you defeat the hardship of labor*
arctus, -a, -um: narrow, limited
districtus, -a, -um: severe, strict
rudimenta: the basics, the rudiments
fervidus: aflame, zealous (ly), eager (ly)
impleo, implere: satisfy, fulfill

strages, -is: rock-slide, deadly pile (Cf Cap 11 of the *Dialogues*)
mox ut: as soon as
prex, precis: prayer
suscito, suscitare: raise, restore to life
hinc: hence, and so
sanitas: health (*sense to flesh and flesh to health*)
reddo, reddere: restore (as if *redduntur*. Subj = *sensus, caro*)
aeque: alike, equally

8. Gemma caelestis pretiosa Regis

Jure sub blandae specie columbae,
Nesciam fellis animam sororis
Summa stellati penetrare caeli
Culmina cernis.

Ipse post clarum referens triumphum,
Celsa devicto petis astra mundo;
Luce flammantem radiante caelum
Pallia sternunt.

jure (Adv): rightly
species, -ei: appearance, form
blandus, -a, -um: soft, gentle
columba: dove (cf Dialogues II:34)
nescius, -a, -um: unknowing, unaware, ignorant of (+ gen)
fel, fellis: gall, bitterness, spite
stellatus: starry
penetro, -are: reach, enter
culmen, culminis (neut): height, summit
cerno, cernere: see, perceive

ipse: (*tu ipse*)
clarus, -a, -um: famous, evident
refero, referre: withdraw, go homeward
celsus a um: high, heavenly
devinco, devincere, devictus: overcome, conquer
flammans (< flammare): ablaze, burning
radio, radiare: gleam, beam, shine
pallium: pallium, monastic garment, habit, cowl
sterno, sternere, stravi, stratus: bestrew, bedeck, be spread over
caelum pallia sternunt: *monastic garments* (ie monks) *bedeck the sky*

9. Gertrudis arca numinis
   Hugo Vaillant OSB, ob. 1678

Gertrudis arca numinis,
Sponsoque juncta virginum,
Da nuptialis pangere
Castos amores foederis.

Quadrima Christo nubilis
In claustra prompte convolas;
Spretoque nutricis sinu,
Sponsi requiris oscula.

Candentis instar lilii
Odore mulces sidera,
Et virginali caelitum
Regem decore pertrahis.

Gertrudis arca: *O Gertrude, ark* (Both vocative)
sponsus, -i: bridegroom
juncta (< jungere): pledged, wedded, joined
pango, pangere (+ acc): sing of, sing about (cf *Pange lingua*)
da…. pangere: *give (us the grace) to sing, let (us) sing*
castus, -a, -um: chaste, pure
foedus, foederis: bond, covenant

quadrimus, -a, -um: having lived four winters, four years old
nubilis: destined to be wed (*to Christ*)
claustrum: cloister, convent, monastery
prompte: quickly, willingly
convolo, -are: fly together, fly swiftly
sperno, spernere, sprevi, spretus: disdain, leave, abandon
nutrix, nutricis: nurse
sinus, -ūs: lap, bosom
requiro, requirere: seek, look for
osculum: kiss, embrace

candens, -entis: radiant
instar (neut, indecl): image, likeness
lilium: lily
odor, odoris: fragrance (*with your fragrance*)
mulceo, mulcere: delight, charm (*you charm the stars*)
caeles, caelitis: heavenly *dweller*, heavenly *being*
pertraho, pertrahere: entice, attract

9. <u>Gertrudis arca numinis</u>

Qui vivit in sinu Patris
Cinctus perenni gloriā,
Amanter ut sponsus tua
Recumbit inter ubera.

Amore Christum vulneras,
Hic te vicissim vulnerat,
Tuoque cordi propria
Inurit alte stigmata.

O singularis caritas,
Et mira commutatio!
Hic corde respirat tuo,
Tu vivis huius spiritu.

qui: (Antecedent is *regem*, ie Christ)
cingo, cingere, cinxi, cinctus: gird, encircle, robe
amanter: fondly, affectionately, lovingly
ut: like, as
recumbo, recumbere: lie down, repose, recline
uber, uberis (Neut): breast (Δ *uber, uberis* adj = *abundant, plentiful*)

vulnero, -are: wound
vicissim: in turn, in return
propria….stigmata: *his own stigmata, his own marks*
inuro, inurere: burn into, brand, imprint
alte: deeply

mirus, -a, -um: wondrous
commutatio, -nis: exchange
Hic….huius: *He….His*
respiro, -are: breathe, sigh
spiritus: breath, Spirit

9. Gertrudis arca numinis

Te, sponse Jesu virginum,
Beata laudent agmina;
Patri, simul Paraclito,
Par sit per aevum gloria.

Te: (The person here changes from Gertrude to Jesus.)
sponse Jesu virginum: *O Jesus bridegroom of virgins*
agmen, agminis (Neut): throng, column, multitude
simul: and likewise, and at the same time
par, paris (Adj): equal

Note

Saint Gertrude was a writer in the medieval school of *Brautmystik*, or bridal mysticism. Hugo Vaillant employs her own imagery in this hymn. Similar language is found in the poetry of Saint John of the Cross in the 1500s. Another poet from whom Vaillant borrows is Pope Urban VIII. Cf the hymn *Haec est dies qua candidae*, written by the latter. The hymn-writers borrow freely from each other, and from Sacred Scripture. The origin of this genre of mystical lyric is of course the *Song of Songs* in the Bible. Consider, for example:

Dum esset rex in accubitu suo,
nardus mea dedit odorem suum.
Fasciculus myrrhae dilectus meus mihi,
qui inter ubera mea commorabitur.
(Cant 1: 11-12, ClemVulg)

The word *quadrima*, meaning "four winters old", in the second strophe is exact. Nothing is known of Gertrude's family. At the age of five she became a child oblate in the convent of Helfta, and she was thereafter raised by the nuns.

10. Hymnis angelicis ora resolvimus
Hugo Vaillant, ob 1678

Hymnis angelicis ora resolvimus,
Dum terrena fluunt nocte silentia;
Caelestes modulos virgo Scholastica
Puris mentibus imperat.

Gentis Nursiadum stemmate nobilis,
Agni virgineo foedere clarior,
Sponsi perpetuis fragrat odoribus,
Cordis vulnere pulchrior.

ora resolvimus: *we loosen our tongues, we open our mouths*
terrenus, -a, -um: earthly
silentium: silence
fluo, fluere: flow, flow on, continue
modulus: melody, rhythm
impero, -are: (+ dat pers and acc rei, eg *imperas aliquid mihi*, "from me")
puris mentibus: (dative)

gentis (genitive): *among the people, in the nation*
Nursiades, Nursiadum: the people of Nursia, Nursians
stemma, stemmatis: pedigree, family, origin, birth
nobilis, -is: noble, well-born, distinguished, famous (nominative)
clarior: *more illustrious* (in comparison to *stemmate nobilis*)
agni virgineo foedere: *by reason of the virginal covenant of the Lamb*
fragro, fragrare: be fragrant with, smell sweetly of
odor, odoris: fragrance
cordis vulnere pulchrior: *lovelier still by the wound of His (her) heart*

Meter

This meter is called "the Asclepiadic strophe" or the "Lesser Asclepiad". The fourth line is called "Glyconic". The dominant foot — ~ ~ — is a choriambus.

— — | — ~ ~ — | — ~ ~ — | ~ — (lines 1-3, dodeca-syllabic)
— — | — ~ ~ — | ~ — (line 4, octo-syllabic)

10. Hymnis angelicis ora resolvimus

Fervens innocuis pascitur ignibus,
Et majora petit pabula caritas;
Ut frater superum gaudia disserat,
Virgo fortior impetrat.

O noctis placidae dulcia tempora!
Quae caeli dapibus pectus inebriant,
Dum pandit cupidis sermo vicarius
Jesu numen amabile.

fervens.... pascitur: *burning with passion she is fed, ardently she is nourished*
innocuus, -a, -um: innocent, unharmful (the fires of love)
pabulum: nourishment, food
frater: *her brother* (St Benedict)
gaudia superum (= *superorum*): *the joys of heaven*
dissero, disserare: expound, wax eloquent about (+ acc)
fortior: *so boldly, with increasing boldness*
impetro, -are: gain, obtain, receive (his words), *perh* hear

placidus: peaceable, quiet
tempora: (Acc of exclamation. cf Cicero, *O tempora, o mores*!)
inebrio, -are: intoxicate, inebriate , make drunk
pectus, pectoris: *lit* chest, *metaph* heart (accusative)
daps, dapis: banquet, banqueting, foods
vicarius a um: vicarious, of another
sermo vicarius: *the words of another* (ie of her brother, not of the Lord)
pando, pandere: open, disclose, reveal
cupidis (Dat plu): *for the eager, for those who desire*
Jesu: (Genitive)
numen: (Dir obj of *pandit*)

10. Hymnis angelicis ora resolvimus

Cordis vera quies, inclita Trinitas,
Quae vultūs satias lumine caelites:
Sit te dulce loqui, dulcius assequi,
Et per saecula perfrui.

quies, quietis: rest, repose
inclitus a um: glorious, noble, exalted
vultus.... lumine: *with the light of your face, by the light of your face*
caelites (Acc plu): *those in heaven, the inhabitants of heaven*
loquor (+ acc): speak of, talk about, mention
sit: *Let it be sweet to speak of you, sweeter still....*
assequor, assequi: follow, follow after, imitate (supply *te*)
perfruor, perfrui: enjoy, possess

11. Inter aeternas superum coronas
Saint Peter the Venerable, ob 1156

Inter aeternas superum coronas,
Quas sacro partas retinent agone,
Emicas celsis meritis coruscus,
O Benedicte.

Sancta te compsit puerum senectus,
Nil sibi de te rapuit voluptas,
Aruit mundi tibi flos, ad alta
Mente levato.

superum: (= *superorum*, ie the saints in heaven)
retineo: hold, possess, retain, keep (Subj of *retinent* is *they = superi*)
partus, -a, -um (pario): born, gained, obtained
agon, agonis: struggle, agony, combat
emico, emicare: shine forth
coruscus, -a, -um: glittering, gleaming, radiant

como, comere, compsi: embellish, grace, adorn
te puerum: *the boy who you were, you from when you were a boy*
senectus, senectutis (fem): old age (*a holy old age has graced you*)
voluptas, voluptatis: pleasure
rapio, rapere, rapui: seize, steal, snatch (sibi: *for itself, unto itself*)
aresco, arescere, arui: dry up, wither
ad alta: to higher things, on high, to the heights
mente: *in your mind, in your heart*
levo, levare: raise (nb: *tibi....levato*, not *mente levata*)

11. Inter aeternas superum coronas

Hinc fugā lapsus patriam, parentes
Deseris, fervens nemorum colonus;
Edomas carnem subigisque Christo
Tortor acerbus.

Ne diu tutus latebras foveres!
Signa te produnt operum piorum;
Spargitur felix celeri per orbem
Fama volatu.

hinc: hence, from here
labor, labi, lapsus: slip away, escape
fuga lapsus: *in flight escaping, having made good your escape*
desero, deserere: abandon, forsake, desert
colonus, -i: dweller, colonist, farmer
nemus, nemoris: forest, place of solitude, *plu* woods
edomo, edomare: conquer, subdue
subigo, subigere: subdue (*you conquer the flesh and subdue it to Christ*)
tortor, tortoris: tormentor (ie B himself, because of his severe mortification)
acerbus: harsh, severe, cruel

foveo, fovēre: cherish, favor, prefer
diu: for long, for a long time
latebra: concealment, solitude, *plu* solitary places
tutus, -a, -um: safe, secure, in safety
ne…. foveres: *you could not for long safely prefer solitude*
prodo, prodere: disclose, reveal, display (Δ *prodeo, prodire*)
spargo, spargere: spread, scatter
celer, celeris: swift, rapid
volatus, -ūs: flight, course
celeri…. volatu: *in swift flight*
felix fama: *the happy story*

12. <u>Jam noctis umbrae concidunt</u>
Hugo Vaillant OSB, ob. 1678

Jam noctis umbrae concidunt;
Dies cupita nascitur,
Quā virgini Scholasticae
Sponsus perennis jungitur.

Brumae recedit taedium;
Fugantur imbres nubibus,
Vernantque campi siderum
Aeternitatis floribus.

Amoris auctor evocat,
Dilecta pennas induit;
Ardens ad oris oscula
Columba velox evolat.

cóncido, concidere: fall away, disappear
cupio, cupitus: long for, desire
perennis: everlasting, immortal

bruma, -ae: depth of winter, winter-dark
taedium, -ii: weariness, oppression
fugo, -are: put to flight
imber, imbris: storm, rain storm
imbres nubibus: *rainstorms with clouds, cloud-swollen storms*
verno, vernare: flourish, spring to life
campi siderum: *the fields of the stars, the fields of starry heaven*

evoco, evocare: call out
dilecta, -ae: beloved
pennae, -arum: wings
pennas induit: *puts on her wings,* perh *takes wing*
ardens ad oris oscula: *longing for the kisses of his mouth*
velox, velocis: swift, swiftly
evolo, evolare: fly forth, hasten upward

12. <u>Jam noctis umbrae concidunt</u>

Quam pulchra gressum promoves,
O cara proles Principis!
Nursinus abbas adspicit,
Grates rependit Numini.

Amplexa Sponsi dexteram,
Metit coronas debitas,
Immersa rivis gloriae,
Deique pota gaudiis.

Te, Christe, flos convallium,
Patremque cum Paraclito,
Cunctos per orbis cardines,
Adoret omne saeculum.

pulchra: *beautifully* (*quam pulchra tu*)
gressus, -ūs: step, stride
promoveo, promovēre: advance, extend
cara proles principis: *darling daughter of a prince*
Nursinus: of Nursia, Nursian
abbas, abbatis: abbot
grates, gratium: thanks, thanksgiving
rependo, rependere: pay, repay, requite, give

amplector, amplecti, amplexus: hold, embrace, entwine
meto, metere, messui, messus: gather, reap (Δ *metior, metiri, mensus*)
metit: *she gathers, she collects*
coronae, -arum: crown, floral crown, *perh* flowers of her crown
immersus, -a, -um (< immergere): awash, submerged
rivus, -i: stream, river
potus, -a, -um (+ abl): intoxicated by, drunk on, inebriated on

flos, floris: (vocative)
convallis: valley
cardo, cardinis: pole, corner (of the universe), hinge
adoro, adorare: adore, worship

13. Jam regina discubuit
Anon, c. 1300

Jam Regina discubuit,
Sedens post Unigenitum;
Nardus odorem tribuit,
Bernardus tradens spiritum.

Dulcis reginae gustui
Fructūs sui suavitas;
Dulcis ejus olfactui
Nardi Bernardi sanctitas.

Venit sponsa de Libano
Coronanda divinitus,
Ut Bernardus de clibano
Veniret Sancti Spiritūs.

discumbo, discubui: sit down, recline
nardus, -i: nard, fragrant oil
Bernardus: (Not a nominative absolute, but word play: *nardus* = *Bernardus*)

gustus, -ūs: taste
dulcis: agreeable, pleasant, sweet (Nominative: *dulcis est suavitas*)
fructus sui: (Genitive: *of his fruit*)
suavitas, -tatis: sweetness, goodness (of the fruit)
ejus: her (*reginae*)
olfactus, -ūs: (sense of) smell

Libanus: *Mount* Lebanon
divinitus (Adv): in heavenly manner, divinely
ut: (Purpose clause, because St Bernard now meets the BVM.)
clibanus: furnace, cauldron

Note

The feast of Saint Bernard occurs during the Octave of the Assumption. In the imagery of this hymn the death of Saint Bernard is depicted as an encounter with the Queen of Heaven. She sits down beside her Son, or comes forward to be crowned, just as Bernard emerges from the cauldron of the Holy Ghost, namely from his mystical union with God during this life. The hymn is full of overtones, or cross-references, to the *Song of Songs*, upon which Bernard wrote a commentary. Cf Lessons 9-12 at Matins. In the next two strophes of the hymn, *Quae, ista,* and *haec* refer to the Queen of Heaven. *Quis, iste,* and *hic* refer to Bernard.

13. Jam regina discubuit

Quae est ista progrediens
Velut aurora rutilans?
Quis est iste transiliens
Colles, sanctis conjubilans?

Haec gloria terribilis
Sicut castrorum acies;
Hic gratia mirabilis
Ut Assueri facies.

Ora pro nobis Dominum,
Praedulcis fumi virgula;
Inclina Patrem luminum,
Pastor ardens ut facula.

rutilo, rutilare: be golden-red, shine red, grow red
transilio, transilire: leap over, leap across
collis, collis: hill

haec: *she is, hers is a, this is a*
castrorum acies: *an army encamped*
hic: *he is, his is a (wondrous grace)*
Assuerus: Assuerus, Ahasuerus (cf Esther 1:1)

virgula: rod of incense
fumus, -i: smoke
praedulcis: very sweet, sweetest
inclina: (*inclina nobis Patrem*)
pastor: (Vocative)
facula: torch

Notes

1. *Pulchra es amica mea suavis et decora sicut Jerusalem, terribilis ut castrorum acies ordinata*. Song 6:3

2. Vocabulary: In general *suavis* is a sensory term: pleasant-smelling, sweet to taste, pleasing to the senses. *Dulcis* is a more general term, for example: *aqua dulcis,* fresh water, *dulcissimus amicus,* best friend. Where both words are employed, as in this hymn, the distinction will remain awkward in English.

14. Jesu corona caelitum
Anon, c. 1600

Jesu, corona caelitum,
Maria, caeli gaudium,
Deo fruentes angeli,
Audite vota supplicum.

Vos, patriarcharum chori,
Vatumque turmae nobiles,
Vos, principes Apostoli,
Vos, purpurati martyres,

Vos, juncta confessoribus
Amoena castra virginum,
Anachoritarum greges,
Nostris favete plausibus.

fruor, frui (+abl): enjoy, enjoy (the presence of)
votum: prayer
supplex, supplicis (adj used as noun): on one's kness, bowing, begging, praying

vates, vatis: prophet, seer
turma, -ae: throng, band
principes Apostoli: *prince-Apostles*

castra. –orum: camp, army, camps
amoenus, -a, -um: pleasant
anachorita, -ae: hermit
plausus, -ūs: applause, congratulation, words of praise
faveo, favere, favi: favor, look with kindness on (+ dat)

14. <u>Jesu corona caelitum</u>

Vestris enim concivibus,
Nostram professis Regulam,
Haec jubilantis ordinis
Dicata sunt solemnia.

His inclitis parentibus
Congratulamur filii….
Illustre quos consortium
Vestri beat collegii.

Sit laus Patri cum Filio,
Et utriusque Flamini,
Quos vestra felix civitas
Hymno celebrat perpeti.

concivis, concivis: fellow citizen, compatriot
profiteor, profiteri, professus: profess, acknowledge, follow
haec solemnia (neut plu): *this solemn rite, this solemn office*
dico, dicare: devote, dedicate

congratulor, congratulari: wish joy to, rejoice with (+ dat)
filii: *(we your) sons*
illustris, -e: illustrious, glorious
consortium: company, fellowship
quos (antecedent is *parentibus*): *you whom,* perh *and you*
beo, beare: bless, call blessed, consider blest
collegium: college, order

flamen, flaminis: wind (*Spiritus*)
perpes, perpitis (adj): continual

His inclytis parentibus et seq:

> With these renowned forefathers
> We sons rejoice….
> And the glorious fellowship
> Of your order calls you blessed.

15. Jesu salvator saeculi
Cento from *Jesu salvator saeculi*, qv

Jesu salvator saeculi,
Redemptis ope subveni,
Et, pia Dei Genitrix,
Salutem posce miseris.

Monachorum suffragia,
Omnesque cives caelici
Annuant votis supplicum,
Et vitae poscant praemium.

ops, opis: aid, support
subvenio, subvenire (+ dat): help, come to the help of

suffragium: intercession, support
caelicus, -a, -um: heavenly, of heaven, in heaven
annuo, annuere: nod (ie nod favorably, show a sign of favor)
praemium: reward

16. Jucunda patrum rediit
Anon, c. 1100

Jucunda patrum rediit
Festivitas illustrium,
Confessione cordium,
Qui respuerunt saeculum.

Quorum colentes annuam
Solemnitatem candidam,
Ipsos precamur humiles,
Ut nostras mundent maculas.

Oratione sedulā,
Votisque nostris subditis,
Det nobis indulgentiam
Eorum intercessio.

jucundus, -a, -um: pleasing, happy
festivitas, festivitatis: feast, festivity, celebration
illustris, -is, -e: glorious, illustrious
respuo, respuere, respui: reject, despise, spit upon

colo, colere, colui: keep (a feast), observe, celebrate
candidus, -a, -um: white, luminous

sedulus, -a, -um: earnest, diligent
votum: prayer
subditus, -a, -um: humble, submissive

17. Lacte quondam profluentes
Anon, c. 1200

Lacte quondam profluentes,	*Flowing once with milk*
Ite montes vos procul;	*Go ye mountains far away;*
Ite colles fusa quondam	*Go ye hills, from which once*
Unde mellis flumina;	*Were poured rivers of honey.*
Israel, jactare late	
Manna priscum desine.	
Ecce cujus corde sudant,	
Cujus ore profluunt	
Dulciores lacte fontes,	
Mellis amnes aemuli;	
Ore tanto, corde tanto	
Manna nullum dulcius.	*No manna is sweeter*

Quaeris unde duxit ortum
Tanta lactis copia,
Unde favus, unde prompta
Tanta mellis suavitas,
Unde tantum manna fluxit,
Unde tot dulcedines?

jacto, jactare (+ acc): boast about, take pride in
manna: (Neuter indecl. = *manna, -ae* fem)
priscus, -a, -um: ancient, earlier
desino, desinere (+ infin): cease, stop

ecce cujus corde: *behold one from whose heart*
sudo, sudare: drip, distil
amnis, -is: stream, river
aemulus, -a, -um (+ gen): rivalling, better than

quaero, quaerere: seek, ask
ortum duxit: *found its origin, took its rise*
favus: honey, honeycomb
promo, promere, prompsi, promptus: send forth, produce

17. <u>Lacte quondam profluentes</u>

Lactis imbres Virgo fudit	*The child-bearing Virgin from heaven*
Caelitus puerpera;	*poured out the showers of milk.*
Mellis amnes os leonis	*The mouth of the now dead lion*
Excitavit mortui.	*was the source of the streams of honey.*
Manna silvae, caelitumque	*Woods and the heavenly solitude*
Solitudo proxima!	*so near [to us] produced the manna.*

Doctor o Bernarde, tantis
Aucte caeli dotibus,
Lactis hujus, mellis hujus,
Funde rores desuper;
Funde stillas, pleniore
Jam potitus gurgite.

Summa summo laus Parenti,
Summa laus et Filio;
Par tibi sit Sancte manans
Ex utroque Spiritus;
Ut fuit, nunc et per aevum
Compar semper gloria.

imber, imbris: rainfall, shower
caelitus (Adv): celestially, in a heavenly manner
puerpera: child-bearing
leonis mortui: *of the lion in death, of the lion that has died* (ie Bernard)
excito: give rise to, stimulate, be the source of (*amnes* = dir obj)
caeles, caelitis: dweller in heaven, heavenly

doctor: (In the schools Bernard was styled *Doctor Mellifluus*)
auctus (< augere): increased, enlarged,endowed
dos, dotis: dowry, endowment, gift
ros, roris: dew, *metaph* rain (*rores*: plu for sing)
stilla: drop, raindrop, dew-drop
potior, potiri, potitus (+ abl): acquire, possess
(tu) jam potitus: *now that you possess*
gurges, gurgitis: river, torrent

mano, manare: flow, emanate (*Sancte manans Spiritus*, vocative phrase)

18. <u>Laudibus cives resonent canoris</u>
Anon, c. 1400

Laudibus cives resonent canoris,
Templa solemnes modulentur hymnos;
Hac die summi Benedictus arcem — Aureā summi Benedictus arce
Scandit olympi. — Gaudet olympi. *TP*

Ille florentes peragebat annos,
Cum puer dulcis patriae penates
Liquit, et solus latuit silenti
Conditus antro.

civis, civis: citizen
resono, resonare: sound forth, sing out, resound with (+ abl)
canorus, -a, -um: melodious, harmonious
modulor, modulari: measure, sing, perform (music) (subj = *templa*)
arx, arcis (fem): castle, citadel
scando, scandere (+ acc): mount, climb, ascend
aurea arce gaudet: *rejoices in (over, by reason of) the golden citadel*

ille: *Benedictus*
florens, florentis (< floreo): flowering, flourishing (ie the years of his youth)
perago, -ere: complete, finish, pass through
puer dulcis: *as* a sweet child, a charming lad
patria, -ae: fatherland, ancestry, family
penates: household gods, home (pre-christian reference)
linquo, linquere, liqui: leave
solus, solius (adj): alone, in solitude
lateo, latere, latui: hide, go into hiding, be hidden
conditus (< condo): buried, concealed, immured
antrum: cave, cavern, den

18. Laudibus cives resonent canoris

Inter urticas rigidosque sentes
Vicit altricem scelerum juventam;
Inde conscripsit documenta vitae
Pulchra beatae.

Aeream turpis Clarii figuram,
Et nemus stravit Veneri dicatum,
Atque Baptistae posuit sacrato
Monte sacellum.

urtica: nettle
sentes, sentium: thorns, brambles
rigidus: stiff, hard
juventa: boyhood, youth
altrix: sustainer, source, foster-parent, fomenter, wet-nurse
scelus, sceleris: sin, crime, misdeed
vicit: *conquered his young manhood, that source of sinfulness*
conscribo: write, commit to writing, draw up
documenta, -orum: document (plu for sing)

aereus, -a, -um: of bronze
turpis, turpis: shameful, filthy
figura: image, statue
Clarius: the Clarian, *Apollo Clarius* (the Apollo of Klaros)
nemus, nemoris (neut): grove
Venus, Veneris: *the goddess* Venus
dico, dicare: dedicate, devote
sterno, sternere, stravi: knock down, flatten
sacellum: chapel, sanctuary
sacro, sacrare: make holy, consecrate
pono, ponere: set up, build, install
sacrato monte (abl absol): *the mountain having been made holy*

18. Laudibus cives resonent canoris

Jamque felici residens olympo,
Inter ardentes Seraphim catervas
Spectat, et dulci reficit clientum
Corda liquore.

resideo, residēre (+ dat): reside in, dwell on, dwell in
Seraphim: (gen pl)
caterva: throng, crowd, assembly
reficio, reficere: renew, refresh, restore
clientes, clientum: *his* followers (ie the monastic order)
cor, cordis (neut): heart
liquor, liquoris: liquid, fluid, water
dulci liquore: *with(the) sweet dew (of prayer)*

19. Mella cor obdulcantia
Saint Peter Damian, 1007- 1072

Mella cor obdulcantia
Tua distillant labia;
Fragrantum vim aromatum
Tuum vincit eloquium.

Scripturae sacrae mystica
Mire solvis aenigmata;
Theorica mysteria
Te docet ipsa Veritas.

mel, mellis: honey (*mella*: plu for sing)
obdulco, obdulcare: sweeten
distillo, distillare: drip, drop, distil (subj = *labia*; obj = *mella*)
fragro, fragrare: smell sweetly, be fragrant
aroma, arómatis: incense, perfume
arómatum: (accent on antepenult)
vis, vis: power, force
eloquium: word(s), speech, eloquence
vinco, vincere: conquer, surpass, exceed

mysticus, -a, -um: hidden, dark, mystic
mire (Adv): wondrously, wonderfully
solvo, solvere: unlock, resolve, explain
aenigma, aenigmatis: riddle, mystery, obscurity
theoricus: contemplative, speculative

19. Mella cor obdulcantia

Tu nactus apostolicam
Vicem simul et gloriam,
Nos solve culpae nexibus,
Redde polorum sedibus.

O pontifex egregie,
Lux et decus Ecclesiae,
Non sinas in periculis,
Quos tot mandatis instruis.

Sit Patri laus ingenito,
Sit decus Unigenito,
Sit utriusque parili
Majestas summa Flamini.

nanciscor, -i, nactus: reach, obtain
(vicis) -is: role, rank, position
nexus, -ūs: bond
solvo, -ere: free, release (c acc pers, c abl rei, ie *us from*)
culpa: fault, sin
reddo, reddere: restore (*us to*)
poli, polorum (< polus): *caelum*

sino, sinere: allow, leave
non sinas: *ne sinas (nos esse) in periculis*
tot: so many (indeclinable)
mandatum: precept, instruction
instruo, instruere: teach, inform

parilis, -is: equal, like
flamen, flaminis: wind, Spirit

20. Mira nocturnis modulante lingua
Hugo Vaillant, ob. 1678

Mira nocturnis, modulante linguā,
Gesta Gertrudis celebremus horis,
Quae sacris instans precibus peregit
Tempora noctis.

Illius votis Deus obsecundans,
Mox repentinas pluvias profudit,
Moxque suspensos gravidis coercet
Nubibus imbres.

Arva jam dudum glacie rigebant,
Corde cum maesto miserans colonos,
Fervidis virgo lacrimis resolvit
Frigora brumae.

nocturnus, -a, um: of the night, night-time (adj), nocturnal
modulor, modulari: make music, sing
gesta, -orum (< gerere): deeds, life
Gertrudis, Gertrudis: (Here genitive, antecedent of *quae*)
instans, instantis (< instare): present at, attentive to (+ dat), devoted to
perago, peragere, peregi: pass, spend (of time)
tempora noctis: *the night-time, the hours of night*

obsecundo, -are: comply with, look favorably upon, grant (+ dat)
repentinus a um; sudden, immediate, at once
pro-fundo, -ere, profudi: pour forth (transitive), pour down, rain down
coerceo, coercēre: check, restrain
imber, imbris (masc): rain-storm, rain
suspensus, -a, -um (< suspendere): hanging, uncertain, ominous
gravidus, -a, -um: heavy, full, laden
gravidis….nubibus imbres: *rainstorms with their heavy clouds*

arvum: field, crop
jam dudum: for a while, for a long time
rigeo, rigēre: stiffen, be hard, be frozen
glacies, glaciei: ice
maestus, -a, -um: sad, sorrowful
colonus: farmer, peasant (*miserans* + acc)
resolvo, -ere, resolvi: dispel, loosen, unbind
frigus, frigoris: cold, cold weather, chill
bruma, brumae: winter, winter-time

20. Mira nocturnis modulante lingua

Ne seges largo vitietur imbre,
Sedulis caelum precibus serenat,
Et graves laesi gemebunda placat
Numinis iras.

Igneis mentes penetrat sagittis,
Languidis confert animis medelam,
Atque succendit scelerata castis
Pectora flammis.

Virginum Sponsum superumque Regem
Virginum sanctae celebrent choreae,
Et sacram supplex Triadem per aevum
Orbis adoret.

seges, segitis: crop, harvest
largus, -a, -um: abundant, heavy (rainfall)
vitio, vitiare: damage, spoil, ruin
sedulus a um: earnest, diligent, passionate
caelum: sky
sereno, serenare: make clear, make calm
placo, placare: assuage, appease, pacify
gemebundus a um: groaning (in prayer), sighing
Numen, Numinis: divinity, God
laedo, laedere, laesi, laesus: injure, offend, wound

igneus a um: fiery, of flame, of fire
sagitta: arrow
penetrat, etc: (subj = *He,* scil. *Numen*)
languidus a um: sick, ill
medela: medicine, cure, treatment
succendo, succendere: set on fire, set ablaze
sceleratus, -a, -um: defiled, polluted, damaged by sin
castis….flammis: *with pure flames, with flames of purity*

chorea, choreae: chorus (of dancers), *perh* choir
supplex, supplicis: bowing down, kneeling, prayerful, humble
Trias, Triadis (fem): = *Trinitas*

21. <u>Omnis sanctorum concio</u>
Anon, c. 1200

Omnis sanctorum concio
Matrem collaudet Virginis,
De cujus puerperio
Salus processit hominis.

Haec prolem devotissime
Petiit a Patre luminum.
Et meruit dignissime
Mariam decus virginum.

Ex Joachim, quem habuit
Vitae virum eximium,
Anna Mariam genuit
Matrem Regis justitiae.

Stirps Jesse clara deluit
Evae matris opprobrium,
Dum Anna prolem genuit,
Florem sanctorum omnium.

concio, concionis: gathering, assembly
puerperium: travail, child-bearing
procedo, procedere, processi: come forth, emerge

Haec: *Anna*
prolem petiit: *sought (to have) a child* (elision: [petsit])
meruit Mariam: *she was worthy of Mary, she was worthy to bear Mary*
decus, decoris: beauty, loveliness, glory
decus virginum (appos): *glory of virgins*, perh *most beautiful of virgins*

ex Joachim: *by Joachim, with Joachim*
quem habuit virum: *whom she had as her husband*
eximius, -a, -um: distinguished, excellent
vitae eximium: *distinguished in life, of excellent life*

stirps, stirpis (fem): lineage, stem
deleo, delēre, delui: delete, remove, cancel
Evae matris: *of mother Eve, of Eve (our) mother*
dum: when

22. <u>O vos unanimes Christiadum chori</u>
Anon, c. 1650. Asclepiadic meter cf *Sanctorum meritis inclita gaudia*

O vos unanimes Christiadum chori,
Sanctorum tumulos et cineres Patrum,
Caras exuvias, pignora caelitum,
Laetis dicite cantibus.

Caelo quando piis aequa laboribus
Felices animae gaudia possident,
Poenarum sociis debita redditur
Hic laus, et decus ossibus.

Passim sparsa Deus, polliciti memor
Custos, ne pereant, pignora colligit,
Electosque suis providus aggerit
Aptandos lapides locis.

unanimis, unanime: of one mind, unanimous
Christiades, -um: Christians (Δ *Christiadum, -i = Christendom*)
tumulus: tomb, grave, burial mound
exuviae, -arum: remains, relics, mortal remains
pignus, pignoris (neut): pledge, promise, warranty
caeles, caelitis (Adj: neut gen plu *caelitum*): perh *pledge of heavenly promise*
dico, dicere (+ acc): tell of, speak of
cantus, -ūs: song, singing, chant

caelo: *in heaven*
socius, socii: sharer (*sociis* = ind obj of *redditur*)
poenarum sociis: (ie those who share in, or mitigate, our punishment)
decus, decoris: honor (*and honor is shown to their bones*)

passim: here and there, everywhere
spargo, spargere, sparsus: scatter, sow, fling
pollicitum, -i: promise
Deus polliciti memor custos: *God, mindful keeper of his promise*
pignora: *pledges,* ie. *relics*
colligo, colligere: gather, collect, assemble
providus: far-sighted, with foresight
aggero, aggerere: add to, increase, heap up
lapides: (ie altar stones, altars, stone reliquaries)
electos….aptandos lapides: *chosen stones to be made ready*
suis…. locis: *for their places, to hold them, to put them in*

22. O vos unanimes Christiadum chori

Quin et reliquias et tumulos sibi
Aras ipse Deus consecrat hostia;
Conjungensque suis se caput artubus,
Hos secum simul immolat.

Vos, quorum cineres supplicibus pia
Tutum praesidium plebs colit osculis,
Si vos nostra movent, subsidium boni
Vestris ferte clientibus.

Ut cum nostra novis splendida dotibus
Surget juncta choris spirituum caro,
Indivisa Trias sit Deus omnia
Nobis semper in omnibus.

quin et: *yea verily, nay even*
reliquias et tumulos: (Dir obj of *consecrat*)
aras: *as altars*
hostia: *Deus....hostia, God....as victim*
artūs (masc plu), artuum, artubus: limbs, members
hos (Antecedent is *artubus*): *them, these relics, these saints*

supplicibus....osculis: *with humble kisses*
pia....plebs: *a devout people*
praesidium: defense, protection
tutus, -a, -um: safe, secure
cineres (< cinis): *lit* ashes, *metaph* mortal remains
cineres.... tutum praesidium: *mortal remains as a secure defence*
nostra: "our things", *our concerns, our prayers*
subsidium boni: "reinforcement of good", *increased protection*
cliens, clientis: client (one who seeks the protection of another)

cum: when (+ fut indic, *surget*)
dos, dotis: dowry, endowment, gift
(nostra) caro, carnis (fem): our flesh
juncta choris spirituum: perh *joined with the choirs of the blessed souls*
indivisa Trias sit Deus omnia: *God the undivided Trinity may be all*

23. Puellus Placidus quem pater obtulit
Dom Le Bannier OSB, c. 1850

Puellus Placidus, quem pater obtulit,
Illibata Deo sistitur hostia,
Et tirocinii jam decus inclitum
Exemplar datum aemulis.

Abbati docilis, fictile vasculum
Immittens in aquas, parvulus amphoram
Incautus sequitur, litora deserit
Demersus fere fluctibus.

Quo sic, Maure, lacūs dum teris aequora,
Gressūs acceleras? O vir obediens,
Insuetum per iter vox te pii patris
Ad magnalia dirigit.

sisto, sistere: convey, place, present
tirocinium: novitiate, (group of) beginners
exemplar, exemplaris (neut): model, example
aemulis: *to the envious, to his rivals*

abbas, abbatis: abbot
docilis, -e: attentive, obedient
fictilis: earthen, (of) clay
vasculum: pot, small vessel
parvulus: small boy, little boy
amphora: jar, jug
incautus: careless, heedless
litus, litoris (neut): shore, shoreline, land (plu for sing)
demergo, demergere, demersus: sink, be overwhelmed
fere: nearly. almost

quo: whither? where to?
lacus, -ūs: pond,lake
tero, terere: tread upon, step on
gressus, -ūs: step
accelero, accelerare: speed up, quicken, hasten
insuetus: unusual, unfamiliar, strange
magnalia: *great things, wondrous deeds*
dirigo, dirigere: direct, draw forward

23. Puellus Placidus quem pater obtulit

Raptum restituit mox Placidum lacus:
Sed cujus meritis? Maurus an abstulit
Nursinusve pater gurgitis e sinu?
Solvit quaesita parvulus.

Praesta, summa Trias, per Placidi preces,
Angusto monachi tramite Regulae
Caelorum properent atria consequi,
Immixti Superum choris.

an: whether, if (in implicit indirect question)
aufero, auferre, abstuli: remove, snatch, rescue
-ve: or
Nursinus: of Nursia (ie Benedict)
gurges, gurgitis: waters, waves
sinus, sinūs: breast, lap, inside, perh *middle*
quaesitum: question, inquiry

Soon the lake gives back the stolen Placid.
But by whose merits? Did Maurus rescue (him)
From inside the waves, or (our) father from Nursia?
The little boy answers the question. (See Dialogues Bk II, Cap 7)

angustus: narrow, difficult
trames, tramitis: path, way
monachi: (Nom plu. Subj of *properent*)
propero, properare: make haste, hasten
consequor, consequi: reach, arrive at, obtain
immixtus (< immiscere): mingling with, joined by (+ dat)
Superum (< superus): (Gen plu. = *superorum*)

Notes:

1. The description of any saint as an *illibata hostia*, may seem improper. Father LeBannier means that the boy was very young, and had therefore committed no mortal sin since his baptism.

2. Placid fell into the lake. The waves pulled him away from shore. Maurus, upon the command of Benedict, raced across the water to save him.

24. Quiquid antiqui cecinere vates
Anon, c. 1450

Quidquid antiqui cecinere vates,
Quidquid aeternae monimenta legis….,
Continet nobis celebranda summi
Vita Monarchae.

Extulit Moysen pietas benignum,
Inclitum proles Abraham decorat,
Isaac sponsae decus et severi
Jussa parentis.

cano, canere, cecini: (*cecinere* = *cecinerunt*)
vates, vatis: seer, prophet
monimentum: (= *monumentum*)
contineo, - ēre: contain, possess, recapitulate, display
monarcha (Masc): prince, ruler

The life of the highest monarch contains to be celebrated by us whatever the ancient prophets said in song, and whatever the monuments of the law (said).

efferro, efferre, extuli: raise up, exalt
pietas, pietatis: devotion, obedience, holiness
benignus: loving, gracious
proles, prolis: (Nom sing, subject of *decorat*, [*his*] *off-spring*)
inclitum….Abraham: *the renowned Abraham* (Dir obj of *decorat*)
decoro, decorare: grace, adorn, honor
Isaac: (Accusative. Dir obj of implicit *decorant*)
decus sponsae: *the beauty of his bride*
jussum, jussi: command (*decus* and *jussa* are subjects of implicit *decorant*)
severus: stern, strict, harsh (refers to the sacrifice of Isaac)

24. <u>Quiquid antiqui cecinere vates</u>

Ipse virtutum cumulis onustus,
Celsior nostri Patriarcha coetūs,
Isaac, Moysen, Abraham sub uno
Pectore clausit.

Ipse, quos mundi rapuit procellis,
Hic pius flatu statuat secundo,
Pax ubi nullo, requiesque gliscit
Mixta pavore.

ipse: (ipse patriarcha, ie Benedict)
cumulus, -i: pile, heap
onustus a um: bearing, laden with, heavy with
celsior….patriarcha: *sublime patriarch, so lofty the patriarch*
nostri….coetūs: *of our family, of our order*
claudo, claudere, clausi: enclose, include
sub: under, within, inside (*neath a single heart*)

quos: *those whom*
procellis: (Abl of separation without a preposition)
rapuit: *those whom he snatched from the storms of the world*
hic: here (ie in a monastery)
statuo, statuere: settle, establish, locate
secundus: favorable, following (wind)
flatu secundo: *where the breeze is favorable, with a following wind*
requiesque: (*pax et requies* both nom, altho *gliscit* remains in the sing.)
glisco, gliscere: grow, spread, swell
nullo: (*requies mixta nullo pavore*)
pavor, pavoris: fear, terror

25. Qui te posthabitis omnibus
Hugo Vaillant, OSB, ob. 1678

Qui te posthabitis omnibus ambiunt,
Horum praesidium, dux, Deus et decus….
Quas Mauri meritis, muneribus tuis,
Laudes pangimus accipe.

Hic gentilitiis major honoribus,
Spretis laetus adit claustra palatiis,
Calcat delicias, praedia, purpuram,
Ut Christi subeat jugum.

posthabeo, -ēre: esteem less, belittle, neglect
ambio, ambire (+acc): strive for, press after, follow
praesidium: protection, defence (perh supply *tu es*)

hic: (He, ie Maurus)
gentilitius a um: ancestral, of one's family
major: *greater* [ie than other men], *distinguished*
gentilitiis honoribus: perh *by the excellence of his family*
palatium: palace
sperno, spernere, sprevi, spretus: reject, spurn
adeo, adire (+ acc): go to, approach, enter
claustra < claustrum: cloister, cloisters, monastery
calco, calcare: trample on, tread on, *metaph* despise
delicia, -ae: delight, pleasure, luxury
praedium: estate, land, farm (Δ *praeda, -ae*)
purpura: (the color of worldly success)
subeo, subire (+ acc): go beneath, put oneself under
jugum: yoke

Those who press after you to the exclusion of all else....
Of these men you are guardian, leader, God, and beauty....
By the merits of Maurus and by your gifts,
Receive the praises which we sing.

Meter: Asclepiadic, or "choriambic".
Cf *Sanctorum meritis juncta sint gaudia* (M), p287 supra.

25. Qui te posthabitis omnibus

Sancti propositam Patris imaginem
Gestis comparibus sedulus exprimit;
Spectandis pueri lucet in actibus
Vitae norma monasticae.

Se sacco rigidus conterit aspero,
Frenat perpetui lege silentii;
Noctes in precibus pervigil exigit,
Jejunus solidos dies.

propositus (< proponere): offered, held out, shown (as an example)
patris: (ie Benedict)
imago, imaginis (fem): likeness, example, figure
gesta, -orum (< gerere): deeds, actions
compar, comparis: equal, similar, comparable
sedulus, -a, -um: diligent(ly), zealous(ly)
exprimo, exprimere: express, represent, display
specto, spectare: observe, perh *imitate*
lucet: *shines, is clearly seen*
norma, -ae: standard, rule, norm, model (Subj of *lucet*)

rigidus, -a, -um: strict(ly), rigid(ly), unbending
contero, conterere: crush, bruise, hurt
saccus: sack-cloth
freno, frenare: restrain, bridle (supply *se*)
pervigil (adj): ever watchful, fully awake
exigo, exigere: spend, pass (of time)
jejunus, -a, -um: fasting, in fasting, hungry
solidus, -a, -um: whole, complete (*jejunus solidos dies exigit*)

25. Qui te posthabitis omnibus

Dum jussis patriis excitus advolat,
Sicco calcat aquas impavidus pede,
Educit Placidum gurgite sospitem,
Et Petro similis redit.

Laudum jugis honor sit tibi, Trinitas,
Quae vultūs satias lumine Caelites;
Da sanctae famulis tramite Regulae,
Mauri praemia consequi.

patrius, -a, -um: fatherly, paternal
jussis patriis: *by the command of his father* (ie of Benedict)
éxcitus (< éxcio): summoned, roused
advolo, advolare: fly off, hasten, race (to the rescue)
calco, calcare (+ acc): walk across, tread upon
gurges, gurgitis: waters, *gurgite* "from the waters"
impavidus: without fear, undaunted, intrepid
sospes, sospitis: safe, uninjured
Petro similis: (How so? Peter sank.)

jugis, jugis: unceasing, continual
caelites: (Acc plu. Dir obj of *satias*)
satio, satiare: fill, nourish, satisfy
da famulis: *grant to (your) servants* (+ infin)
trames, tramitis: path, way (*by the path of the holy Rule)*
Mauri praemia: *the same rewards as Maurus*

26. <u>Sacrata nobis gaudia</u>
Anon, c. 1300

Sacrata nobis gaudia
Dies reduxit annua,
Quā patres nostri optimi
Coluntur laude alacri.

Qui purā mentis acie,
Mundi devicto principe,
Amara dantes semina,
Jam messis tenent gaudia.

Scutum sumentes fidei,
Juxta dictum Apostoli,
Mucrone Sancti Spiritus
Hostes prosternunt invidos.

Ut vera Christi lilia
Fulgentes in Ecclesia,
Commissa sibi agmina
Pascebant dape gemina.

álacer, álacris, álacre: ready, quick (*laud*e a*lacri*, hiatus, ie no elision)
reduco, reducere: bring back, restore
acies, aciei (fem): sharpness, clarity
amarus, -a, -um: bitter
messis, messis: harvest (cf Psalm 125: 5-6)
mucro, mucronis: (spear) tip, blade, sword (cf Eph 6: 16-17)
prosterno, prosternere: knock down, overthrow
invidus, -a, -um: envious
ut + indic: as, like
lilium: lily
pasco, pascere (+ acc): nourish, feed, shepherd (vb)
agmen, agminis: column (of soldiers), troops
daps, dapis (fem): banquet, food

Notes:
1. *dantes semina*: anomalous. *Mittentes semina* in the liturgical text of Ps 125; *portantes semina* in the ClemVulg. Niermeyer does not record this use of *dare*.
2. *dape gemina*: perhaps = Word and Sacrament, or Body and Blood.

27. <u>Salvete, cedri Libani</u>
Anon, before 1700. Feast of All Saints OSB.

Salvete, cedri Libani,
Plantae virentes Ordinis,
Quae prata nunc caelestia
Impletis almo germine.

Vos Trinitatis gloria
Aeterna circumplectitur;
Vos aura Matris Virginis
Mulcet piis favoniis.

Libanus, -i: (Mount) Lebanon (*Libani* is genitive; and nb *cedri* is feminine)
planta. plantae: young plant, sapling, new vine
vireo, virere: be green, grow, flourish
pratum: meadow
impleo, implēre: fill, fill up (ie populate)
almo germine: perh *from a loving seed*

vos: (accusative)
circumplector, plecti, plexus: enfold, surround, encircle
aura, aurae: air, breath, breeze
mulceo, mulcere: charm, delight
favonius: a favorable wind, wind of good omen

27. Salvete cedri Libani

Vos angelorum curiae
Cingunt choreā perpetim,
Et irrigant purissimi
Aeternitatis rivuli.

O inclitae propagines,
Vestros juvate filios;
In valle maestā debiles
Nos roborate surculos.

Sit laus Patri cum Filio,
Sumulque dulci Flamini;
Laeti quibuscum vivitis
In sempiterno lumine.

chorea, choreae: chorus, dance
perpetim: continually, without cease

propago, propaginis: off-shoot, generation, fruit
juvo, juvare: help, support
maestus, -a, -um: sorrowful, afflicted
debilis, debile: weak, feeble
roboro, roborare: strengthen
surculus, -i: twig, sprout, branch (*nos surculos,* "us twigs")

laeti: (*laeti sunt illi cum quibus vos vivitis*)

28. <u>Signifer Invictissime</u>
Saint Peter Damian, 1007-1072

Signifer invictissime,
Sacraeque dux militiae,
Nos, Benedicte, valido
Precum defende brachio.

His armis exsecrabilem
Leonis vince rabiem,
Quibus olim teterrimam
Pellis ab ore merulam.

militia, militiae: army, soldiers (ie monks)
validus, -a, -um: strong, mighty
prex, precis: prayer (*with the mighty arm of [thy] prayers*)

arma, armorum: weapons, arms
exsecrabilis: accursèd, abominable
rabies, rabiei: madness, rage
leo, leonis: (cf *adversarius vester sicut leo rugiens etc*)
quibus: (*his armis....quibus*) (ie the preces SPN Benedicti)
teter, tetra, tetrum: foul, filthy, offensive
pello, pellere, pulsi: (*pellis* for *pulsisti*)
ab ore: *away from (your) mouth*
merula, merulae: blackbird, merle, bird of ill-omen

Note

The blackbird, or merle, is mentioned the life of Saint Benedict in the *Dialogues* of Gregory the Great, Book Two: Chapter 2. Both the *merula* and the *leo* are images of the devil. See also Isidore, *Etymologiae*, sv "merula".

28. Signifer Invictissime

Urticae junctae vepribus
Vulnus curant vulneribus;
Flammata mens divinitus
Ignem exstinguit ignibus.

Crucem mittens ut lapidem
Veneni frangit calicem;
Non valet mortis vasculum
Vitae ferre signaculum.

Frater, quem tunc nequissimus
Vagum raptabat spiritus,
Dum tuā virgā caeditur,
Stabilitati redditur.

urtica, urticae: nettle
vepres, vepris: thorn-bush, briar
curant: *cure the wound (of lust) with wounds (to the flesh)*
mens, mentis: soul (This usage is common in the hymns.)
divinitus (Adv): *divinely, in a heavenly manner*
flammata mens divinitus: *his soul aflame with divine grace*
ignem exstinguit ignibus: *puts out fire with fire*

crucem mittens: (ie. by making a sign of the cross. *Dialogues,* Cap 3)
ut lapidem: *like a stone*
venenum, veneni: poison
vasculum, vasculi: vessel, cup
fero, ferre: endure, bear (not *carry*)
signaculum, -i: sign

nequissimus: = *iniquissimus*
vagus a um: wandering, astray, vagabond
quem etc: *whom a most wicked spirit had sent a-wandering*
caedo, caedere: beat, strike
stabilitas: (ie *stabilitas monastica.* cf Rule, Cap 58)

29. Succedit nocti lucifer
Anon, c. 1200

Succedit nocti lucifer,
Quem mox aurora sequitur,
Solis ortum praenuntians
Lustrantis orbem lumine.

Christus sol est justitiae,
Aurora Mater gratiae,
Quam Anna praeit rutilans,
Legis propellens tenebras.

Anna radix uberrima,
Arbor et salutifera
Virgam producens floridam,
Quae Christum nobis attulit.

succedo, succedere, successi (+dat): follow, succeed
lucifer, luciferi: Light-Bearer, morning star
praenuntio, -are: announce, foretell
lustro, lustrare: purify, illuminate

Mater: *(His) Mother (is the) dawn of grace*
prae-eo, prae-ire: precede, go before (+ acc)
rutilo, rutilare: grow red, glow
rutilans: *red-lovely, in the red of dawn*
propello, -ere: expel, dispel, drive out

radix, radicis (fem): root (*virga, radix, flos,* cf Isaiah 11:1)
uber, uberis (adj): abundant, fertile, fruitful (Δ *uber, uberis = breast*)
virga, -ae: rod, branch (The BVM is *virga florida* and also *virgo*.)
floridus, -a, -um: with flowers, flourishing
affero, afferre, attuli: bring, give

Note:

The morning star appears in the night sky before dawn. In the iconography of the hymns, just as the rising sun represents the coming of the Lord, so likewise the morning star may represent the Precursor of the Lord. In this hymn, the morning star also refers to Anna.

30. Te beata Sponsa Christi
Hugo Vaillant OSB, ob 1678

Te, beata Sponsa Christi,	
Te, columba virginum,	
Siderum tollunt coloni	*the settlers of the stars*
Laudibus, Scholastica;	*extoll you with praise*
Nostra te laetis salutant	
Vocibus praecordia.	
Sceptra mundi cum coronis	
Docta quondam spernere,	
Dogma Fratris insecuta	
Atque sanctae Regulae,	
Ex odore gratiarum	
Astra nosti quaerere.	*you knew how to seek the stars*
O potens virtus amoris!	
O decus victoriae!	
Dum fluentis lacrimarum	
Cogis imbres currere….,	*you compel the rains to come*
Ore Nursini parentis	
Verba caeli suscipis.	
Luce fulges expetitā	
In polorum vertice,	*at the summit of the heavens*
Clara flammis caritatis	
Cum nitore gratiae;	*with the radiance of grace*
Juncta Sponso conquiescis	
In decore gloriae.	*in the beauty of [his] glory*

praecordia, praecordiorum: hearts
docta (< docēre): *taught, learnéd, wise*
insequor, insequi, insecutus: follow
nosti: *you know* (= *novisti*)
fluentum, fluenti: stream, river (cf Dialogues II:33)
parens, parentis: *spiritual* parent, father, ie *brother*
expeto, expetere, expetītus: desire, seek out
conquiesco, -ere: rest, rest together

30. Te beata Sponsa Christi

Nunc, benigna pelle nubes
Cordibus fidelium,
Ut serenā fronte splendens
Sol perennis luminis,
Sempiternae claritatis
Impleat nos gaudiis.

Gloriam Patri canamus
Unicoque Filio;
Par tributum proferamus
Inclito Paraclito,
Nutibus cuius creantur
Et reguntur saecula.

serenus a um: clear, calm, serene
frons, frontis (fem): forehead, brow, *perh* face
splendens, splendentis (< splendēre): resplendent, shining
claritas, claritatis: brilliance, glory
nutus, -ūs: nod, command

Meter:

Trochaic tetrameter, with alternating "catalectic" li
line the final measure is one syllable shorter. As always
optionally long or short.

Te be a ta sponsa Christi
— ~ | — ~ | — ~ | — —

In de co re glori ae c
— ~ | — ~ | — ~ | —

Spondee permitted in second measure

Nostra te lae tis sa lutant
— ~ | — — | — ~ | — —

Vo ci bus prae cordi a
— ~ | — — | — ~ | ~

Made in the USA
Middletown, DE
20 December 2024

67645331R00239